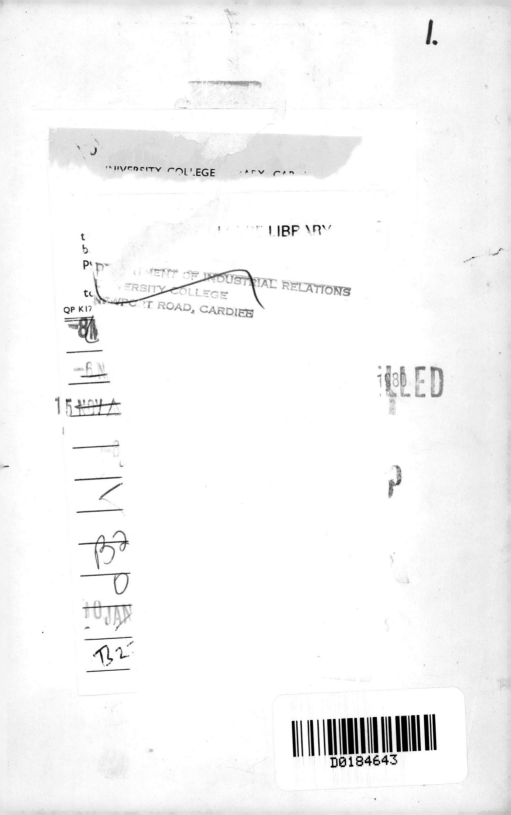

STUDIES IN MANAGEMENT

EDITED BY

ANDREW ROBERTSON

Senior Research Fellow, University of Sussex
Formerly British Institute of Management and the
National Institute of Economic and Social Research

No. 5

BRITISH MANAGEMENT THOUGHT

JOHN CHILD

Senior Research Officer, London Business School

BRITISH
MANAGEMENT
THOUGHT

A CRITICAL ANALYSIS

London
GEORGE ALLEN AND UNWIN LTD
RUSKIN HOUSE · MUSEUM STREET

PRINTED IN GREAT BRITAIN
in 11 on 12 pt. Baskerville
BY T. & A. CONSTABLE LTD
EDINBURGH

PREFACE

THE content and purpose of this book are discussed towards the close of Chapter 1. Much of its substance derives from my thesis on *British Management Thought and Education: Their Interpretation of Industrial Relationships* which was approved by the University of Cambridge for the award of the degree of Doctor of Philosophy. For purposes of publication it has proved necessary to reduce considerably the number of historical references given in support of the text. Any reader who might wish to examine the complete material upon which this book is based is advised to consult the original dissertation. However, essential sources and quotations are referenced, and I am greatly indebted to those who have given me permission to quote from their work.

I am particularly grateful to my former research supervisor, Mr John H. Goldthorpe, for the constant advice and encouragement which he freely devoted to the research underlying this book. Professor A. B. Cherns, then at the Department of Scientific and Industrial Research, provided valuable advice at several points. My work has also benefited from discussions with Messrs H. Blezinger, C. L. Fletcher, G. K. Ingham, and former colleagues at the Oil Engine Division of Rolls-Royce Ltd. My wife, Elizabeth, has throughout lent encouragement and constructive criticism to this study.

J. C.

CONTENTS

PART I

INTRODUCTION

MANAGEMENT AND MANAGEMENT THOUGHT

Management and its Emergence – The Nature of Managerial Problems – British Management Thought and its Functions – The Scope of Some Previous Studies – The Scope of This Study.

MANAGEMENT AND ITS EMERGENCE

MANAGEMENT may be regarded from at least three different perspectives: first as an economic resource performing a series of technical functions which comprise the organizing and administering of other resources; secondly as a system of authority through which policy is translated into the execution of tasks; and thirdly as an élite social grouping which acts as an economic resource and maintains the associated system of authority.[1] Definitions of management may be based on any one of these perspectives. For instance, Henri Fayol's classic definition is couched in terms of managers' technical functions – to forecast and plan, to organize, to command, to co-ordinate, and to control. Wilfred Brown's more recent definition, on the other hand, stresses managerial authority and hierarchy.[2]

Some commentators have deplored what they call this 'confusion in the use of terms' on the grounds that it prejudices an objective analysis of managers' technical functions by what they believe to be extraneous considerations of status.[3] However, as the present study proceeds it will become evident that a recognition of the different linked aspects of management in terms of technical functions, social status and organizational authority is of considerable analytical importance. For the development of management thought, and the awareness of the managerial role which it reflects, cannot be understood merely through reference to the technical aspects of managing.

Management as a purely technical factor has always been

pursued to some degree wherever work activities have been organized. In this respect there is little distinction to be drawn between the managerial functions of the owner-entrepreneur, the civil administrator and the salaried industrial manager. The chief difference lies in the social characteristics and context of these three roles. It is a series of distinctive social attributes in terms of property ownership, training, personal objectives, organizational goals, and so on, that enable us to distinguish the industrial manager from other roles to which similar technical functions may also be attached.

British management thought developed in step with the appearance of a distinct occupational grouping. During the course of this century, management has become progressively differentiated from both business owners and from other employees. Separation from ownership has been expressed by the concept of a 'divorce of ownership from control'. This process was one which we shall see was given considerable prominence at an early stage in management thought. The differentiation of management from ownership has been associated with a diffusion of shareholding, and it is much more evident in larger organizations.[4]

Managers have become set apart from other employees. This process has been manifest not only in the elongation of organizational hierarchies separating senior managers from lower-level employees, but also in an increasingly selective entry to managerial ranks especially in terms of required educational qualifications. Thus the proportion of senior managers possessing a university education has risen considerably faster over the last few decades in both Britain and the United States than has the proportion of graduates in their populations as a whole.[5] In Britain there appears to be a long-term movement away from managers starting their careers as manual workers or clerks, and towards starting as personnel already possessing some technical or managerial training.[6]

These trends, resulting in the development of an increasingly distinct managerial social stratum, have been associated with growing organizational size and administrative complexity and with an increasing sophistication of available industrial techniques. For example, the following figures indicate how in Great Britain the average size of establishments in manufacturing industry has been rising:[7]

Table 1

Great Britain: *Average size of establishments in
manufacturing industry, 1935, 1955 and 1961*

	1935	1955	1961
Number of establishments	64,649	56,313	55,161
Employment in these establishments	7,203,000	7,833,000	8,178,000
Average employment per establishment	111·4	140·1	148·3
Number of establishments employing 1,000 persons and over	553	1,129	1,206

Statistics on the proportion of administrative, technical and clerical employees in manufacturing industry provide some guide to the relative increase in managerial numbers during the present century, and this proportion has been increasing in most industrial societies throughout the world. The following table gives figures for Great Britain:[8]

Table 2

*The proportion of administrative, technical and clerical workers
employed in manufacturing industries, 1907-1966*
(expressed as percentages of total numbers in employment)

1907	1924	1935	1948	1959	1966
7·9%	11·8%	13·1%	16·6%*	21·3%†	24·3%
			16·0%†	21·1%‡	

Standard Industrial Classification

* pre-1948
† 1948
‡ 1958

Figures up to and including 1948 (old S.I.C.) relate to the United Kingdom; those from 1948 (new S.I.C.) relate to Great Britain.

A further pointer to the development of a distinct managerial stratum is the foundation of specialized institutes catering for a specifically managerial membership and concerned with various aspects of industrial administration. Such institutes reflected a growing consciousness that management required its own associations separate from employers' organizations. The latter were in any case more concerned with political than technical issues, oriented more towards a defence of industrial property rights than towards the search for new managerial methods. The more prominent management institutes were founded in:[9]

1911 – Sales Managers' Association
1913 – Welfare Workers Association (This was at first strictly
    speaking not a 'management' institute; after the First
    World War, however, it became increasingly identi-
    fied with management and in 1931 adopted the title
    'Institute of Labour Management'.)
1915 – Office Managers' Association
1919 – Institute of Cost and Works Accountants
1920 – Institute of Industrial Administration
1931 – Works Managers' Association

Finally, and closely related to the foundation of management
institutes, there was from the close of the First World War a
rapid growth of attention to industrial administration as a
distinct area of study. A specialized literature emerged, and
some of this will be reviewed in subsequent chapters. There
were also early examples of training courses and conferences
devoted to the subject. For instance, in 1919 the Manchester
Technical College began teaching on industrial administration,
while in the same year the first of the 'Oxford' management
conferences, was organized by Seebohm Rowntree. A school
on management was run at Cambridge, in 1919 under C. S.
Myers, and some lectures from this were subsequently published.[10] Moreover, the work of new and independent research
organizations such as the Industrial Welfare Society (founded
1918) and the National Institute of Industrial Psychology
(founded 1921) was largely concerned with managerial problems.

THE NATURE OF MANAGERIAL PROBLEMS

In order to appreciate the content and development of British
management thought it is necessary to review briefly, albeit in
the form of an 'ideal type', the problematic nature of management in work organizations. It is useful here to return to the
threefold distinction of management as a technical function, a
social group, and a system of authority. For it is evident, both
at the level of industry as a whole and within particular organizations, that the technical function of managing is intimately
bound up with the social situation of a managing group, and
that this relationship has important consequences for the
acceptance of managerial authority.

When a distinction is made between management as technical

function and as social grouping, it serves to draw attention to the paradox of conflict and consensus facing management in British industry today. On the one hand, there can be few people who do not now accept that the maintenance of the living standards afforded by a highly complex and developed industrial society requires a competent, carefully organized management of resources. The National Economic Development Council expressed this point when it stated that 'to achieve the increase in productivity necessary for growth will call for highly skilled management throughout the economy'.[11] In other words, there is a general social *consensus* over the value of management as a technical resource, which derives from a wider social agreement on the benefits of pursuing, or at least maintaining, national economic prosperity.

On the other hand management as a social grouping is liable to be involved in *conflict* with other sectors of society. It is possible to analyse this conflict on two levels. First, there may be dispute over the ultimate goals of the industrial enterprise, particularly as the processes of production and trade will frequently entail a range of what welfare economists term 'social costs'. For management in the private sector of British industry is not directly accountable to the 'public interest', a point which Factory Acts and the more recent restrictive practices legislation have served to underline. Indeed, there are some who would question even the effectiveness of public accountability over the nationalized industries.[12] Secondly, there are features associated with the everyday operation of industry that tend to place managements in conflict with other groups through which they have to work. We shall elaborate on these features shortly. In sum, managerial groups may find themselves challenged, both in respect to the policies which they (or their controlling boards) lay down for industry, and over the procedures they adopt in fulfilment of those policies.

This linked but opposing relation of consensus and conflict has direct implications for the authority which management, as the initiative and co-ordinative force in industry, has by definition to exercise over other resources. While in principle a system of managerial command over other groups may be considered as socially legitimate, in practice managers can face opposition to the actions they decide to pursue. Thus, as a technical prerequisite for economic efficiency, managerial

authority is generally acceptable as an area open to objective
analysis and study. But as a social group, managers might well be
seen by others as using that authority in a far from impartial
manner, to achieve ends which are peculiar to themselves rather
than to the groups they aspire to control.

This is the paradox which the commentator we quoted
earlier over-simply ascribed to a 'confusion in the use of terms'.
It implies that it is ultimately not useful to review managerial
operations in ignorance of the social relationships which inhere
in any particular organization and its environment, and which
managers themselves to some extent structure further through
their own policies and actions. That is to say, industrial relationships affect the nature of managers' technical problems.

At the level of a particular business organization, it is possible
to distinguish between managerial relationships with groups that
are to a large extent external to the organization, and those
relationships which concern management action within the
organization. In the former case, largely external groupings such
as financiers, customers, and labour organizations may possess
considerable sanction over the directions of managerial action
by virtue of their power to resist and even vitiate change.[13]
Moreover, government agencies possess considerable influence
over organizations in certain industries which rely heavily on
the State for subsidies, contracts or protection. The State is also
in a position to challenge management policies if it feels these
are contrary to the 'public interest'.

The fact that the maintenance of a business enterprise
requires a contribution from a variety of social groups means
that managers work within a web of competing interests. For
although the various factors of production and customers all
have a stake in the sustained and efficient performance of the
enterprise, they compete at the same time against each other
in the division of benefits from that performance. Furthermore,
the maximization by these groups of their own short-term gains
could well be to the detriment of the long-term growth of the
enterprise. In other words, this situation presents another facet
of the conflict-consensus paradox with which management has
to reckon. Indeed, this forms part of the wider phenomenon of
conflicting interests within a basically co-operative and nor-
matively integrated system which sociologists have discerned
in society at large.[14]

Within private industry, the balance which managements are able and willing to strike between these competing interests may depend to some extent upon the degree to which they have been affected by the 'divorce of ownership from control'. This trend has now an extensive, mainly American, literature.[15] It has in a sense been a 'voluntary' abdication of day-to-day industrial control by ownership and is associated with the formalization of advancing managerial expertise into separate administrative structures and with the spreading out of shareholding over more (and often smaller) units. Their accumulation of expertise in the control of increasingly large and complex enterprises has tended to place managers in a strategically superior position, *vis-à-vis*, a growing number of 'absentee' owners. For a similar reason, ministerial control over managerial operation in public enterprise may also be tenuous.   This situation is comparable to that analysed by Max Weber of the 'expert' bureaucrat and his 'dilettante' political master.[16]

As managers (including those at director level) may be free in many cases to act independently of ownership, it has frequently been assumed that they are placed in a central role for determining the objectives of a business organization, over and above the mere execution of policies designed to fulfil those objectives. Consequently, the question has been raised, not least by management spokesmen themselves, whether management should continue to regard itself as responsible primarily to legal ownership, or whether as a new 'professional' group, it has the right and obligation to assume wider responsibilities. In these situations of 'managerial enterprise' it is thus a matter of social concern to ascertain the nature of the managerial goals which are, or could be, followed.[17] Given the range of competing claims upon business organizations, one of the chief problems with 'managerial enterprise' is the decision as to where and in what order of priorities, managerial responsibilities lie. It is therefore not surprising, as we shall find, that management apologists recognized the growing divorce from ownership well before most social scientists (Marx and Veblen's early recognition of the development was exceptional among social scientists[18]). Moreover, management writers were acutely aware of the way the divorce from ownership held implications for the source of managerial authority and for the direction of its responsibilities.

The relationships which concern managerial action within

organizations may broadly be said to embrace both those with non-managerial employees and those within the administrative structure itself. Indeed, in this second area the process of functional specialization in larger organizations has tended to differentiate between line and specialist roles, and between departments, in such a way that consequent conflicts and divergent attitudes may be sufficiently severe as to cast doubt on the analytical wisdom of using the term 'the management' with its suggestion of a monolithic entity.

The problem of managerial authority is accentuated within business organizations, where power is distributed differentially between persons and groups enjoying close and highly interdependent relationships. On the inter-personal level, psychologists point out that hierarchy may encourage feelings of hostility and aggression among subordinates. At another level of analysis, management faces the problem brought out by Weber when he indicated that authority to be freely accepted had to rest upon a system of shared values.[19] Thus managements may be presented with hostility stimulated by the structuring of industrial control, and with challenges to the exercise of this control resulting from groups holding different interests and associated values. There is a similarity between this distinction and that of Simmel's, which Coser has elaborated in terms of 'non-realistic' and 'realistic' conflicts.[20]

It has already been suggested that in Britain today there is a considerable agreement on the need in industry for effective management authority. That is, while management's accountability may still be a matter of concern, its right to final control over matters of administration is no longer seriously challenged as a principle. Nevertheless, within the process of administration there may occur either temporary breakdowns in managerial authority or a more subtle subversion of its requirements. The former case will take the form of 'open conflicts', strikes being a prime example. The latter will proceed as 'hidden conflict', examples of which are output restriction and rivalry between different administrative departments.

The divergences in values which may underlie organizational conflict frequently relate to affiliations of organizational members within the wider society. For instance, a different assessment of legitimate organizational objectives between senior managers on the one hand and manual workers or technical specialists on the other, may be influenced by a markedly different position in the social class hierarchy in the first case or by membership of professional communities in the second. Consciousness of these social differences may well be reinforced by restrictions on promotion from either specialist, clerical, or operative positions up to senior managerial level. These cleavages will also tend to be accentuated by objective differences of interest between managements and other organizational groups. In the case of all employees there is the well-known problem of wages as both costs to the organization to be minimized and as rewards to employees to be maximized. In addition, the nature of the employment contract is such that it leaves open for future bargaining how much work or responsibility is to be undertaken in return for how much remuneration and other rewards. The 'effort-bargain' (Behrend) or the 'contributions-inducements balance' (Simon) is thus conducive to conflict with management.[21] Further conflicts between managerial goals and those of other employees may also arise, such as over the managerial requirement of organizational adaptability and the employee's requirement of job security. In the case of the technical specialist, the commercial requirements of a business organization as defined by senior management may cause funds to be withheld from areas of research that professionally trained specialists wish to pursue for their intrinsic scientific interest.

Conflicts of this nature are an inherent feature of business organizations, though they will not necessarily be overt and they may frequently be tempered by prevailing goodwill or accommodated by appropriate organizational procedures. Nor is conflict in organizations necessarily wholly detrimental to their effectiveness, particularly if it is a necessary inducement towards, or accompaniment of change. The important point is that it illustrates how the pattern of organizational social relationships will have a direct effect upon the execution of management's technical functions.

Our brief review has indicated how strains within an organization may relate to institutional factors outside its physical or legal boundaries. It clearly supports the notion of business organizations as 'open systems'. It is on the basis of an analysis such as the one we have presented that commentators are coming increasingly to view such organizations as 'plural societies'[22], operating in a state of 'collective schizophrenia', as one put it vividly.[23]

Under these conditions, the managerial function – of 'getting things done' – entails not only regulation but also reconciliation. In Etzioni's terms, managers must secure the 'compliance' of others.[24] The techniques of taking action through others presuppose a minimum acceptance of managers' authority to initiate this action in the first place. However, our analysis so far leads reasonably to the proposition that these techniques will lack effect if they overlook the nature of social relationships prevailing within an organization and across its boundaries. It is here that we begin to touch upon perhaps the most fundamental dilemma which has confronted management thought. Namely, that a search for the legitimation of managerial authority by claiming a community of interests within the enterprise and a pursuit of social responsibility outside it, can readily prejudice an objective appraisal of the social constraints imposed on the operation of that authority. In short, the dilemma is that the ideological purposes of management thought may weaken its capacity to afford managers a balanced assessment of the social organizations within which they have to work.

BRITISH MANAGEMENT THOUGHT AND ITS FUNCTIONS

An appreciation of the social context of management problems enables British management thought to be placed in some perspective, while it also allows for a critical review of the assumptions and propositions contained in that thought. British management thought comprises the body of writings and other recorded material which has been directed towards the assessment and improvement of managerial authority, performance and status. The present study is concerned to record and analyse the main interpretations offered by British management thought of social relationships in industry. It will give attention to the broader organizational and social concerns of management thought rather than to writing on particular functional techniques, though it has to take account of the relative weight given to the latter.

It will become apparent that British management thought was a quite highly structured system of ideas which themselves possessed a high degree of complementarity. This thought derived mainly from managers or consultants, although social scientists sharing similar objectives have made a significant contribution. Those who formulated management thought were active members of what is sometimes called the British 'management movement'. As the proponents of managerial professionalism, the leading members of management institutes, and the chief contributors to management conferences, they formed a relatively cohesive intellectual élite. They were concerned to assess leading contemporary opinion, with particular reference to the occupational status of management. They also attempted to assess new academic and scientific thinking in order to derive concepts and methods applicable to managements' functional requirements.

These activities of management thinkers indicate respectively that management thought possessed functions in regard to managerial social status and managerial technical activities. We shall seek to elaborate on this double function of management thought in Chapter 7 following the presentation of relevant descriptive material in the preceding chapters. The analytical proposition which we are advancing and which derives from our earlier analysis of management itself, is that management thought held a *legitimatory* function and a *technical* function. The legitimatory function related to the status position (in the broadest sense) of managers, while the technical function related to the improvement of their performance. Both functions can readily be seen to be associated with the question of managerial authority. The legitimatory function was primarily linked to the securing of social recognition and approval for managerial authority and the way in which it was used, while the technical function was primarily linked to the search for practical means of rendering that authority maximally effective. In so far as the legitimatory function was concerned with securing social approval, it tended to be associated with the presence within management thought of claims to adopt socially acceptable values; so far as the technical function was concerned with operational effectiveness, it tended to be associated with statements of effective managerial techniques.

This scheme of analysis, which will be fundamental to our study, indicates that in the sense of comprising both 'ideological' and 'scientific' elements, British management thought was a comprehensive body of knowledge. It is somewhat more than the management 'ideologies' which have been the subject of some previous studies (which we review shortly). Although the concept of 'management thought' cannot be given precise boundaries, it is normally distinguishable from a less defined and less sophisticated 'business ideology', from more specific and rigorous contributions of a primarily academic nature, and from the personal views held by the general run of practising managers. We shall subsequently find a number of indications that the intellectuals responsible for management thought were frequently far removed in their ideas from most British management practitioners. Moreover, an analysis of the overall 'developmental cycle' of British management thought will clarify its relationship to business ideology and academic contributions. For it will become apparent that the emergence of management thought was associated with a process of role differentiation between business spokesmen and management intellectuals, while its recent decline has been associated with a role convergence between management intellectuals and those academics concerned with management and organizational studies.

THE SCOPE OF SOME PREVIOUS STUDIES

The objectives of available studies on management thought have not necessarily been the same as our own, and there has been relatively little analysis of the British case. Urwick and Brech's *The Making of Scientific Management* contains valuable material, but its sections on Britain are devoted mainly to the development of managerial techniques. In so far as these authors have themselves been prominent members of the management movement, their work lacks a critical dimension.[25] *Management in Britain*, by McGivering and others, is the work of sociologists and it does adopt an analytical framework in its brief section on 'the new managerial ideology'. The authors relate this ideology to associated social-structural conditions. They note how trade union pressures have borne on management, and they are concerned to trace how management ideology has changed since the inter-war years alongside advancing technology and industrial concentration.[26] However, the McGivering *et al.* study takes the writings of but one prominent industrialist as indicating all the ramifications of 'management ideology', a limitation we discuss at the close of Chapter 4. It is not concerned to work out in any detail the likely relationships between the ideology and relevant structural processes. Moreover, this study does not distinguish between management intellectuals and managers in general when discussing the sources of the ideas it reviews. We shall argue later that this is to miss an important distinction, and one which even today is reflected in the reservations that many practising managers hold concerning the value of management education. Both these British studies will be referred to again in subsequent chapters.

The most substantial analysis of management thought is to be found in a collection of works by Bendix, particularly his comparative historical study covering different periods in Britain, East Germany, the United States and Russia, *Work and Authority in Industry*.[27] In one paper, Bendix makes a distinction between the various functions of business ideology which has provided a valuable guide to our own analysis in terms of legitimatory and technical functions.[28] He clearly recognizes how what he calls 'ideologies of management' relate both to the growing size, complexity and formalization of industry, which required that employees accept an 'ethic of work performance', and to pressures from trade unionism reinforced by 'the ideological attack of the muckrakers'.[29] Bendix, however, adopts a somewhat Marxist analysis of the determination of management thought, which we later suggest understates the autonomous influence of already available ideas. He is concerned in *Work and Authority in Industry* primarily with broad international and historical comparisons, which are ambitious in so far as he relies on only four cases. Therefore, he is not able to pursue each 'managerial ideology' beyond a certain level of detail, and this means that he does not follow up his earlier distinction between legitimatory and technical elements so fully as would otherwise be possible. While at various points Bendix does distinguish between management spokesmen and practising managers, or between owner-entrepreneurs and managers, these distinctions are also subordinated to his wider analytical scheme which takes in totalitarian versus democratic, and developing as opposed to industrially mature societies.

Sutton and his colleagues in *The American Business Creed* are not strictly speaking concerned with management thought, least of all with its technical aspects. However, they posit an interesting relationship between the form taken by American business ideology and largely psychological 'strains' in business-men's occupational roles. Apart from this important contribution, their analysis suffers from the absence of a historical dimension. Nor does it distinguish clearly between managers and 'business-men' generally, or between either of these groups and business spokesmen.[30] Both Bendix and Sutton's work will be referred to again in Chapter 7.

Finally, two further studies require mention for their analytical contributions. Mitrani, in a poorly documented study of French managers' modes of thought and action, has outlined a distinction between ideological and technical elements comparable to that offered by Bendix. However, Mitrani does not consider the likely interaction between these elements in managerial orientations, and unlike Bendix he shows relatively little awareness of the close links between patterns of industrial behaviour and managements' technical problems.[31] None of the studies mentioned so far is concerned with the possible distortions that ideology could bring to management writing and thought designed to solve rather more technical problems. However, to some extent Harbison and Myers in their *Management in the Industrial World* do illustrate the influence of ideology upon the methods chosen to manage labour in their section on 'managerial philosophies toward workers'.[32]

THE SCOPE OF THIS STUDY

The intention of the present study, as already mentioned, is to record and analyse the main developments in British management thought with particular reference to the various organizational and social relationships that are of managerial concern. There are a number of continuing themes within management thought upon which it will be necessary to concentrate. The first theme centres upon the notion of management as a 'profession'. This referred to the justification of managerial aspirations and actions in terms of socially approved values (especially the concept of 'service'), and to the quality of managerial relationships with other social groups who were party to, or affected by, the operations of business organizations. A second continuing theme was represented by various formulations of a 'human relations' approach towards employees. This approach had its origins well before the work of Elton Mayo and his school with which it is popularly associated. Thirdly, there was a continuing concern in management thought with the search for optimum 'principles' of organization. These three themes were highly interdependent, since the latter two formed part of the development of generally applicable managerial knowledge that was an essential basis for professionalism, while the ethical aspects of professional aspirations had a bearing upon the new methods of treating employees which were advocated by management writers.

The following descriptive review of British management thought will concentrate on *industrial* management. In this it adheres to the predominant emphasis within management thought. It will also be evident that management writers tended to make little distinction in their use of terms such as 'manager', 'worker' and 'enterprise' between the great variety of roles and types which may be subsumed within those over-generalized concepts. This qualification is mentioned here by way of explanation, but it will be seen to relate to the extensive recent criticism of management thought as over-simplified and naïvely universalistic in outlook. Such criticism is referred to in Chapters 6 and 8. Two points need to be made regarding our own use of terms. First, we shall employ the terms 'ideas', 'notions', 'concepts' and the like in a neutral sense to refer to the structural constituents of British management thought. Second, we shall use that much disputed term 'ideological' only to refer to those value elements within management thought which tended to serve a legitimatory function on behalf of management.

Chapters 2 to 6 trace the historical process of emergence, maturity and decline through which British management thought has passed. These chapters assume that the reader has some familiarity with the pioneering contributions to management thought made by writers of international stature such as Taylor, Fayol, Follett and Mayo. To the extent that their ideas were incorporated into British management thought, we shall make reference to them, but it is not possible in the present study to elaborate fully on their work.[33] In following the historical development of British management thought, attention will be given to the balance between its 'ideological' and technical content, and to how this balance changed over time. We shall attempt to locate this changing balance in relation both to the environment within which the British management movement operated and to the development of the ideas available to management thinkers. The presence of ideological and scientific strains within management thought also raises the question of whether the former could distort the latter. Chapter 6 in fact reviews the way in which recent social science research has suggested the intrusion of ideology into management techniques, and into the analysis of organization and social relationships upon which these techniques were founded. The same chapter also contains a critical review of the Glacier writings, which represent a recent and novel development within British management thought.

There are two chapters in the conclusion to this book. Chapter 7 draws together some threads of the analysis underlying our historical review. This chapter considers the nature of management thought's overall 'developmental cycle', discusses the internal structure and the functions of that thought, and reviews the way in which management thought was received by practising managers. The general failure of practising managers to welcome or accept much of management thought is related to a major problem in management education today, namely finding an approach to the analysis of the 'human aspects' of industry which is both immediately useful to managers and based upon reliable research findings. This kind of problem, and how it is illustrated by recent developments in management thought and social science, forms the subject matter of Chapter 8. This chapter closes the study by drawing out some of its wider and more controversial implications for the nature of management education today, including the question of teaching content and the role of the universities in supporting management studies.

NOTES

1. F. Harbison and C. A. Myers, *Management in the Industrial World*, New York: McGraw-Hill 1959, pp. 19-20. Cf. W. H. Wesson, 'Management' in eds. J. Gould and W. L. Kolb, *Dictionary of the Social Sciences*, New York: Free Press 1964, pp. 403-404.

2. H. Fayol, *General and Industrial Management*, London: Pitman 1949, p. 6; W. Brown, *Exploration in Management*, London: Heinemann 1960, p. 50.

3. L. Urwick, Forward to Fayol, *op. cit.*, p. xiii.

4. P. Sargant Florence, *Ownership, Control and Success of Large Companies*, London: Sweet & Maxwell 1961.

5. Acton Society Trust, *Management Succession*, London 1956, p. 15; W. L. Warner and J. C. Abegglen, *Big Business Leaders in America*, New York: Harper 1955, p. 47.

6. D. G. Clarke, *The Industrial Manager: His Background and Career Pattern*, London: Business Publications 1966; R. V. Clements, *Managers: A Study of their Careers in Industry*, London: Allen & Unwin 1958.

7. I. C. McGivering, D. Matthews and W. H. Scott, *Management in Britain*, Liverpool: The University Press 1960, p. 14; *Annual Abstract of Statistics*, no. 104, London: H.M.S.O. 1967.

8. S. Melman, *Dynamic Factors in Industrial Productivity*, Oxford: Blackwell 1956, p. 73; *Annual Abstract of Statistics*, nos. 99, 101, 104, London: H.M.S.O. 1962, 1964, 1967.

9. H. Whitehead, 'The Changing Environment of Management', *British Management Review*, VI, 2, 1947, pp. 9-11; T. G. Rose, *A History of the Institute of Industrial Administration*, London: I.I.A. 1954, chapter 1.

10. Ed. B. Muscio, *Lectures on Industrial Administration*, London: Pitman 1920.

11. N.E.D.C., *Conditions Favourable to Faster Growth*, London: H.M.S.O. 1963, p. 3.

12. N. Ross, 'Workers' Participation and Control', *Scientific Business*, II, 8, Feb. 1965, p. 353.

13. W. Brown, *op. cit.*, pp. 222-223.

14. D. Lockwood, 'Some Remarks on "The Social System"', *British Journal of Sociology*, VII, 2, June 1956, pp. 134-146.

15. W. L. Baldwin, 'The Motives of Managers, Environmental Restraints, and the Theory of Managerial Enterprise', *Quarterly Journal of Economics*, LXXVIII, May 1964, pp. 238-256, reviews some of this literature.

16. Eds. H. H. Gerth and C. W. Mills, *From Max Weber: Essays in Sociology*, New York: Oxford University Press 1946, chapter VIII, section 12.

17. W. L. Baldwin, *op. cit.*; R. Marris, *The Economic Theory of 'Managerial' Capitalism*, London: Macmillan 1964.

18. T. Veblen, *The Theory of Business Enterprise*, New York: Scribner 1904, chapter VI; Eds. T. B. Bottomore and M. Rubel, *Karl Marx: Selected Writings in Sociology and Social Philosophy*, London: Watts 1961, pp.150-154.

19. *From Max Weber, op. cit.*, p. 295 ff.

20. L. Coser, *The Functions of Social Conflict*, London: Routledge & Kegan Paul 1956, p. 48 ff.

21. H. Behrend, 'The Effort-Bargain', *Industrial and Labor Relations Review*, X, 4, 1957, pp. 503-515; H. A. Simon, *Administrative Behavior*, New York: Free Press 2nd ed. 1957, chapter VI.

22. N. S. Ross, 'Organized Labour and Management – the United Kingdom', in ed. E. M. Hugh-Jones, *Human Relations and*

Modern Management, Amsterdam: North Holland Publishing Co. 1958, pp. 100-132.

23. W. J. Gore, *Administrative Decision Making*, New York: Wiley 1964, quoted in a review by T. Lupton, *Journal of Management Studies*, II, 1, Feb. 1965, p. 105.

24. A. Etzioni, *A Comparative Analysis of Complex Organizations*, Glencoe: Free Press 1961.

25. L. Urwick and E. F. L. Brech, *The Making of Scientific Management*, London: Management Publications 1945-49, esp. vol. II.

26. I. C. McGivering *et al.*, *op. cit.*, pp. 91-101.

27. R. Bendix, *Work and Authority in Industry*, New York: Wiley 1956; idem, 'Industrial Authority and its Supporting Value Systems', paper of 1954 in R. Dubin, *Human Relations in Administration*, Englewood Cliffs: Prentice-Hall 2nd ed. 1961, pp. 270-276; *idem*, 'Industrialization, Ideologies and Social Structure', *American Sociological Review*, 24, 5, Oct. 1959, pp. 613-623.

28. R. Bendix, *op. cit.* 1961, p. 271.

29. *Ibid.*

30. F. X. Sutton, S. E. Harris, C. Kaysen and J. Tobin, *The American Business Creed*, Cambridge: Harvard University Press 1956.

31. N. Mitrani, 'Les Organisateurs d'Entreprise: Leurs Modèles, Maîtres à Penser et Conduites', *Année Sociologique*, 3rd series 1955-56, pp. 480-491.

32. F. Harbison and C. A. Myers, *op. cit.*, chapter 3.

33. For further reference see *inter al.*: S. Krupp, *Pattern in Organization Analysis*, New York: Holt, Rinehart & Winston 1961; D. S. Pugh, D. J. Hickson and C. R. Hinings, *Writers on Organizations*, London: Hutchinson 1964. Also J. Child, 'Quaker Employers and Industrial Relations', *Sociological Review*, XII, 3, Nov. 1964, pp. 293-315, for the formative influence of British Quaker employers.

PART II

THE DEVELOPMENT OF BRITISH
MANAGEMENT THOUGHT

CHAPTER 2

IN THE MAKING
(to World War I)

The Management of Labour – The Foundations of Managerial Knowledge – Towards a Social Legitimation of Industrial
Authority – Summary

As the mid-Victorian boom drew to a close in the 1870s, the
dominant British entrepreneurial philosophy was founded upon
the concepts of self-help and laissez-faire economics. It held
that anyone could attain wealth and status through diligence
and thrift. The possession of these attributes indicated moral
fibre, and it was concluded that entrepreneurs, having risen to
higher social positions, could legitimately control employees on
the grounds of their moral superiority.* Although this was an
individualistic creed, it allowed no fundamental conflict of
interest between masters and men.' For it was the employer
himself who provided the opportunities for workpeople to
better themselves through merit and work. Entrepreneurial
initiative was considered the foundation for the nation's
unprecedented economic prosperity, and trade unionism in
challenging both individualism and the system promoting it
was seen to spell disaster for the common good.[1]

The literature of the time indicated that British employers
were in general hostile to trade unionism for its supposed interference with the market system.[2] The correct wage was that of the
competitive market, which worked according to 'that grand law,
which we all believe to be of divine origin, by which every one
who promotes his own true interest necessarily promotes, at
the same time, the interests of society at large'.[3] The competitive division of labour was thus assumed automatically to
promote social co-operation and benefit. Hence economists,
who were the main source of such theories, joined with manu-
facturers in attacking trade unions for injecting an artificial
rigidity into the system, for stressing class rather than individual-

c   33

istic perspectives, and for promoting conflict at the expense of co-operation. 'What are the economic effects of any effort to monopolize or regulate labour. Are they not to cripple production, which in turn must react on wages?', asked one economist of a working-man audience.[4]

This individualistic outlook was laissez-faire in the sense that it regarded labour as a commodity whose price was set by the market, rather than as a factor which would respond to higher incentives (not all monetary), and which in fact could be consciously 'managed'. Such a philosophy continued to prevail among many British employers right to the First World War, although as early as 1872 a writer like Brassey was able to give numerous examples of the practical benefits following a deliberate above-market 'high wage' policy.[5] Nevertheless, towards the end of the century entrepreneurial philosophy was becoming less uniform. There had, for instance, been a keen advocacy in some circles of profit-sharing, or 'industrial partnership', as a means to enlist workers' loyalties to their firm. A pioneering scheme was that of Henry Briggs in the 1860s, and the economist Jevons had great faith in the idea.[6] In the main, the motive behind these early ventures was an attempt to prevent workers from joining trade unions. This was certainly true of the Briggs experiment, and also of the well-known Metropolitan Gas scheme which the chairman of the company admitted 'was to protect ourselves against the union by attaching the men to the company'.[7] Co-partnership at Lever Brothers had a similar purpose, and in this case formed part of a pioneering, carefully designed policy of labour management.[8] More exceptional was the scheme devised by Theodore C. Taylor, whose sense of religious altruism restrained him from any attempt to prevent employees from joining unions.[9]

Similarly, the 1892 Royal Commission on Labour provided evidence that some employers were coming to reject the extreme anti-union and laissez-faire point of view. The Commission found that industrial relations tended to be most favourable when both sides were strongly organized, and it received many replies from employers recommending co-operation with unions with respect to arbitration, conciliation, and sliding-scale wage schemes.[10] Thus by the 1890s, some employers were prepared to treat wage levels not as given by the market but as a variable, which could be manipulated to increase worker co-operation. Piece-rate systems came into operation particularly in engineering and railway workshops.[11] By 1914 even a few economists supported this move away from laissez-faire.[12]

However, these were by no means the opinions of all employers replying to the Royal Commission. Those faced with the militant 'new unionism', the dock employers for example, remained much more hostile to trade unions. In any case the evidence submitted to the Commission probably over-represented those employers who had found some means of accommodation with unionism. There were, indeed, many spokesmen who reacted strongly to the 'new unionism' and who after 1889 formed part of what one writer has called 'a developing counter-attack . . . against the industrial organizations of the working people'.[13] Thus, although some commentators view the falling profit-margins of the 1880s as a watershed which led many employers to devote attention to labour as a variable in productivity, it is also important to remember that any idea of comprehensively managing the worker had captured the attention of but few and very exceptional employers in the years to 1914.[14] The great majority of firms remained indifferent to working conditions and labour management.[15]

The rest of this chapter will be concerned with these exceptions, the early pioneers who, following motives peculiar to themselves, provided a number of antecedents for British management thought. Their work and opinion foreshadowed three broad aspects of this thought – the control and motivation of labour, the compilation of a body of knowledge appropriate to management, and a wider social legitimation of industrial authority in terms of something approaching a professional ethic.

THE MANAGEMENT OF LABOUR

This area contained the most notable precedents for British management thought before 1914. Most early labour management policies developed from the 'industrial betterment' principle, which had entailed a decisive rejection of laissez-faire indifference to working conditions and standards of reward. While in some cases the impetus for these experiments may have derived from growing trading difficulties, it is clear that they were frequently inspired by religious motives as in the case of the Quaker employers, Sir William Mather, and a few others.[16] For while Robert Owen had, early on, insisted that 'welfare' paid material dividends, there was little scientific evidence for this until the physiological experiments in munitions factories during the First World War. Indeed, it appears that some Quaker employers incurred appreciable losses in maintaining such benefits for their employees.[17]

Schemes of industrial welfare divided into two broad types. First were those which aimed merely at improving employees' standards of living and culture; second those which went further and developed into the nucleus of labour management policies oriented towards increasing efficiency as well as human well-being. Examples of the former type – model villages, public baths, recreation clubs, libraries – can be found in the early nineteenth century.[18] Many of these schemes represented a formalization of entrepreneurial benevolence once increasing factory scale had rendered it impracticable to provide perquisites informally. In a sense, this first kind of welfare was extraneous to the actual process of managing. It did not necessarily involve new methods of labour management and could simply serve as a compensation for the deficiencies of the old system.

In the case of firms such as Lever's, Hans Renold, Mather & Platt, and the larger Quaker companies, welfare had by the late nineteenth century developed significant labour management features. Among the provisions in such firms were regular selection and training schemes (which in companies like Cadbury's were also intended to facilitate promotion), high wage policies, below-average hours of work, and methods of improving communications to keep step with the growth of factory size. Joint consultation and even employee counselling were foreshadowed at Port Sunlight, York and Bournville.[19] Mather & Platt in 1893 conducted a pioneer experiment into fatigue and hours of work, while Edward Cadbury's description of Bournville practice in 1912 reads much like a modern personnel management manual.[20] Quaker employers were in fact particularly active in establishing the Welfare Workers Association, the forerunner of the present Institute of Personnel Management.[21] This whole group of employers shared a high regard for efficiency, which increasingly they believed to follow from a careful attention to labour management. Lever's motto for his co-partnership scheme was 'waste not, want not'. A major role in the thinking of Quaker employers was undoubtedly played by their secular ethic which condemned waste and emphasized the careful use of resources for the benefit of others. They believed that these goals would in the first place be achieved by ensuring that their own employees benefited from good conditions of work. As Edward Cadbury put it in terms of Bournville policy:

'The supreme principle has been the belief that business efficiency and the welfare of the employees are but different sides of the same problem.'[22]

Industrial welfare may also be distinguished according to whether it was designed to close the enterprise to trade unions or whether a more open-minded policy was adopted. Welfare that was little more than an arbitrary dispensation of favours could lead to the worst aspects of paternalism when, as with some railway companies, it represented an attempt to suppress unionism.[23] On the other hand, it appears that those employers who pioneered regular systems of labour management were also more favourable to trade unionism than most. Even Lever on occasion spoke in favour of unions and the right to strike, despite the avowed intention of his profit-sharing scheme.[24] Mather & Platt's reply to the 1892 Royal Commission stood alone in the extent of its support of trade unions. The Renolds from an early date worked in full co-operation with the unions, while Seebohm Rowntree spoke out for their right to present employee grievances.[25] Cadbury very clearly acknowledged that workers could possess a 'dual allegiance' both to their own representative organizations as well as to their place of work, when he stated in 1912 that:

'The test of any scheme of factory organization is the extent to which it creates and fosters the atmosphere and spirit of co-operation and good-will, without in any sense lessening the loyalty of the worker to his own class and its organizations.'[26]

THE FOUNDATIONS OF MANAGERIAL KNOWLEDGE

After the Civil War in the United States there had been a considerable study of managerial methods as a means to raising productivity and coping with growing organizational scale and technological complexity. Discussion centred particularly on modes of organizational control and structure, on executive recruitment and training, on new costing techniques and on incentive wage payments. These developments and the socio-industrial change which had stimulated them, form the backcloth to the 'scientific management' movement primarily associated with the name of F. W. Taylor. As a number of commentators have pointed out, the concept of 'scientific management' was a creative synthesis of elements already known. What was new about scientific management was that it brought together existing advances in managerial knowledge in the form of a complete system, based on a powerful philosophy of the 'mental revolution' in industry, which was more inclusive, integrated and codified than previous writings.[27]

F. W. Taylor was to exercise a profound influence on British management thought, yet his writing made little overall impact on British industry before the First World War. Pioneering employers such as the Cadburys, Renolds, and Rowntrees gave scientific management an attention that was both receptive and critical. On the one hand, scientific management was equally at odds with laissez-faire indifference towards the planning of work, the selection and the motivation of employees. For scientific management involved a search for optimum principles of industrial operation and a conscious endeavour to inject a new philosophy of relationships in industry. Yet, on the other hand, it lacked that sympathetic view of workers and their representative organizations upon which Quaker employers particularly insisted. This led men such as Edward Cadbury to foreshadow the critiques of scientific management subsequently offered by British industrial psychologists. These critiques condemned the physical strain of 'speeding-up' associated with scientific management, its treatment of the worker as a 'living tool' allowing him minimal discretion and variety in work, and its attempt to win employees away from their allegiance to trade unions.[28]

In parallel with American developments, there was in Britain shortly before the First World War a synthesis of costing, production planning, stock control and other administrative techniques evident particularly in the work of J. S. Lewis and E. T. Elbourne.[29] The advances under way in labour management were, if anything, more far-reaching than those across the Atlantic. One of the first and most remarkable systematic presentations of new labour management methods was Cadbury's *Experiments in Industrial Organization* (1912), from which we have already quoted.

TOWARDS A SOCIAL LEGITIMATION OF INDUSTRIAL AUTHORITY

The sharp rise in industrial unrest immediately before 1914, and the growing force of socialist demands which accompanied it, encouraged some of the more perceptive employers to go some way beyond ownership of industrial property as legitimation for their authority. While there was as yet little conception of a 'professional' ethic for those exercising industrial control, there were already moves in that direction resulting from an attempt to meet labour's demand for a new moral order in industry. For instance, although Sir William Lever had said quite bluntly that 'an untrained rank and file wage-drawer cannot make any useful suggestions or aid in high management', he nevertheless professed himself keen to open senior management to promotion on merit. Moreover, he regarded an efficiently managed co-partnership system as a means to the common good, and as early as 1909 he spoke of 'efficient service to the public' as the foundation of a business enterprise.[30]

Employers professing close religious connections appeared particularly pained by the mounting class struggle of this period. They were thus the more concerned to find some moral justification beyond mere ownership for their positions. For example, Sir Benjamin Browne addressing an Anglican Congress in 1912 put forward a claim of service based upon expertise:

'It is absolutely self-evident that nothing is more injurious to the interests of the working classes than to worry, frighten or interrupt the only man who finds the capital, organizes the industry and gets the orders – the only man in fact who can give employment.'[31]

The Quaker employers also inclined towards the principle of employers' 'duties as well as their rights', as Edward Cadbury put it. Surveys such as those of Joseph Rowntree on drink, Seebohm Rowntree on poverty, and Edward Cadbury on sweated labour, led them to the view that industrial organization should be efficient enough to afford employees adequate

*Soc.
Resp.
IV*

living standards. In their opinion industry had a social function beyond that of profit-seeking, and production itself was a means to wider ends. Moreover, at this time they recognized that industrial conflict had some real social foundation and could not just be ascribed to the activities of 'agitators'. The mitigation of conflict implied changes in the prevailing mode of running industry. Seebohm Rowntree called for some material sacrifice on the part of entrepreneurs if further unrest were to be avoided. Edward Cadbury singled out the pressures of control over employees and attempts at 'driving' them as major sources of conflict, and likewise stated the need for better ways of management.[32]

SUMMARY

By the early twentieth century a few British employers, dismissed as sentimentalists by most of their peers, were challenging the practical and moral bases of laissez-faire. They initiated a move away from legitimating industrial authority solely on the grounds of ownership rights. Although their approach to industrial control remained primarily autocratic, it was of a paternalistic rather than a dictatorial kind. Moreover, they recognized that this control should be accompanied by expertise and a sustained search for improvement. The Renolds, for example, are well known for their early attempts to supplement their personal direction of a family firm by a carefully designed organization structure. The experiments of other firms in the field of labour management also involved the establishment of appropriate organizational arrangements, including the creation of additional functional roles.

These employers pioneered regular procedures of selection, recruitment and promotion; they set new standards for rewards and conditions of work. While their initiatives placed great stress on increasing material rewards through greater efficiency (for poverty was still an acute social problem), they nevertheless recognized the limitations in a crude and harsh 'engineering' approach to higher productivity which at this time was associated with some less enlightened sections of the American 'efficiency movement'. In contrast to most American management writers, the British pioneers tended to acknowledge the trade union movement as a legitimate institution. At the same

time, within their own companies, they moved from adopting
a purely contractual view of relationships towards a more
solidary and communal emphasis.

In short, these early developments represented new thinking
on matters both of legitimation and technical operation. In
particular, the growing stress on service, which was intended to
point the way to a solution of industrial unrest, was seen as
interdependent with efficient performance. This perspective
was the foundation of British management thought.

NOTES

1. R. Bendix, *Work and Authority in Industry*, New York: Wiley
1956, chapter 2, esp. p. 109 ff.
   2. *Royal Commission into the 'Organization and Rules of Trades Unions
and Other Associations'* 1869, appendix: replies of employers to
written questions, esp. pp. 97, 103; W. R. Greg, *Mistaken Aims and
Attainable Ideals*, London: Trubner 1876; F. Smith, *Workshop
Management*, London: Wyman 1878.
   3. F. Hill, 'Identity of the Interests of Employers and Workpeople' in *Lectures on Economic Science*, arranged by the National
Association for the Promotion of Social Science, London: Longmans,
Green 1870, p. 45.
   4. L. Levi, *Work and Pay*, London: Strahan 1877, p. 73. Also cf.,
National Association for the Promotion of Social Science: Resolutions
on '*Labour and Capital*', passed July 1868 (pamphlet); F. Hill, *op. cit.*
and W. S. Jevons, 'On Industrial Partnerships' in the same volume;
W. S. Jevons, *The State in Relation to Labour*, London: Macmillan
1882, esp. p. 109 in the 3rd edition.
   5. C. Watney and J. A. Little, *Industrial Warfare*, London:
Murray 1912, pp. 239-240; T. Brassey, *Work and Wages*, London:
Bell & Daldy 1872, 3rd edition.
   6. W. S. Jevons, *op. cit.* 1882, chapter VI; on the Briggs scheme
see A. Williams, *Co-Partnership and Profit-sharing*, London: Williams
& Norgate 1913, pp. 67-68.
   7. Sir G. Livesey, evidence to the *Royal Commission on Trade
Disputes and Trade Combinations* 1906, Q. 4569.
   8. Sir William Lever, quoted in A. Williams, *op. cit.*, pp. 96-97,
106-107, 109-114.
   9. Theodore C. Taylor, quoted in A. Williams, *op. cit.*, pp. 22-23,
91.
   10. *Royal Commission on Labour* 1892, employers' written replies,
p. 320 ff; E. H. Phelps-Brown, *The Growth of British Industrial
Relations*, London: Macmillan 1959, p. 184.
   11. E. J. Hobsbawm, 'Custom, Wages and Work Load in Nineteenth-Century Industry', in eds. A. Briggs and J. Saville, *Essays in
Labour History*, London: Macmillan 1960, pp. 132-137.

12. E.g., J. A. Hobson, *Work and Wealth*, London: Macmillan 1914, pp. 250-251.

13. J. Saville in eds. Briggs and Saville, *op. cit.* 1960, p. 317.

14. For a view of the 1880s as a watershed see: A. Briggs, 'Social Background' in eds. A. Flanders and H. A. Clegg, *The System of Industrial Relations in Great Britain*, Oxford: Blackwell 1954, p. 20 ff; E. J. Hobsbawm, *op. cit.*

15. E.g., A. Williams, *Life in a Railway Factory*, London: Duckworth 1915.

16. A. Vernon, *A Quaker Business Man: the Life of Joseph Rowntree*, London: Allen & Unwin 1958, chapter 10 and p. 198; P. W. Kingsford, 'Pioneers of Modern Management, 5 – Sir William Mather 1832-1920', *The Manager*, June 1957, pp. 460-465.

17. L. Urwick and E. F. L. Brech, *The Making of Scientific Management*, vol. II, London: Management Publications 1947, pp. 55-58; Society of Friends, *London Yearly Meeting 1913*, Proceedings, p. 158.

18. N. P. Gilman, *A Dividend to Labor*, Boston, Mass.: Houghton Mifflin 1899; E. D. Proud, *Welfare Work*, London: Bell 1916, p. 3; C. Walton, *Welfare Study*, Glasgow: Maclure & MacDonald 1917; anon., 'Some Early Examples of Industrial Welfare', *Welfare Work*, VI, 62, Feb. 1925, pp. 22-24; Urwick and Brech, *op. cit.*, vol. II, pp. 179-180.

19. Sir William Lever, quoted in A. Williams, *op. cit.* 1913, pp. 109-110; A. Briggs, *Social Thought and Social Action*, London: Longmans 1961, p. 99 ff; A. Vernon, *op. cit.*; E. Cadbury, *Experiments in Industrial Organization*, London: Longmans 1912; B. N. Reckitt, *The History of Reckitt and Sons*, London: Brown 1951; *Clarks of Street 1825-1950*, Street: C. & J. Clark Ltd. n.d.; E. H. Phelps-Brown, *op. cit.*, p. 76 ff.

20. *Industrial Fatigue Research Board, 1st Annual Report*, London: H.M.S.O. 1920, p. 4; E. Cadbury, *op. cit.*

21. *Labour Management*, XIV, 153, Sept. 1932, p. 158; M. M. Niven, *Personnel Management 1913-63*, London: Institute of Personnel Management 1967.

22. E. Cadbury, *op. cit.*, p. xvii.

23. N. P. Gilman, *op. cit.*; B. Meakin, *Model Factories and Villages*, London: Fisher Unwin 1905; A. Shadwell, *Industrial Efficiency*, London: Longmans 1906, indicated labour's hostility to this kind of welfare.

24. A. Williams, *op. cit.*, 1913, p. 104.

25. *Royal Commission on Labour* 1892, *op. cit.*, p. 362; C. G. Renold in a recorded discussion, *Sociological Review*, VII, 2, April 1914, pp. 123-124; B. S. Rowntree, *The Way to Industrial Peace*, London: Fisher Unwin 1914, pp. 93-94.

26. E. Cadbury, *op. cit.*, p. xvii, also p. 270.

27. F. W. Taylor, *Scientific Management*, New York: Harper 1947 edition; H. G. J. Aitken, *Taylorism at Watertown Arsenal*, Cambridge, Mass.: Harvard University Press 1960, chapter 1.

28. A. Briggs, *op. cit.* 1960, p. 119; E. Cadbury, 'Some Principles

of Industrial Organization: the Case For and Against Scientific Management', *Sociological Review*, VII, 2, April 1914, pp. 99-117; Urwick and Brech, *op. cit.*, vol. II, chapters VII and XI.

29. J. S. Lewis, *The Commercial Organisation of Factories*, London: Spon 1896; E. T. Elbourne, *Factory Administration and Accounts*, London: Library Press 1914.

30. Lever, quoted in A. Williams, *op. cit.*, 1913, pp. 96, 111.

31. Sir B. C. Browne, *Selected Papers on Social and Economic Questions*, Cambridge University Press 1918, p. 221.

32. E. Cadbury, *op. cit.*, 1912 and 1914; B. S. Rowntree, *op cit.* p. 97.

CHAPTER 3

EMERGENCE
(to the early 1920s)

The Reactions of Employers: (1) service; (2) control; (3) human needs of labour – The Emergence of Management Thought: (1) management a distinct profession; (2) management expertise and industrial control; (3) the management of labour, the beginnings of 'human relations' – A Summary of the New Thought by 1921, John Lee's 'Management' – Summary.

THE swift and dramatic course of industrial events which accompanied the First World War and its aftermath had a profound effect in hastening the spread of new thinking on industrial control which, we have seen, had its foundations before 1914. Labour circles came to challenge both the principle of private industrial ownership with their demand for nationalization, and employers' rights of management within factories. In the first place, the development of the shop stewards' movement during the war lent substance to the demand for workers' control; the authority of some employers was fast being challenged in real terms.[1] While the notion of 'reconstruction' also found a place in the writings of a few employers, it had for labour implications which were far more revolutionary and which held distinct moral connotations.[2] Secondly, the experiments of the Health of Munition Workers Committee and propaganda from the Munitions Ministry's Welfare Department under Seebohm Rowntree pointed out the need for new techniques and working conditions in industry.[3] Thirdly, these developments were reinforced by the nebulous yet powerful sense of a 'comradeship of the trenches' which lent itself as a censure of older and harsher methods of managing labour.[4]

In 1916 the independent Garton Foundation recommended the establishment of joint employer-worker committees in order to give labour a 'voice in matters directly concerning its special interests, such as rates of pay and conditions of employment'.[5] A year later the Whitley Committee set up by the Government put forward essentially the same proposals in its interim report.[6] This report had shortly been preceded by two meetings between a group of leading employers and trade unionists, held at Penscot House on the initiative of the Quaker brothers Seebohm and Arnold Rowntree. These meetings also formulated similar recommendations.[7] Some industrialists at this time, Lord Sydenham among them, feared an absolute overthrow of power in their factories. Even Seebohm Rowntree was apprehensive of 'the demand of the extremists for a complete recasting of the industrial system'.[8] Whitleyism, the officially sponsored compromise, on paper suggested significant modifications to prevailing systems of industrial control. However, it by no means presented an extreme solution, and was in fact justly summed up by the then Minister of Labour: 'Such a plan is typically British. It does not make for revolution.'[9]

These years saw an expanding, new body of thinking on industrial administration distinguished by a self-emphasized contrast with older, more laissez-faire concepts. It carried the work of earlier pioneers still further, and dealt more explicitly with novel ethical claims and techniques. This new thought showed more awareness of the growing differentiation between legal ownership and specialized management. The very speed with which new concepts were developed in this short period indicates the role played by the pressure of immediate events over and above the underlying, longer-term trend towards industrial bureaucratization. It is difficult to separate out writings concerned primarily with management from the wider reactions of a property-owning industrial group now set sharply on the defensive. We shall in this chapter attempt first to review the more general reactions of employer spokesmen and then, second, to trace the emergence up to about 1921 of a more specifically 'management' thought.

THE REACTIONS OF EMPLOYERS

Towards the close of the war, a number of prominent employers advocated a new start in industrial aims and methods, in the hope that this would re-create a greater unity in British industry. Apart from the sources we shall refer to directly, the opinions of these men can be found in proceedings such as those of the 'Industrial Reconstruction Council' and of the 'National Alliance of Employers and Employed' which published the journal *Industrial Unity*. In broad terms, these employers claimed three things. First, a willingness to acknowledge a wider public responsibility in the form of service to the community. Second, to renounce autocratic methods of managing employees. Third, to treat labour on the basis of human rather than commodity market criteria.

(1) *Service*

The Quaker employers at their 1918 Conference were among the first to propose that business should adopt an ethic of service as a means to better industrial relations. They advocated that the postulate of laissez-faire economics, whereby labour and capital both attempted to maximize their rewards, should be superseded by a philosophy of restraint. This would allow both parties to shift their attention towards co-operation for the benefit of the whole community.[10] Other industrialists, among them W. L. Hichens (chairman of Cammell, Laird's), Lord Leverhulme, and Seebohm Rowntree, repeated the claim that they now regarded industry as a 'national service'. The same group of employers with a few others simultaneously recommended various schemes of profit-limitation, with any surplus to be divided among the parties to production. These renunciations of profit were generally expressed in moral terms.[11]

It was not a great step further for these employers to claim that they were in fact acting not so much for their own interests but rather as 'trustees' of the nation's productive resources. Sir Benjamin Browne, for instance, expressed this point of view in 1916:

'Position, influence, money and property are not given to us for our own pleasure and profit; they are talents to be used for the glory of God and the help of our fellow-men.'[12]

Business as a trust or profession implied that the right to industrial authority was now being claimed on the basis of effectiveness and capacity in the administrative function, as Browne himself recognized in the same paper. Indeed, from the employers' point of view any notion of trusteeship had to embrace administrative expertise otherwise there would be little reason why the State should not fulfil this role, which was precisely the argument of Socialist writers. Seebohm Rowntree was another who constantly urged fellow employers to use newly available techniques in order that increased efficiency should enable firms to afford the minimum material benefits to labour which he felt were necessary for industrial peace and human dignity.[13] The notion of trusteeship in turn implied that recruitment to positions of industrial control should be based on merit rather than on inheritance; this opened the door to distinctly managerial claims to industrial authority.

(2) Control

These somewhat hasty apologies for industrial authority suggest by and large correctly that British employers were determined to resist the principle of workers' control. Nevertheless, some employers treated the idea of 'joint' control, or a *share* in administration, with greater respect. Up to about 1920 these particular employers paid considerable lip-service to 'industrial democracy'. For Whitleyism at this time still retained the force of a new idea, and it took time for failings in its practical operation to become apparent. Moreover, and probably most important of all, the immediate post-war boom continued to afford considerable bargaining power to labour.

Thus during these few years around the close of the war, it is possible to find even Leverhulme (formerly Sir William Lever), otherwise well-known as an industrial autocrat, writing in favour of 'democratic' management.[14] He was joined by several others who advocated that labour be accorded an increased share in the process of factory management.[15] These spokesmen believed this was a necessary basis for better 'understanding', given the prevailing industrial conditions. Quaker employers, urged on by the Society of Friends, accepted the principle of democratic industrial relationships with something approaching genuine enthusiasm. Works councils were established in many of their factories, and where these had previously existed merely as 'social committees' they were now extended to cover matters of material substance such as remuneration. At their 1918 Conference these employers stated their acceptance of an advanced form of industrial democracy:

'It is fully realized that experience on Works Councils may and should train the members for greater participation in the control of

the business, and enable them ultimately to take part in the commercial and financial administration.'[16]

However, this potentially explosive question of control was
treated with caution even by so-called 'enlightened' employers.
In practice, it was still rare that workers were granted one of
the first necessary steps towards a share in control, namely some
voice in the selection of foremen, their immediate superordi-
nates. Two notable exceptions were at Hans Renold's and
Rowntree's.[17] In fact we shall notice how, over time, the more
that management thought laid emphasis on specialized
administrative expertise, the more any notion of sharing in
control took the form of merely communicating information
down to employees rather than allowing for any substantial
joint decision-making. This broad shift in emphasis away from
the ethical and legitimatory principle of 'democracy', and
towards an overriding concern with the minimum requirements
of administrative expertise (a technical principle), will be seen
more clearly once we have reviewed the development of
management thought during the inter-war years.

Even before 1920, it was becoming obvious that some
employers had only dealt with the idea of shared control as a
device to buy time. For instance, as early as 1918 Hichens had
confided to his shareholders that 'the talk of the democratization of industry was very largely overdone nowadays'. In a
lecture of the same year, he severely qualified his earlier views
by stating that the idea of workers sharing in management was
unsound. Instead of this, he urged employers to pay greater
attention to service, to their code of industrial morality, and
to a spirit of unselfishness. He thought that these sentiments,
rather than arguments of 'pure-reason' would lead to industrial
peace.[18] The Federation of British Industries, while admitting
in 1919 that workers had genuine grievances, listed the technical
disadvantages of any encroachment on managerial functions.
It concluded that commercial management should be staffed
by those 'possessing the requisite qualifications', and that it
could not be subject to any control by manual workers.[19]
Employers' associations had taken stands against Whitleyism
as early as 1917 which differed only in the degree of their hostility. The coal-owners in 1919 reacted violently against those
who sought to impose shared control upon them.[20] The great
majority of employer spokesmen vehemently criticized schemes

for appointing workman directors such as that established by
John Dawson's of Newcastle-on-Tyne.[21] At another level of
argument, nationalization newly embodied in the Labour
Party's 'clause four' also provoked strong reactions from employers.[22] In short, Whitleyism might lead to idealistic professions of a new and joint spirit of service in industry,[23] but for
all save the most exceptional employers it was not going to
mean any reduction in their authority.

(3) Human needs of labour

If prevailing demands for a better industrial order were not
going to be allowed expression in terms of any revolution in
control, then an alternative outlet for them which carried much
less risk to authority lay in the granting of improved conditions
of employment. This alternative was in fact adopted with more
apparent enthusiasm by leading employer spokesmen. Indeed,
a reaction against the older laissez-faire attempt to treat labour
as but another commodity was now quite in keeping with the
results of experiments into fatigue and monotony, with governmental opinion, and with the aspirations expressed in the
Treaty of Versailles.[24] Pre-war attitudes and methods were the
bane of Capital's social legitimation, and more thoughtful
employers were now keen to disassociate themselves from these.
We have seen how welfare provisions, and superior conditions
of work had been introduced by a few pioneers before 1914.
The wartime investigations of the Health of Munition Workers
Committee had meanwhile added the weight of evidence to
the view summarized by a Ministry of Reconstruction pamphlet
that 'the good employer profits by his "goodness" '.[25] Thus it
appeared that the provision of adequate working conditions
for labour would be a main factor in quietening unrest and
increasing productivity. The group of progressive employers –
Hichens, Leverhulme and Rowntree again prominent among
them – strongly advocated minimum wage levels, shorter
working hours, improved security of tenure, and similar proposals.

While these spokesmen were of the view that some industrial
unrest could be met by an adequate satisfaction of workers'
'primary' material needs, a few of them went further and began
to give some attention to the question of 'secondary' social needs
as these might be satisfied by new ways of managerial leadership.

D

Thus the 'new humanity' towards labour came to include a consideration of social psychological factors in factory relationships, a field that has continued to interest writers to the present day. We shall consider these conceptual developments shortly in assessing 'management' writing during this same period. It is enough here to mention that this growing attention to leadership had two aspects. In the first place, it was part of the general philosophy of a new start in industrial practice – a contrast and reaction to the petty tyranny of foremen and managers popularly associated with the pre-war period. Secondly, it rapidly took on a more positive aspect, and came to be recognized as a new motivational approach moving in line with the recommendations of that fast-developing subject, psychology.

In general, this new concept of leadership aimed at restoring that 'personal touch' which growing industrial scale had threatened, and it is not altogether surprising to find Quaker employers among the first to take the idea up. In 1918 they recommended a 'careful choice of overlookers and managers, who should be able both to lead and inspire'. Seebohm Rowntree had urged much the same to an audience of employers and welfare supervisors in October 1917. Administration in Quaker factories had always attempted to follow the ethical precept of 'the kindly spirit'. At the close of the First World War, other employers were beginning to recommend much the same methods, recognising them to be technically, as well as morally, valuable.[26]

THE EMERGENCE OF MANAGEMENT THOUGHT

With the onset of slump and widespread unemployment in 1920, and with the associated decline in the power behind labour demands, British industrialists could emerge from the defensive. Although there was a new heightening of unrest again in the mid-1920s, unemployment remained the major long-term social problem. The stand against joint control on the part of the coal-owners in 1919 was reinforced by that of the engineering employers in 1922, and these encouraged other industrialists to stiffen against trade union demands. Thus at the national level, the number of Joint Industrial Councils in operation fell from 73 in 1921 to only 47 by 1926, and this

development was paralleled by the breakdown of many works
committees. That the initiative for breakdown generally came
from the employers' side is strongly suggested by the fact that
in the first place the majority of requests for the establishment
of works committees had come from workers and not from
employers.[27] In other words, the release of pressures on
employers gave them a choice between continuing the 'new
spirit' and the search for new administrative methods, or
reverting back to older ways. Urwick and Brech have indicated
how all but a few chose the last alternative.[28] In any case, apart
from the few more progressive spokesmen, British employers
had probably never forsworn their former opinions. For instance,
back in 1917 Sir Robert Hadfield had complained bitterly
against the attempts of other employers to boycott and injure
firms which granted improved conditions to labour.[29] The
reaction which ensued by 1921 was quite startling. One indicator
of its extent was the fall in membership of the Welfare Workers'
Institute from around 700 in 1919 to only around 250 in 1921.[30]

After about 1921 it is therefore relatively easy to distinguish
what may be called a 'management movement', the writings
and speeches of which can be taken as comprising 'management
thought' proper. This movement consisted of the intellectual
spokesmen who continued the new thinking of the Reconstruction period, and who sought to combine the growing fund of
management techniques with some legitimation for their use
by industrial administrators. Although the management movement emphasized how these administrators were coming to
form a new property-less group exercising an increasingly
distinct industrial function, and although it identified with this
group, its membership did not necessarily exclude men from
owning families. Indeed, some of the latter, such as Seebohm
Rowntree and C. G. Renold, played a leading part in the
management movement's activities.

We now pause in our historical narrative, in order to pick up
some threads of the new management thought as it emerged
up to around 1921.

(1) *Management a distinct profession*
An early distinguishing mark of management thought was the
recognition of a separate managerial function in industry, and
even more the realization that the perceived interests of

managers might diverge from those of ownership. This divergence immediately raised a question of responsibility and
legitimation of authority.

The divorce from ownership had attracted the attention of
British commentators from about 1916 onwards. In his prophetic *The Works Manager To-day*, which is also noteworthy
because of the author's political background, Sidney Webb was
by 1917 quite clear that managers formed a distinct occupational
group:

'In my opinion, the profession of the manager, under whatever
designation, is destined, with the ever-increasing complication of
man's enterprises, to develop a steadily increasing technique and
a more and more specialised vocational training of its own.'[31]

The Institute of Industrial Administration was founded in
April 1920 as the central organization of the newly conscious
management movement, and several contributors to its journal
(among other writers) began to stress that managers were the
new 'third party' in industry.[32] In fact, some interesting evidence
to the 1919 Coal Industry Commission had shown how conflict
could frequently arise between technically qualified management and legal ownership.[33]

Alongside the idea of business as a 'trust' which some employers were putting forward at the time, the managerial
function was coming to be accorded a label of 'professionalism'.
On the one hand, Webb was probably using the term in its
narrower sense when he referred to 'the quite distinct profession
of organising men', and Casson likewise used it in antithesis
to the older type of business amateurism. Yet, on the other
hand, by 1919 Deeley, who was one of the first management
lecturers at the Manchester Technical College and formerly a
manager at Hans Renold's, wrote of the 'professional' manager
inspiring his colleagues to undertake 'such schemes of social
well-being as are not unworthy of being compared with those of
the Church', over and above their pursuit of production.
Seebohm Rowntree felt that 'the way to the Promised Land'
lay with 'the public-spirited managers and over-lookers, who,
so to speak, have to hold the scale between the rights and interests
of labour and those of capital'. Elbourne similarly put forward
the claim that managers held the 'balance of interests' in
industry, and others repeated the same idea. In other words,
there soon developed a professional claim of the wider kind

for management, involving the concept of impartiality in the pursuit of a public or social responsibility.[34]

Apart from these ethical legitimations, professionalism also derived support from the development of a body of specialized knowledge and techniques which in fact accompanied the recognition of management's distinctive nature. Although Hilton had in 1917 complained that the work of managers was poorly recognized and ill-paid, Sidney Webb for one, fully appreciated the role they were to perform. 'Under any social order, from now to Utopia,' he stated, 'management is indispensable and all-enduring.'[35]

(2) Management expertise and industrial control

Even before 1914, one or two British textbooks on management techniques had appeared, and some of these had contained sections on organization. By the war period, the work of Taylor, Emerson and others was beginning to have an impact among British thinkers.[36] The British school of industrial psychology, which derived largely from the impetus of wartime experiments, began by 1920 to supplement the limitations of the 'engineering' approach followed by many American consultants. Writers such as Cadbury, Casson, Elbourne, Renold, and Webb pointed out that a use of this growing knowledge held great potential for the increase of industrial efficiency.[37] One of the most remarkable summaries of newly available management techniques was the Ministry of Reconstruction's *Scientific Business Management*, published in 1919. This gave a full list of welfare and efficiency techniques, and it strongly urged employers to adopt them.[38] In 1920, H. T. Wright published a work on organization as a guide for firms wishing to adapt themselves to scientific management methods, including the functional division of tasks. This book also treated welfare as a necessary and remunerative managerial responsibility.[39]

These early writings on techniques and organization contained a number of interesting implications. Firstly, several authors believed that a serious study of management could help solve what Casson called the 'main problem' in industry; namely, 'how to prevent industrial warfare – how to establish a right relationship between workers, managers, and owners'. Seebohm Rowntree viewed efficiency as essential to achieve the minimum standards of remuneration necessary to remove material causes for worker dissatisfaction. Cadbury urged labour not to oppose the new management methods but instead to see that it received 'a fair share of the gains'. John Lee later admitted that 'attention has been directed to this science (of industrial administration) largely by evidence of industrial unrest'.[40]

Secondly, however, even those who had been relatively keen supporters of 'industrial democracy' were by the early 1920s coming to the opinion that after a point the devolution of authority on to workers could prejudice the attainment of full efficiency. C. G. Renold, whose firm in fact continued to maintain an active system of formal consultation with shop stewards, provides an instance of this shift in opinion. He also argued that effective managerial organization – rules and procedures – must supersede haphazard autocratic control before joint action with employees was possible.[41] F. W. Taylor himself appears to have conceived of a similar point when he claimed that scientific management 'substitutes joint obedience to fact and laws for obedience to personal authority. No such democracy has ever existed in industries before'.[42] x

The real implication behind all these arguments was that a management based on expertise would in fact be in the legitimate and most effective position to define just what the industrial situation required. It is therefore not surprising to find that eventually most management writers joined in the reaction against the idea of joint manager-worker decision making, particularly once labour pressures for that idea became less intense. This rejection of effective joint control was, as with employer spokesmen generally, excused in terms of the technical prerequisites for efficient industrial performance. For example, Wright held that 'It must be recognized that the work-bench is not a suitable training ground for management'. He along with other writers insisted that managerial posts required appropriate qualities and qualifications although they were still hoping, in this period, that workers could be given some chance of promotion after suitable company training.[43]

(3) *The management of labour – the beginnings of 'human relations'** The Reconstruction period saw the beginnings of one of the most important and paradoxical features about the analysis of

* The meaning we attach to the term 'human relations' should become apparent as this study proceeds. At the level of managerial technique, we use it to refer to

labour relations contained in British management thought. For on the one hand, interested academics and management writers with a keen eye to prevailing social problems, sources such as Baillie, Myers, Rowntree, and the Garton Foundation, were quite aware of the numerous and complex causes of the industrial conflict then so much in evidence. These writers between them put forward a comprehensive list of causes such as fatigue, monotony, speeding-up, lack of worker autonomy on the shop floor, gross inequalities of economic reward in society, class consciousness, the disparity between the ideal of political democracy and the absence of democracy in industry.[44]

On the other hand, we shall find that management thought tended increasingly to place its main hopes for worker motivation and the resolution of conflict not on an attempt to mitigate the factors just listed, but rather on the persuasive powers of personal managerial leadership. It is probably true to say that this emphasis derived in large part from a feeling that features such as class consciousness, the absence of industrial democracy, monotony, and inequalities of reward or dispute over remuneration, were either beyond the power of individual managements to control or were part of the price that had to be paid for technical efficiency in many industries. In other words, it appeared most promising to concentrate attention on motivational techniques which managers could readily use. What is interesting is that this perspective through its own logic tended to restrict the analysis of industrial conflict to causes that were 'controllable' in managerial terms. In short, it encouraged a

---

attempts at raising levels of employee performance and co-operation with managerial objectives by means of improving the quality of managers' and supervisors' personal interaction with subordinates, by improvements in communication, and through other appropriate modifications of 'informal' organization. At the level of the associated philosophy, human relations stresses the desirability of co-operative and solidary relationships, the importance of group activities, non-material rewards, and either a participative or manipulative style of managerial leadership. At an extreme, human relations analyses the enterprise as a closed system, minimizes the relevance of conflict as a rational course of action, and virtually ignores the role of occupational interest groups such as trade unions.

The description 'human relations school' is often applied to the writings of Elton Mayo and his associates at the Harvard Business School. We indicate eventually that Mayoism represented the extreme and most cogent exposition of an approach contained in much earlier writings.

We do not therefore employ the term 'human relations' as it is sometimes used, to mean 'the day-to-day relations of managers and employees at all levels'. (John Marsh, *People at Work*, London: Industrial Welfare Society 1957, p. 12.)

solidary view of the enterprise, a concentration on workers' social rewards, an emphasis on leadership style, and other features commonly associated with 'human relations'.

We shall suggest later on that this human relations viewpoint by minimizing more deep-seated causes of conflict accorded well with the professional claims of the new management movement, which in themselves implied that managers possessed no intrinsic conflicts of interest with labour. Indeed, it is also probable that the essentially legitimatory claim of professionalism, which involved a notion of impartial expertise, itself encouraged the shift over time in management thought towards human relations. Although even in the Reconstruction period reference was made to psychology as a support for the new views on leadership, it will become evident how non-scientific and question-begging notions of 'fairness' and the like were applied at the same time to assume away complex economic and social issues. From a modern sociological standpoint it becomes clear that these developments allowed important values and conceptual limitations to enter the analysis of industrial relationships in management thought.

In the years immediately after the First World War propositions of a human relations nature were just beginning to be advanced. In many cases they derived initially from the notion of the 'personal touch' which itself looked back to the days of small workshops which had allowed close and 'natural' interaction between employers and workers. In the first place, writers agreed that management had to follow principles of 'fairness' and 'justice' in its dealings with labour, particularly by doing its utmost to provide adequate remuneration and working conditions.[45] Having accepted these provisos, it is not surprising that the repeated talk of a new 'joint purpose' in industry should have led management thinkers to expect that enlightened personal leadership on the part of managers would then go far to eliminating industrial conflict altogether. Seebohm Rowntree, for instance, thought that conflict constituted 'a serious reflection on the ability of the employers to do their job efficiently'. He looked to managers and welfare supervisors, 'to introduce the new outlook, the new spirit, and the new understanding which will ultimately make serious strife impossible between capital and labour'.[46]

Wright thought that a programme of education should be

undertaken to convince both capital and labour that their interests were 'identical', while it was also suggested that once industrial control was vested in managers, themselves employees, the old bases for conflict in industry no longer applied. At least one writer argued that conflict over wages was itself merely a legacy of pre-war laissez-faire competition.[47]

One or two writers pointed to military experience during the was as providing a model for managerial leadership.[48] In addition the harmony prevailing at factories under Quaker management, together with the development of empirically-based psychology, lent further support to the view that improved personal interaction could provide a solution to labour troubles. Thus the welfare supervisor who put forward the following opinion in 1920 was expressing the view held by many members of the management movement: 'A great deal of the industrial unrest is due to the *attitude* with which masters and management approach men . . . the problem is mainly *psychological*' (author's italics).[49]

Occasionally a writer became over-enthusiastic for the potentialities of psychology and plunged into what was both offensive and ridiculous: 'The wonderful results obtained with the deaf, blind and dumb, with defective or criminal material is such as to remove the despondency of those who consider labour difficulties.'[50]

Supervisors were consequently urged to concentrate on the human leadership aspects of their tasks, and Taylor's principle of functional foremanship appeared to make possible this task specialization.[51] It was already being said by 1920 that foremen should devote most of their attention to *personal* relationships, and in particular should understand worker psychology. Their leadership was thus to be employee- and group-centred: phrases such as 'team work', 'group mind' and the 'psychology of crowds' were already in currency among management writers by the beginning of the 1920s.[52] In fact their use indicates that at least some management thinkers were coming at that time to regard worker action in social terms rather than following the individualistic explanations usually associated with Taylorism and early industrial psychology. Moreover, one may find already even the implication that managers should have as much, or even more regard for workers' sentiment than for their manifest rationalizations. For example, in 1917 Seebohm

Rowntree had said that 'If they (workers) find one who can lead and inspire them they will follow him anywhere'. And in an article of the same year he elaborated on this view:

' . . . we must create among the workers an enthusiasm and an esprit de corps. . . . A thousand "hands" are simply a thousand human beings, each with his own personality, his own peculiar temperament. . . . Employers must give far more thought to the whole question of personal relationships. . . . They must now learn to concentrate on practical psychology (and) sympathetic leadership.'[53]

This argument was frequently repeated. 'Treat them as people, that is the keynote of good management. Why do workers strike? Is it not, in most cases, to prove that they are people and not things?' asked Casson.[54] As a corollary it was also argued that managers and foremen would now have to be carefully selected for their abilities to lead – they would have to possess 'character' and 'personality'.[55] Once this view was added to an insistence on the complex managerial techniques required by large-scale industry, it inevitably supported the conclusion that only a restricted range of recruits was suitable for managerial positions. Also by implicitly emphasizing differences in personal quality between managers and workers, this view added point to the claim that for technical reasons workers could not be allowed any extensive share in decision-making. And in this way an interesting circular argument was reached. For it was apparent that the new emphasis on securing industrial co-operation via the influence of personal leadership was to some extent a compensation for the rejection of industrial democracy as the means to this co-operation. There was contained in all this an inextricable mixture of technical and legitimatory purposes: concern for optimum performance on the one hand, and concern to expound the superior expertise and morality of the new managers in dealing with workers, on the other hand.

Although this growing solidary emphasis on team work and esprit de corps within factories caused management thinkers to regret the centralization of collective bargaining following the First World War, they did not as a rule admit of any design to win workers' allegiance away from their own chosen representatives. The fact that in this sense they still regarded enterprises analytically as open systems placed their policies in sharp contrast to what we shall see were later versions of human relations. Indeed, some writers at this time argued that worker representation at plant level should be strengthened in order to allow as full a contribution from labour as was possible within the technical constraints imposed upon shared control. For instance, factory practice at Rowntree's and Hans Renold indicated considerable willingness to maintain discussions of a 'constitutional' kind.[56] For we have in any case seen that the enlightenment professed by the management movement after the war included some sympathy with trade union aspirations for higher standards of remuneration and similar industrial reforms. Moreover, the militancy and strength of the labour movement up to the early 1920s would have made any idea of subverting unions and worker representatives extremely long-term and somewhat academic. In the event a claim to support labour aspirations was to remain with management thought through much of the 1920s. It was consistent with the management movement's affirmation of greater impartiality, rationality, and moderation as compared with pre-war 'laissez-faire' capitalism.

A SUMMARY OF THE NEW THOUGHT BY 1921 –
JOHN LEE'S 'MANAGEMENT'

John Lee was Director of the London Telegraph and Telephone Centre, and he remained a prominent figure in the British management movement until his death in 1928. A remarkable, yet long-neglected work of his – *Management: a Study of Industrial Organisation* – was published in 1921.[57] This contains all the main strands of the new management thought, and is probably the best available review of the development it had reached at the close of the post-1918 Reconstruction period. We shall outline the main arguments contained in this work, providing illustrative quotation where possible.

Firstly, Lee was quite clear that industrial managers had emerged as a distinct occupational group whose 'scientific' approach was superior to the arbitrary rule of ownership:

'They are an expert professional class, and the new science of industrial management is coming to recognize them as that factor in industry which is calling for study and consideration. This evolution of a separate management . . . brings experience and special training and leadership to bear on the work of management in a way which was never possible to the old-fashioned owner who "could do what he liked with his own".'

Promotion and selection to managerial levels should be restricted to those suitable for the new scientific nature of administrative tasks; Lee recognized that this implied considerable recruitment from outside a firm rather than from its own lower employees. In fact he argued that the universities should take up the task of instructing management recruits both in 'the synthesis of sciences' that comprised management knowledge and in suitable ethics to safeguard the proper use of managerial authority. These ideas precede the recent establishment of university business schools by 40 years. Lee's aim, in short, was: 'a trained body of administrators, proud of their calling as professional men'. . . themselves reasonably paid but not personally benefiting in the profits'.

Managers should be trained in a number of subjects ranging from accountancy to psychology. Among these Taylor's scientific management was of value, but Lee recognized that it required qualification in the light of industrial psychology. As he concluded, 'The truth is that human nature is too complex for the crude Scientific Management'. Moreover, he emphasized that the principles suggested by Taylor should be applied to managerial organization as well. For instance, a functional model of organization at all levels would help to create a sense of unity throughout the enterprise for two main reasons. First, it would motivate subordinates to a sense of common purpose by granting them more initiative. Second, it would place authority on to a basis of collective consensus rather than arbitrary autocracy. This type of managerial operation should thus produce 'an actual and living organism in which each living unit is compelled, and is glad to be compelled, to offer his best . . . a collective expression of ideals or of opinions'. It is interesting to notice how these concepts anticipate Mary Parker Follett's 'law of the situation' and 'collective creativeness', and how in these passages Lee foreshadows Burns and Stalker's recent 'organismic' model of managerial organization. Lee was not specific as to how this functional principle was to be worked out in detail; it was 'a matter of spirit rather than machinery'. Yet nevertheless he felt that it was universally applicable – 'there are no industries, large or small, to which the principle does not apply'.

In Lee's book one can find very clearly illustrated the reasoning we have noted elsewhere whereby a rejection of shared control on technical grounds was compensated for by a claim to accept the new goal of service, and by the growth of interest in a human relations approach to motivation. First, he argued that the need for managers to possess technical expertise not only required restricted recruitment, but also rendered 'democracy' a false analogy for industry:

'The control of an industry calls for immediate pragmatic results, dependent upon skilled purchase, skilled sale, economic organization, and other actual factors which differ in immediacy from the more or less doctrinaire theories of so-called politics.'

Second, Lee would instead urge management to remain impartial as between different interests and to follow an ideal of service, which in fact left the authority to decide policy in managers' own hands. In that case, 'Whitleyism would include a real consideration of the interests of all, and therein lies its value and not in a transference of authority'.

Third, if workers were not to be granted the right to elect their own managers, or co-managers, then their co-operation would have to be induced by other means. Co-operation would in fact now have mainly to depend on the powers of personal persuasion possessed by the 'professional' managers: '. . . the new administrator will not be chosen by the workers. He will be chosen for his professional value, a professional value in which personality is a very important factor, and one which will attract intelligent obedience.'

Hence in Lee's analysis of labour relations there is a strong emphasis on a form of industrial control which in fact is manipulative under a participative guise. Solidary and group conceptions of factory relationships are evident. Apart from being technical motivational alternatives to shared control, these views were also of course in keeping with the more legitimatory assumptions of managerial impartiality and superior personal qualities. Lee's formulations are for 1921 so prophetic of much more recent management thought that they deserve illustration. He begins with the premise that: 'Autocracy is no longer possible either in politics or in industry. . . . It seems clear that the group mind will take the place of the old discipline.' This means that: 'We are probing a new realm of human relationship in effort, which is to take the place of the old relationship of subordination and yet is to include veritable and intelligent subordination, but subordination which will include active and intelligent partaking in the effort towards ultimate efficiency.'

Lee develops the concept of a firm's 'morale', and views the supervisor's role as 'the leader, the guide, the farther-seer'. More explicitly, the new type of manager 'will realize that his control must be rather radiation than domination. He must gather from those over whom he is placed so that his will becomes their corporate will. This will be true industrial democracy.' When, further on in this study, we find almost identical ideas dominating British management thought thirty years later (and still sheltering under claims of 'democracy'), it will become clear that human relations represents one of the most fundamental continuities in that system of ideas.

In his book, Lee makes frequent reference to psychology, particularly that of James, Jung, and McDougall. This is intended to give some quasi-scientific basis for his ideas, but the way in which Lee relies upon this support prejudices a balanced analysis of industrial relationships. For instance, while Lee does discuss wage systems and Whitley Councils, his analysis of labour relations is largely couched in inter-personal terms. His book in fact provides an example of the first stages of the trend we discussed on page 55, whereby an enthusiasm for human relations tends to detract from what present-day sociology would consider an objective and full appreciation of the causes for industrial conflict. It would not, however, be correct to suggest that this trend was far advanced in this period; in fact during the 1920s it is still possible to find relatively comprehensive analyses of conflict in management writings. Moreover, although Lee argues for a kind of company unionism functioning through local factory committees, he remains in step with management thought of his time by not going so far as to claim that a human relations type of management would be able to supplant workers' need for trade union representation.

The *logic* of Lee's book, if taken far enough, would nonetheless imply a view of factories as closed systems. It rests on the desire to enhance managerial control by providing more areas in which it could exercise persuasive leadership to the exclusion of rival interests. For this reason Lee again anticipates subsequent developments in arguing that much of the work performed (and influence held) by welfare supervisors should be incorporated into labour management.

SUMMARY

British management thought emerged in times of social and industrial turbulence. At this early stage, the formative management movement was not always clearly distinguishable from employer spokesmen.

The immediate context of management thought consisted of political and technical developments which presented diametrically opposed implications for industrial authority. Politically, those in control of industry were faced with a severe unrest which labour leaders were channelling into a direct attack on the principle of private ownership and even of management authority itself. A legitimatory problem was therefore posed. At the same time, the practical value of a new body of administrative knowledge deriving from scientific management, industrial psychology and industrial welfare, was becoming recognized by informed employers and managers. A major technical development was under way.

Thus, politically, there was considerable pressure to grant some recognition to the aspirations of a militant labour movement. Such recognition would have to include some acknowledgement of more democratic systems of industrial control. However, the nature of the new management techniques not only militated against any direct industrial democracy, but in fact implied the assumption of even more control by managers over matters previously left to the 'rule of thumb' of the craft worker.

As an additional factor in the situation, not only was management gaining recognition as a distinct and useful function, but also *managers* (or at least their spokesmen) were beginning to recognize themselves as a new and separate power group – a 'third party' – in large-scale industry. There can be little doubt that the alacrity with which management spokesmen developed the idea of separation from ownership had much to do with labour challenges to the old industrial order.

In short, British management thought emerged amid a

mixture of circumstances which possessed important technical and legitimatory implications for management. It is not surprising that, given this background, legitimatory arguments occupied an important proportion of early management thought.

This legitimatory content was distinguished by various combinations of values, half-truths, and factual evidence. For example, management expertise could be discussed relatively objectively as a technical basis for a general improvement in national economic prosperity. At the same time, it could, and did, serve as a major point of justification for separate and unimpeded managerial control in industry. When it was employed in this way, writers such as Lee greatly exaggerated the amount of 'science' underlying that expertise. It is also possible to appreciate the primarily legitimatory purposes behind such notions as 'service' and a 'professional' ethic.

The functions performed by the human relations conceptions developed in this period are somewhat more difficult to distinguish. In the first place, there was some indirect evidence that technical advantages, including a lesser resistance to new methods and lower unrest, had accrued in factories such as those run by Quakers where managerial control was characterized by a greater employee-centredness. Further, psychologists were starting to suggest that a less autocratic and more sympathetic type of personal leadership was generally more effective. Thus there can be little question that management thinkers in this period took human relations methods to be supported by some hard evidence and experience. But in the second place, the early examples of human relations also formed part of a legitimatory and value-inspired claim to abide by a 'new humanity' in the treatment of industrial labour. This claim suggested that managers were prepared to institute moral reforms in industry, and to discard pre-war conditions. Moreover, notions such as 'esprit de corps', 'team work', and 'corporate will', signified the extension of a hand of fellowship to labour, particularly as a compensation of the managerial rejection of shared control. These ideas were backed up by claims to provide higher minimum working conditions, and to pursue goals of impartiality and public service. The management movement in these ways claimed that it could work in sympathy, common interest, and harmony with labour. Its underlying legitimation was a technical and moral superiority over an older system of direct ownership control which, it suggested, had caused so much industrial unrest. Human relations implied a solidary conception of the enterprise, with emphasis placed on rewarding social needs and on an approach to productivity through a personal motivation of employees. It suggested that conflict was open to control by appropriate managerial leadership. Its slogan of team work in fact begged both the causes of much conflict and legitimate dispute over the structure of industrial authority. These patterns of thought were encouraging for the management movement, and presumably close to its heart. However, so long as prevailing industrial conditions forced it to pay heed to militant labour demands, it was also induced to take some account analytically of the contractual aspects of industry, the role played by material rewards, and the constitutional approach to industrial government. And in this way a conceptual tension was set up within British management thought, which we shall see only relaxed later on when its environment changed.

NOTES

1. B. Pribicevic, *The Shop Stewards' Movement and Workers' Control 1910-22*, Oxford: Blackwell 1959; M. Bloomfield, *The New Labour Movement in Great Britain*, London: Fisher Unwin 1920, pp. 76-77.

2. Cf., R. H. Tawney, *The Acquisitive Society*, London: Bell 1921, *passim*.

3. *Industrial Fatigue Research Board, 1st Annual Report*, London: H.M.S.O. 1920; A. Briggs, *Social Thought and Social Action*, London: Longmans 1961, chapter V.

4. W. L. Hichens, *Some Problems of Modern Industry*, London: Nisbet 1919, p. 61; M. Bloomfield, *op. cit.*, p. viii; E. H. Phelps-Brown, *The Growth of British Industrial Relations*, London: Macmillan 1959, pp. 347-348.

5. The Garton Foundation, *Memorandum on the Industrial Situation after the War*, London July 1916, reprinted in ed. D. Bloomfield, *Problems of Labor*, London: Pitman 1920, p. 14.

6. *Interim Report on Joint Standing Industrial Councils*, Cmd. 8606, London: H.M.S.O. March 1917.

7. A. Bullock, *The Life and Times of Ernest Bevin*, London: Heinemann 1960, vol. I, pp. 68-71; cf., similar recommendations also reached by the British Association, reproduced in ed. A. W. Kirkaldy, *British Labour 1914-1921*, London: Pitman 1921, esp. pp. 184-185.

E

8. Lord Sydenham, preface to H. Chellew, *Human and Industrial Efficiency*, University of London Press 1919, p. xiv; B. S. Rowntree, *Industrial Unrest: a Way Out*, London: Longmans 1922, p. 35.

9. Quoted n.d. in M. Bloomfield, *op. cit.*, p. 102; also G. J. Wardle, *Industrial Unity*, London: Industrial Reconstruction Council 1919, pp. 5-6 for a similar official view.

10. *Quakerism and Industry 1918*, ed. J. E. Hodgkin: Report of the Conference, para. 5, p. 131.

11. Ed. H. Carter, *Industrial Reconstruction*, London: Fisher Unwin 1917, essays by E. Cadbury and W. L. Hichens; W. L. Hichens, *op. cit.* 1919, pp. 49-50; *idem, The New Spirit in Industrial Relations*, London: Nisbet 1920; T. B. Johnston, *Industrial Peace, Capital, Labour and Consumer*, Bristol: Arrowsmith 1919, p. 11; Lord Leverhulme, in ed. S. J. Chapman, *Labour and Capital After the War*, London: Murray 1918, pp. 38-39; *idem, The Six-Hour Day and Other Industrial Questions*, London: Allen & Unwin 1918, p. 250; and many writings by B. S. Rowntree.

12. Sir B. C. Browne, *Selected Papers on Social and Economic Questions*, Cambridge University Press 1918, p. 265.

13. B. S. Rowntree, chapter X in ed. S. J. Chapman, *op. cit.*; *idem, The Human Needs of Labour*, London: Nelson 1918, esp. appendix G; A. Briggs, *op. cit.*, chapter IV.

14. Lord Leverhulme, *The Six-Hour Day, op. cit.*, pp. 185-191, 252.

15. Anon., 'Industrial Reconstruction – an Employer's View', *The Athenaeum*, March 1917, p. 137; articles in ed. H. Carter, *op. cit.* by E. Cadbury p. 71, W. L. Hichens p. 50, E. Benn pp. 80-82 and W. Hazell pp. 84-85; H. N. Casson, *Labour Troubles and How to Prevent Them*, London: Efficiency Magazine 1919, pp. 155-163; G. J. Wardle, *Industrial Unity, op. cit.*, p. 6; 'The head of Britain's largest rubber works', quoted by M. Bloomfield, *op. cit.*, p. 153.

16. *Quakerism and Industry 1918, op. cit.*, Report of the Conference, para. 26, p. 136. Cf., B. S. Rowntree, *op. cit.* 1922, p. 38; Joseph Rowntree, quoted in A. Briggs, *op. cit.*, p. 144; D. Chapman, 'Seebohm Rowntree', *Scientific Business*, II, 7, Nov. 1964, p. 325; Cadbury Brothers Ltd., *A Works Council in Being*, Bournville 1921.

17. C. T. Goodrich, *The Frontier of Control*, London: Bell 1920, pp. 120-121.

18. W. L. Hichens, reported in *Industrial Unity*, I, 7, Nov. 1918, p. 50; *idem, Some Problems of Modern industry, op. cit., passim*.

19. Federation of British Industries, *The Control of Industry*, London, July 1919, pp. 5, 6, 7-8.

20. M. I. Postgate, *The Whitley Reports and their Application*, London, Fabian Research Dept. 1918, p. 3; *Coal Industry Commission*, Minutes of Evidence May 1919: evidence of Lord Gainford, vol. II, p. 810; R. H. Tawney, 'Recent Thought on the Government of Industry' in *Labour and Industry*, Manchester University Press 1920, esp. p. 201.

21. G. H. Humphrey, *Workmen as Directors*, lecture of May 1919, London: Industrial Reconstruction Council 1919, p. 5; F.B.I., *op. cit.*, p. 8.

22. F.B.I., *op. cit.*, pp. 3-5; Lord Gainford, evidence to Coal Industry Commission, *op. cit.*; W. L. Hichens, *op. cit.* 1920, pp. 13-15; Lord Leverhulme, *op. cit.* 1918, pp. 42-43.

23. E.g., J. H. Whitley's speech and his audience's reactions recorded in *Making a New World*, London: Industrial Reconstruction Council 1919, pp. 6, 7.

24. *Interim Report on Joint Standing Industrial Councils*, Cmd. 8606, *op. cit.*, para. 24; Ministry of Reconstruction, *Scientific Business Management*, London: H.M.S.O. 1919, p. 1; The Home Office, *Welfare and Welfare Supervision in Factories and Workshops*, London: H.M.S.O. *1919*, esp. pp. 2-3; *Treaty of Versailles 1919*, article 427.

25. *Op. cit.*, pp. 1, 6.

26. *Quakerism and Industry 1918*, Report of the Conference, para. 37, p. 138; B. S. Rowntree, quoted in A. Briggs, *op. cit.*, esp. p. 131; Sir B. C. Browne, *op. cit.*, pp. 249-250; Sir R. Hadfield in ed. H. Carter, *op. cit.*, p. 30; C. G. Renold, quoted in M. Bloomfield, *op. cit.*, pp. 161-162. Also Bloomfield, pp. 69, 99.

27. *Industrial Relations Handbook*, London: H.M.S.O. 1961, p. 24; C. R. Borland, 'The Committee Movement in Industry', *Welfare Work*, IX, 102, June 1928, pp. 99-100; *Report on the Establishment and Progress of Joint Industrial Councils*, London: H.M.S.O. 1923.

28. L. Urwick and E. F. L. Brech, *The Making of Scientific Management*, London: Management Publications 1947, vol. II, p. 191.

29. Sir R. Hadfield in ed. H. Carter, *op. cit.*, pp. 30-31.

30. M. M. Niven, 'The Beginnings of the Institute', *Personnel Management*, XXXIX, 339, March 1957, p. 33.

31. S. Webb, *The Works Manager To-day*, London: Longmans, Green 1917, pp. 6-7.

32. See contributions to the *Journal of Industrial Administration* (J.I.A.) during 1921 by E. T. Elbourne, J. Fearn, Sir L. Macassey, and O. Sheldon. Also W. J. Deeley, *Labour Difficulties and Suggested Solutions*, London: Benn 2nd ed. 1919, p. 25; E. M. Wrong, 'Some Tendencies in Industry' in ed. B. Muscio, *Lectures on Industrial Administration*, London: Pitman 1920, pp. 40-41.

33. *Coal Industry Commission 1919*, evidence of Sir M. Delevingne, vol. II, p. 724.

34. H. N. Casson, *op. cit.*, chapter III, esp. pp. 29-30; W. J. Deeley, *op. cit.*, p. 25; S. Webb, *op. cit.*, p. 3; S. and B. Webb, Special Supplement on Professional Associations, *New Statesman*, IX, 211, 212, April 21, 28, 1917, pp. 4, 34, 35. Also contributions to the *Journal of Industrial Administration* during 1921 by E. T. Elbourne, Viscount Haldane, Sir L. Macassey, Capt. H. R. Sankey, and O. Sheldon, and to *Welfare Work* in 1920 and 1921 by W. B. Owen. B. S. Rowntree and P. J. Worsley.

35. J. Hilton in ed. H. Carter, *op. cit.*, p. 97; S. Webb, *op. cit.*, p. 157. Also Webb quoted in M. Bloomfield, *op. cit.*, pp. 94-95.

36. Urwick and Brech, *op. cit.*, vol. II, chapters VII and X.
37. E. Cadbury in ed. H. Carter, *op. cit.*, p. 72; H. N. Casson, *op. cit.*, chapters IV, VIII, IX, X; E. T. Elbourne, various contributions, particularly editorials, to the *J.I.A.*, from Jan. 1921; on Renold, cf., L. Urwick and E. F. L. Brech, *op. cit.*, vol. II, chapter XI; S. Webb, *op. cit.*, chapter XI.
38. Ministry of Reconstruction, *Scientific Business Management*, *op. cit.*, esp. p. 1.
39. H. T. Wright, *Organisation, as Applied to Industrial Problems*, London: Griffen 1920.
40. H. N. Casson, *op. cit.*, p. 20; B. S. Rowntree in *Industrial Administration*, *op. cit.*, pp. 10-11; E. Cadbury in ed. H. Carter, *op cit.*, p. 72; J. Lee, *An Introduction to Industrial Administration*, London: Pitman 1925, p. v.
41. C. G. Renold, 'Workshop Committees' in ed. A. W. Kirkaldy, *British Labour 1914-1921*, London: Pitman 1921, pp. 207-210; *idem*, quoted in M. Bloomfield, *op. cit.*, p. 163.
42. F. W. Taylor, quoted in B. Muscio, *Lectures on Industrial Psychology*, London: Routledge, 2nd ed. 1920, p. 260.
43. H. T. Wright, *op. cit.*, pp. 33, 38; *Engineering World*, 'Promotion in Workshops', 19th March 1921, reproduced in *J.I.A.*, I, 4, April 1921, p. 115; J. McKillop, 'A Specification of a Manager', *J.I.A.*, I, 9, Jan. 1922, pp. 285-286.
44. J. B. Baillie, 'Industrial Unrest: Some Causes and Remedies', in *Labour and Industry*, Manchester University Press 1920, pp. 87-93; C. S. Myers, *Mind and Work*, London University Press 1920, chapter VI; B. S. Rowntree, *Industrial Unrest: A Way Out*, London: Longmans, Green 1922. Also other works by Rowntree cited above; Garton Foundation Memorandum, 1916, reprinted in ed. D. Bloomfield, *op. cit.*, pp. 10-12.
45. E. Cadbury, and Sir A. Denny in ed. H. Carter, *op. cit.*, pp. 72 and 40-41; H. N. Casson, *op. cit.*, p. 163; Sir L. Macassey, *op. cit.*, *J.I.A.*, I, 3, March 1921, p. 73; Ministry of Reconstruction, *op. cit.*, p. 6; H. T. Wright, *op. cit.*, p. 225.
46. B. S. Rowntree, *op. cit.* 1922, p. 11; *idem*, *op. cit.*, *Welfare Work*, Jan. 1920, p. 5.
47. H. T. Wright, *op. cit.*, p. 27; J. Fearn and J. E. Powell, comments in *J.I.A.*, I, 2, Feb. 1921, pp. 53, 54.
48. W. J. Deeley, *op. cit.*, pp. 168, 179; J. H. Whitley, speech reported in *Making a New World*, *op. cit.*, p. 7.
49. W. B. Owen, 'Welfare Work Among Men', *Welfare Work*, I, 11, Nov. 1920, p. 166.
50. W. J. Deeley, *op. cit.*, p. 4.
51. *Quakerism and Industry 1918*, *op. cit.*, para. 37, p. 138; W. J. Deeley, *op. cit.*, chapter II, esp. pp. 10-11; M. Bloomfield, *op. cit.*, p. 99; J. Lee, *Management*, London: Pitman 1921, p. 44.
52. H. N. Casson, *op. cit.*, *passim*: W. J. Deeley, *op. cit.*, p. 23; E. T. Elbourne, reported in *J.I.A.*, I, 2, Feb. 1921, pp. 55-56; J. Lee *op. cit.*, pp. 16-17; Sir L. Macassey, *op. cit.*, *J.I.A.*, March 1921,'

p. 72; Ministry of Reconstruction, *op. cit.*, pp. 1-5; H. T. Wright, *op. cit.*, p. 222.

53. B. S. Rowntree, quoted in A. Briggs, *op. cit.*, p. 132; *idem*, 'Labour Unrest', a paper of October 1917, reproduced in appendix G. *The Human Needs of Labour*, *op. cit.*, pp. 164, 165, 166.

54. H. N. Casson, *op. cit.*, p. 11.

55. H. Chellew, *op. cit.*, pp. 90-91; Home Office, *op. cit.*, p. 10; B. S. Rowntree, in ed. S. J. Chapman, *op. cit.*, p. 246; H. T. Wright, *op. cit.*, p. 222.

56. C. G. Renold, *op. cit.*, in ed. A. W. Kirkaldy, *British Labour 1914-1921*, London: Pitman 1921, pp. 224-228; on Rowntree's, see A. Briggs, *op. cit.*, pp. 146-147.

57. J. Lee, *Management: A Study of Industrial Organization*, London: Pitman 1921. Main quotations are from pp. 2, 7-8, 70, 16, 32-33, 3, 8, 10, 16-17, 4, and 10 respectively.

CHAPTER 4

CONSOLIDATION
(the inter-war years)

Management Thought During the 1920s: (1) management as an expert profession; (2) the management of labour; (3) the 'science of industrial administration' and rationalization; (4) the work of the 1920s consolidated in three major publications – Management Thought During the 1930s: (1) the theory of òrganization; (2) the incorporation of Mayoism; (3) other developments in the 1930s – Summary and a Note on the Liverpool University Study of 'The New Managerial Ideology'.

BRITISH management thought had even by 1920 achieved considerable coherence in its conceptualization of industrial relationships. Indeed, it is probably true to say that management thought never again achieved the sheer speed of analytical development which it had shown during the Reconstruction era. With the possible exception of Urwick's work on formal organization theory, there was little produced by British management writing between 1920 and 1940 which did not rely heavily on earlier ideas. Overall, this period may be regarded as one in which initial advances were consolidated and systematized. We shall see that even the pioneering works of Follett and Mayo fitted easily into an already existing British framework of ideas.

A broad view of the inter-war years strongly suggests that, within the management movement, there was a shift of attention away from legitimatory problems towards more technical ones. This development becomes noticeable after the mid-1920s, though its subtle nature prohibits the setting of any precise date for its commencement. Taking the two inter-war decades as a whole, management thought became less concerned with the following: the search for democratic processes of control in factories; the granting of promotion opportunities to factory workers; the claim to espouse managerial social responsibility in terms of service to the community and a humane regard for employee interests; and the denial of profit maximization as a primary managerial goal. At the same time within British management thought a greater emphasis came to be placed on the 'scientific' search for efficiency. This focused discussion on to optimum techniques of labour management and models of organization structure. In conjunction with these shifts of emphasis, the former idea of an equal partnership with labour was slowly transformed into the conception of a relationship in which an expert management played the dominant role.

When illustrating these shifts in Britain management thought, it will be instructive to recall the environment in which they were set. To describe this at all adequately would be a lengthy process. Nevertheless, there are two important features of the inter-war period which particularly help to explain why the management movement should shift its attention away from legitimatory matters and towards technical ones. In the first place, there was some change in trade union orientations, notably after 1926. In the attempt to recoup its strength after the General Strike, the trade union movement paid increasing attention to channels of political influence (particularly with an eye to repealing the 1927 Trade Disputes Act), and to conciliatory dealings with employers' representatives. Moreover, persistent unemployment in those older 'heavy' industrial sectors, where trade union membership was primarily based, also helped to soften labour demands for the restructuring of industrial authority. In a real sense, 'direct action' against plant management tended to give way to wider institutionalized procedures, the very operation of which required at least a de facto recognition of managerial authority. Thus, one of the main pressures which had induced management intellectuals to defend the legitimacy of the occupation they represented was now easing.

Secondly, economic retrenchment during the inter-war period, which again most affected the older industries, typically led employers to reject new management techniques on the grounds of their supposedly costly administration. During the First World War the government's active interest in industrial productivity had induced it to support the introduction of better working conditions and new ways of managing labour. This active encouragement had diminished by the close of the Reconstruction era, just at the time that severe economic difficulties first arose. In these circumstances, the small band of devotees comprising the British management movement was hard pressed enough to get industrialists to see any value in their existing precepts, let alone to formulate new ones at any great rate. In other words, at the same time as there was less necessity to present a moral philosophy for the legitimation of managerial authority, there was every inducement for management thinkers to stress the practical and financial – that is, the technical – value of their ideas.

We now review the course of British management thought in this period, taking the 1920s and 1930s separately for ease of presentation.

MANAGEMENT THOUGHT DURING THE 1920S

(1) *Management as an expert profession*
For much of the 1920s management thinkers continued to feel the need to explain how an independent managerial control of industry was necessitated by increasing scale and technical complexity. Independence from ownership was justified on the basis of the technical expertise required by modern industry. An example is found in a work of 1923, which was to remain one of the most influential books of the inter-war period, when Sheldon in his *Philosophy of Management* argued that:

'. . . the science of business administration, the size of many modern concerns, and the intricate organization of business have shown the need for a marked degree of training and ability in the heads of modern concerns. Such positions cannot be left wholly to the whim of shareholders. . . . Either Capital must accept a direct burden of industrial service, or it must be content to be shouldered out of industry.'[1]

Management spokesmen also continued for a while to place the responsibility for prevailing industrial unrest on to older entrepreneurial attitudes. They went on to claim that industry under managerial control would be conducted impartially, and with an eye to productive efficiency, rather than serving merely the desires and interests of an owning class.[2]

Thus during the 1920s there was a relatively frequent exposition of management as a professional 'third factor in industry', accompanied by various assertions of its new freedom from ownership.[3] It was claimed that 'standing dispassionately free,' the manager performed the disinterested function of 'holding the balance', acting as 'arbitrator', and 'seeing fair play'.[4] This managerial aspiration to play honest broker clearly implied that 'it is no longer to be identified merely with Capital interests', as the Institute of Industrial Administration stated in 1922.[5] It is important to notice how these assertions of a trustee role also implied that managers themselves could safely and legitimately be left to define the interests of other groups concerned with industry, in such terms as to reconcile these with the 'common' interest in maintaining the vigour of the enterprise. It is not hard to discern the close relationship between this derivation of professionalism and the concept of a 'law of the situation' which Follett began to put forward in Britain after the mid-1920s. The notion of professionalism carried strong implications for the way in which management thought should analyse industrial conflict, suggesting as it did the absence under managerial control of necessary divergences in real interests. Developing such views, several writers came during this period to insist that managers were not just an independent factor, but in reality the 'dominating' one in industry.[6]

In its 1922 memorandum, the Institute of Industrial Administration also mentioned the 'standards of knowledge and ideals' to which management aspired. Sheldon later restated this when writing of management's progression towards 'professional standards, both technical and moral'.[7] And in fact, for the greater part of the 1920s, British management thought still gave considerable attention to the formulation of moral standards in terms of public service and social responsibility. A number of spokesmen joined in issuing somewhat extravagant ethical claims for managers, such as leading 'industry into safer and better paths in the future', lending 'ultimate purpose' to an industrial life which they would dedicate to the 'cultivation of mankind', while remaining all the while fired with 'the glory of achievement'.[8] In a work of 1922, directed in part at critical Christian sources, John Lee expressed the hope that 'a profession of management' would 'provide a priesthood in industry just as there is a priesthood in worship'. Sheldon wrote of service replacing the profit motive, which as a prime industrial goal 'becomes increasingly remote and archaic'. Both he and Northcott owed much of their similar views on this matter of industrial goals to the Quaker under whom they worked at York – Seebohm Rowntree.[9]

Nevertheless, as the decade moved on, one or two technically oriented qualifications to this type of legitimatory sentiment came to be noticeable within British management thought. For instance, it was eventually admitted that service, however worthy an aim, had to remain within the bounds of financial realism.[10] Those who worked with Rowntree at York shared his view that no industrial service could be rendered at all without first establishing operational efficiency. In Northcott's opinion, expressed in 1928, managerial responsibility to run a business efficiently and to secure 'a fair wage for capital' overrode others such as that of consultation with workers.[11]

Managerial professionalism may have been a major aspiration of those who wished to draw away from the prevailing climate of industrial strife in Britain, but its implications for worker promotion did nothing to lessen the feeling of cleavage between those in and those out of control. There was widespread agreement among management spokesmen in the 1920s that recruitment to administrative positions in industry should be dependent on the possession of minimum intellectual and personal qualities. These should be scrutinized by means of regular selection procedures.[12] Much of the discussion on entry qualifications was couched in terms of eliminating the nepotism which the management movement liked to associate with ownership control; in fact it was hoped to encourage a recruitment system which would be fairer and more effective in opening managerial posts to anyone who proved suitable. However, whatever these intentions, the level of intellectual qualities that was being put forward tended automatically towards the exclusion of most manual workers from the range of recruitment. Despite Seebohm Rowntree's plea in 1920 for training programmes which could afford workers some chances of promotion, others during the 1920s were coming to assume that university graduates were the most suitable managerial recruits. In fact, some were taking up the suggestion Lee had raised in 1921, and arguing that training in management subjects should come at university or similar level.[13]

It is a little surprising that very few thinkers in the management movement recognized the possible implications for labour relations which might arise from a restriction of entry into management. Or perhaps it is more accurate to suggest that the increasing emphasis on a solidary analysis of factory relationships (which we discuss shortly) did not encourage an objective appraisal of this possible source of perceived social differentiation within the enterprise. One exception was G. H. Miles, a prominent industrial psychologist, who was quite decided that this trend in recruitment heightened the 'breach' between the two sides of industry.[14]

(2) The management of labour

The reaction of management writers against the idea of shared worker control in management, or an active constitutionalism, which became apparent during the Reconstruction period, now crystallised into a clear rejection. F. W. Taylor's early insistence that industrial efficiency required the assumption of even *greater* control over the processes of production by a suitably qualified and selected management, was by the 1920s generally accepted in the British management movement.[15] Even Quaker employers such as Edward Cadbury and Seebohm Rowntree, who had earlier been among the most enthusiastic advocates of a worker share in control, came by the later 1920s to accept that operational effectiveness required important decisions to be left in managerial hands. Similarly, Casson, who in 1919 had shown some considerable support for 'workers' committees', was by 1928 lukewarm towards them because of the way in which they could 'interfere' with managerial authority.[16]

Nevertheless, the 1920s continued to present sufficient industrial strife to discourage any complacency within the management movement on the score of relations with labour. A number of writers indicated that industrial unrest, and the possibility of State intervention in industry which might follow, provided great encouragement to the continued study of 'industrial administration'. They shared Mond's belief that: 'it certainly should be within human capacity to devise some means whereby all people with a common object should work together for a common purpose.'[17]

Consequently, after the shock of 1926 there was some revival of interest in possible methods of reducing industrial conflict. Sir Alfred Mond himself is associated with an attempt at rapprochement with trade unionism on the national level. In fact, nearly all management spokesmen during the 1920s continued to insist that every attempt should be made to co-operate with unionism. However, it is worth noticing that the greater part of discussion was by now given over to possibilities at plant level, where it was felt more opportunities lay for managerial initiative. There was, for instance, a renewed interest in works committees, and those in operation at I.C.I., Hans Renold's, and Rowntree's were given particular publicity.[18]

Although some of these committees followed quite an advanced constitutional pattern, in the sense that employees were represented by shop stewards who were accorded some opportunities for negotiation, most of the discussion given to committees within the management literature by the late 1920s viewed them as *consultative* bodies rather than as any means to afford workers a share in control. In other words, there had already been a shift away from Whitleyism, and the democratic ideal which had first accompanied it, towards a concept of 'joint consultation' which was primarily regarded as a useful technique of labour management. Even the Quaker employers, who ten years earlier had regarded the works council as a stepping stone to a share in administration, now in 1928 considered it merely 'a very convenient body to consult', chiefly because it encouraged the worker to possess 'a real sense of his corporate responsibility.'[19] In fact by the end of the decade, while still claiming that factory committees made some concession to the principle of democracy, exponents of human relations such as Casson, Northcott, and Urwick concentrated on discussing them as mechanisms for communication.[20]

Among other ideas to reduce industrial conflict, profit-sharing and co-partnership enjoyed a new vogue immediately after 1926. Some stressed the importance of disclosing full company financial details to employees so that they might be able to understand better the wider enterprise in which they had a place. Finally, one or two spokesmen expressed the hope that some means might be found to regulate remuneration in such a way that the 'anachronisms and hagglings' of an earlier era could give way to a rational, 'modern scientific outlook'. It is interesting how these aspirations foreshadow Jaques' recent attempts to construct systems of 'equitable payment'.[21]

In the event, the determination of British management writers to restrict the scope of industrial democracy led them to place increasing emphasis, first, on the compensatory notion of treating employees equitably and, second, on the idea of fostering their loyalty by means of human relations styles of managerial leadership. 'Equity' was a precept closely related to the professional ethic claimed by the management movement when it allocated to itself a goal of impartial service. For service to employees derived from the assumption that the new management's 'wider outlook and deeper sensitiveness' made possible the fulfilment of social functions for employees over and above the pursuit of production. 'We are making finer things than the finest engines, for we are making men and women,' wrote Lee in 1925.[22] Three years later the Quaker employers made the same point, defining the aim of business as the creation of 'better citizens, as well as better workers'. 'Business,' they continued, 'should be one of the factors making for the fuller life.'[23] This general trend of thought was summarized by Northcott, the labour manager at Rowntree's:

'Justice, fairness, honesty and equity are fundamental principles in industrial relations. They are ethical in nature, and demonstrate that industrial relations must be approached from the ethical standpoint.'[24]

However inadequate it might be in practice, equity became the leading (non-scientific) principle in management thought's professed aim to find a 'scientific' basis for the regulation of wages and conditions of employment. It was partly due to the inability to find a more precise reference point in these matters that Sheldon in 1923 admitted that in his view the management of men was not susceptible to scientific treatment. He was later to be criticized for this pessimism by Mary Parker Follett, who nevertheless in her writing did not tackle directly the problem of settling industrial remuneration.[25] Certainly, the continued recourse to concepts such as a 'corporate spirit', a 'spiritual sense of mutual dependence', 'motives of love, of devotion, of ideals', 'a spiritual relationship between owner and manager and between manager and worker', 'vision', 'fair play and justice', 'a fair day's wage for a fair day's work', 'a fair return', and 'a most scrupulous sense of fairness and adherence to justice' did not belong to the quantitative realm associated with science.[26] Indeed, they begged the whole problem of wage determination and the conflict of interests that went with it.

The intention of management thought in the field of labour relations was, in Lee's words, 'to discover some co-operative basis of which the pioneer captains of industry could not have

had the faintest idea'.[27] A much more definite move to implement this aim lay in the elaboration of those human relations
methods which had been developed towards the close of the
First World War. Mary Parker Follett's lectures given after
1926 in Britain, attracted considerable attention within the
management movement, and these stressed that, using psychological insights, a 'science' of human relationships could be
developed and learned. In fact, it was in large part on this basis
that she believed industrial management had the makings of
a profession. Her analysis had considerable affinity with the
human relations model, stressing as it did integration, social
functions of group relationships, and participative managerial
leadership. There was during the 1920s a continued concern
that large plant size was destroying the 'personal touch' in
industry. Therefore it was felt that to revive a basis for co-operation in business, management should make every effort to
promote a greater participation by employees in the activities
of their firms. This was in any case necessary if the kind of claim
put forward by Mond, that managers and workers were in
fact 'co-workers', was to have any foundation. Hence by the
later 1920s, the discussion of labour relations was coming to
give increasing prominence to techniques of 'consultation',
'team-play', 'respectful affection' and the like.[28]

Given that formal systems of participation in managerial
operations were no longer admissible, then it is understandable
that management thought turned increasingly to the first-line
supervisor as the point of contact through which workers could
be led to share more willingly in the (managerially-defined)
goals of the enterprise.[29] If the foreman was to fill this role it was
necessary that managers should treat him as an integral part
of their own organization.[30] The foreman was now, as before,
being urged to 'understand the psychology of the worker', and
even to appreciate the human implications of technology.[31]
Moreover, by the late 1920s the analysis of worker behaviour
was slowly coming to include the suggestion, which was to be
fully developed by the Mayo school, that important aspects of
worker behaviour were not of a 'logical' nature. For instance in
1928 one of the founders of the Welfare Workers movement
stated her view that:

' . . . a state of efficiency can never be attained by purely logical
and impersonal methods . . . To be really efficient, management must.

take account of this emotional element. The effect on the rate of output in a department, i.e., on its efficiency, of substituting a foreman who leads his men for one who drives may be as great as that of the installation of a new labour-saving machine, and in the long run is cumulative and incalculable'.[32]

Lee also agreed that reason and material requirements were by no means the only important factors underlying worker motivation.[33] Social and emotive forces were also present behind worker action, and foremen could use these in furtherance of the technical ends of the enterprise. Wardropper, for instance, concluded that 'the mental attitude of the worker to his job is largely determined by the atmosphere the foreman creates in the workshop'.[34] Others took up a similar theme. The model for foremen was 'the democratic leader . . . of the persuasive type . . . knowing how to manage groups and influence them'. This type of foreman, it was thought, would 'get the utmost in production', since industrial co-operation was in essence a question of 'successful communication' and of 'a state of mind'.[35]

Thus by the end of the 1920s the 'democratic leader', in management thought, had as his chief aim the persuasion of workers in order to get the most out of them. This paradoxical use of the primarily ethical label of 'democratic' to refer to a motivational technique, gives some indication of how the body of management literature was moving its attention away from legitimations designed to soften labour demands for shared control, and towards a more open and direct concern for purely technical performance. Whatever the continued claims of service, and these by the late 1920s were becoming less prominently displayed, this shift of emphasis within British management thought towards the mechanics of worker performance is unmistakable.

A further development which formed part of the same process was the transformation of 'industrial welfare work' into 'labour management'. The inception of the Welfare Workers Association in 1913 had been in large part the inspiration of Quaker employers. There is little doubt that at the time this development was viewed in a largely ethical light, as an attempt to protect the interests and needs of individual workers in large firms.[36] In 1920 Seebohm Rowntree was still able to write of welfare work as designed, not merely to combat industrial conflict and to service 'human machinery', but also to safeguard workers' well-being.[37] In the same year the Welfare Workers Institute (as it was then known) regarded itself as professionally independent, 'able to take an entirely free position as between capital and labour'. As late as 1927 the editor of *Welfare Work* could remind members of the Institute that they held 'an independent position as between management and workers . . . and they owe loyalty to both'.[38]

Yet John Lee, for one, was already urging management to incorporate a welfare movement which could both contribute considerable experience in the understanding and control of labour, and provide a means whereby the management movement's desire of giving employees an increased sense of purpose within the firm might be fulfilled.[39] After an agonised period of debate, the Welfare Workers themselves acceded to a move away from the field of social work towards that of labour management proper. Miss E. T. Kelly admitted in 1928 that 'from the welfare supervisor of today is expected good work rather than "good works" '. And in 1931, the year when the title of the Institute and its journal both changed to 'Labour Management', its President could emphasize 'we claim that our work is an integral part of management'.[40]

Although labour management continued to concern itself with so-called 'post-office functions' such as selection, welfare services, and statistics on engagement and labour turnover, its rejection of the welfare work label did indicate a definite shift of emphasis towards the American type of personnel manager. By 1930 this American counter-part had for some time been given a more positive human relations function – this was in Ordway Tead's words 'directed to increasing the interest, skill, enthusiasm, effectiveness, and unity of corporate purpose of the entire personnel of the organization'.[41]

These developments along human relations lines during the 1920s are of considerable significance in the history of British management thought, not least because they heralded a view popular in the 1940s and early 1950s that trade unions performed no necessary role at the level of the individual enterprise. Moreover, they were associated with a growing tendency to exclude from management thought a consideration of those factors conducive to industrial conflict which were normally outside management's area of control. In consequence, over the course of time, prescriptions for successful labour management

were increasingly couched in terms of a restricted analysis which
avoided mention of trade unionism and of those matters of
industrial dispute giving unionism cause for existence. These
trends, one must emphasize, were gradual and subtle. It is
chiefly by viewing their effects over fairly long periods of time
that they may be most clearly discerned, and this we shall do in
Chapter 5 by comparing the different analytical perspectives on
industrial conflict contained within management thought in the
1920s and the late 1940s. Indeed, we shall note that it has been
the task of recent industrial social science to remind students
of management how such features of social structure, comprising
the environment of enterprises, may be of the utmost significance
for industrial behaviour and hence for managerial policy.

There were various indications by the late 1920s of the earlier
stages in this narrowing of analytical perspective. They would
appear to have resulted in much the following way, from the
desire to enhance worker co-operation at plant level. To start
with, most management thinkers during the 1920s favoured a
policy of full co-operation with trade unionism. Generally
speaking, the management movement was in the first half of the
decade prepared to admit that trade unions were the legitimate
representatives of workers' interests. Indeed, during the years
of labour militancy, which in many respects lasted up to 1926,
it did not have much option but to admit this as a realistic
principle. Nonetheless, these management thinkers also felt
strongly that the centralization of union activities should be
offset by a greater interaction between managers and workers
(or worker representatives) at plant level. For this was the level
which really concerned individual managements.[42] Otherwise a
growing distance between the two parties, together with the fact
that at the national level emphasis was generally on industry
wide matters, would render impossible an agreement to formulate common policies appropriate to the local problems of
particular companies. To encourage this atmosphere of co-
operation at local level, it was necessary to improve existing
methods of motivating labour, and for this reason there had
from such an early date been an active discussion of human
relations methods.

In concluding Chapter 3, we suggested that there was some
tension within management thought as long as this attempted
to reconcile a sympathetic appreciation of the demands of a

F

militant labour movement with a developing human relations outlook. It is thus understandable that by the later 1920s, when British trade unionism was both weakened and set further in its centralized outlook, this tension should begin to be resolved. That is, management writers continued their aspirations for plant level leadership, but now paid decreasing heed both to the role of unions in representing factory employees, and to those matters concerning material rewards and industrial authority, with which most union activity was normally associated. In the event, and concurrent with the stress on 'integration' which was given by prominent spokesmen such as Follett, a number of writers began to assume that managers themselves could quite adequately represent workers' interests in the factory. In turn this was felt not merely to obviate the need for unions to adopt a hostile attitude towards management, but also to mean that trade unions no longer performed any necessary function at plant level. As Northcott stated in 1928: 'labour is so inarticulate, and the expression of its aims so biased and imperfect, that sympathetic understanding must be seconded by a willingness at times to become labour's advocate, and state its case.'[43]

In conjunction with this changing view, we have already noted how in management thought the discussion of factory committees had, by the late 1920s, moved away from the Whitley model towards a 'communications' one, with its scope typically restricted to consultation rather than embracing negotiation or shared decision-taking. Developments such as these should, of course, be viewed as part of an extended reaction against the principle of a worker share in control. Moreover, the growing emphasis within management thought on employee motivations of a social nature and at an interpersonal level, implied that it was technically functional for managers to concentrate on meeting these 'secondary' needs, and to discount more awkward claims for material benefits or extended prerogatives that might still be presented by worker representatives. Such discounting was, of course, a more feasible course following the 1926 union defeat, and when a relatively 'loose' labour market prevailed.

We can at this stage already begin to appreciate a feature which is to be discussed in the second main section of this chapter, namely why in the 1930s the British management movement adopted the Mayo school's philosophy so readily and, for a while, gave it relatively little publicity. For Mayoism's practical human relations recommendations on supervisory leadership were anticipated in British management thought at least as far back as the close of the First World War. And we have just seen that several of its salient analytical points, such as the stress on employees' social needs and non-logical actions, the inattention to trade union functions, and the severely restricted perception of conflict, were also foreshadowed by the shifts in emphasis among British writers towards the close of the 1920s.

(3) *The 'science of industrial administration' and rationalization*
During the 1920s there was a steady development of techniques in the fields of costing, work measurement, and production layout, in addition to the continuing activity of industrial psychologists in the study of fatigue, monotony, physical work environment, wage incentives, and so on. These activities paralleled the discussion of methods for managerial leadership which we have just reviewed. In addition, the search had already begun for optimum models of organization structure, and this was accompanied by a growing interest in the analysis of managerial activities within organizational frameworks. These developments were an application of F. W. Taylor's thesis that methods of scientific investigation be utilized for the study of managerial problems, in the hope that certain standardized techniques and 'principles' could be discovered for use in diverse factory situations. As the Institute of Industrial Administration stated in 1922, the new management movement was seeking a 'definition and standardization of its principles, motives, and methods'.[44]

Lee hoped that this 'science of industrial administration', as he called it, would eventually provide a solution to industrial conflict. The growth of managerial technical knowledge, oriented towards the extraction of more from a given amount of effort, promised a general social benefit which would thus be to the workers' good as well. Secondly, although the growth of technical expertise had induced management thinkers to reject the notion of shared control, it at the same time enabled them to formulate an alternative basis upon which managerial decisions should be readily accepted by other employees. This was the concept of authority based upon function, and the idea of co-operation on the basis of the facts of a situation, which were together associated with the work of Mary Parker Follett.

In Follett's view, the technical requirements of an industrial situation constrained the actions of *both* managers and workers. Thus the latter were not so much subject to the control of the former, but rather both were subject to the impersonal control of situational requirements. Managerial expertise provided a means to assess the situation in an objective manner. In this way the development of the 'science of industrial administration' had a further legitimatory function for the acceptance and maintenance of managerial authority. Lee, among others, passed Follett's argument over to his readers in an article on discipline published in 1928.[45] As early as 1923 Sheldon had arrived at much the same idea, which of course suggested that once the facts of a particular issue were known it was unnecessary to enter into any prolonged conflict over its solution. Sheldon, having concluded that management could now operate by 'scientific means rather than by the autocracy of the "boss" ', continued:

'Management is no longer the wielding of the whip; it is rather the delving into experience and the building upon facts. Its leadership is based upon knowledge rather than upon force. Its task is no longer solely that of "getting the job through". Rather, in many of its activities, it operates through the application of a capacity trained in the investigation and solution of problems. Management, in fact, instead of being a law unto itself, has found that there are laws which it must obey.'[46]

The weakness of any assumption that a 'law of the situation' guaranteed the integration of differing interests within organizations was unwittingly exposed by several members of the management movement itself. For instance, it proved necessary for both Renold and Urwick to defend scientific management techniques against the charge that these were contrary to the interests of manual workers. In trying to disassociate these techniques in principle from their abuse by employers in terms of speeding-up, increased monotony, and loss of worker autonomy, these authors in fact were admitting that technical expertise could in practice be used either for or against the worker's benefit by those in industrial control.[47]

A subject of growing interest among students of management

in the 1920s was organization structure and the classification of managerial activities. Following leads given by F. W. Taylor and Henri Fayol, much of the discussion on organization was devoted to the various merits and demerits of the so-called 'line' (which Sheldon called 'departmental') and 'functional' models, to problems of centralization and decentralization, and to the question of whether to organize by process, product, or area.[48] We have, for example, already noted how John Lee in his *Management* (1921) had placed considerable faith in a functional model (derived from Taylor) as the means to create a 'group' feeling within the enterprise. Nevertheless, by 1928 the year of his death, he was coming to admit the force in Fayol's own critique of Taylor, namely that functionalism posed great difficulties for the maintenance of unified control and command.[49]

Both Taylor and Fayol had suggested that systematic study might promote the development of guiding principles of organization, and the definition of managerial tasks to fit into organizational structure. However, these two pioneers quite clearly admitted that their own formulations could be improved upon, and that these did not represent 'one-best ways' which could be applied without modification to varying factory situations. Some writers in the earlier 1920s continued to warn against the natural tendency to allow the new study of industrial administration to crystallise into what Lee called 'a dogmatic series of doctrine'.[50] Elbourne made a similar point in 1922 when he wrote:

' . . . we can allow that Taylor stood for the principle of scientific analysis of the problems of management; a principle to which we can unhesitatingly subscribe without admitting that there is to be only one prescribed outcome of such analysis, as some disciples of Taylor seem to hold.'[51]

However, men such as Sankey, one of the first Presidents of the Institute of Industrial Administration, were already coming to equate the move from 'rule-of-thumb' managerial methods with a search for what he called 'laws of administration'.[52] Accordingly the idea of planning an organization along rational lines was rapidly developing into the assumption that some universally optimum structure of formal managerial roles and procedures was attainable through systematic study – in other words, the notion of an 'ideal' organization was coming into currency. And regardless of his other warnings about dogmatism, John Lee argued as early as 1925 that the managerial span of control should be no greater than five.[53]

The major step towards the construction of *a priori* 'principles of management' came with Urwick's remarkable essay of 1928 on 'Principles of Direction and Control'. In this he admitted his debt to Taylor both for the functional model and for the idea that a search for principles followed naturally from the concept of scientific management. The actual framework for Urwick's principles was heavily influenced by Fayol. In this essay, 'principles' amounted to a rather vague stylization of managerial tasks (for instance, 'investigation', 'direction', 'experiment' and so on) together with an attempt to set down organizational precepts such as the 'correspondence' of authority with responsibility. What is perhaps one of the historically most interesting points about this essay is that while Urwick admitted the 'insuperable difficulties' in proving the validity of management principles, he at the same time proceeded to claim categorically that 'it is possible to lay down certain principles or guides to action which are valid in *all* cases'[54] (our emphasis).

Urwick, who in 1929 became Director of the International Management Institute at Geneva, was for the next thirty years to become the most outstanding and prolific contributor to British management thought. He was already at the close of the 1920s associated with a further extension of the idea of scientifically planned organization and management, which became known as the 'rationalization movement'. Rationalization attracted most attention among management writers from the mid-1920s up to the depth of the slump in 1932-33. It followed on from German experiments in the early 1920s, and was the main subject of consideration at the 1927 World Economic Conference.

Rationalization was viewed as a quite natural extension of the principle of careful managerial regulation beyond the limited scope of individual firms to industry and distribution as a whole. It implied a further turning away from laissez-faire thinking, and an attempt to substitute organization for the rule-of-thumb anarchy of economic life. In Urwick's opinion, 'Every sincere student of rationalization admits frankly his immense debt to the scientific management movement. He is but applying on a greater scale that "mental revolution" of which F. W. Taylor spoke.'[55] Sir Alfred Mond among others joined

Urwick in this view. These managerial spokesmen claimed that the technical economies gained through rationalization would enable industry to enhance its service to the whole community.[56] However, as had been the case with Taylorism, it was left to industrial psychologists to dissent from this claim by pointing out the dysfunctions of rationalization for employees. Myers, in particular, felt that the burden imposed on workers by the introduction of mass production in terms of monotony, rigidly prescribed patterns of working, and redundancy, was ignored by the rationalizers. This burden, together with inter-departmental rivalry promoted by functional management structure, constituted a source of conflict which the organization theorists ignored.[57]

(4) *The work of the 1920s consolidated in three major publications*
There is no question that the culmination of a decade of intense activity among management thinkers, a period stretching back at least to Sidney Webb's *The Works Manager To-day* in 1917, was the *Dictionary of Industrial Administration* edited by John Lee and published in 1928. Many of our references in this chapter have come from this source. A two-volumed work of over 1,000 quarto pages, it drew upon the specialist contributions of over 100 authorities, including several prominent trade unionists. Although it is now generally long-forgotten, there is nothing else to compare with this work in the history of British management thought. Indeed, when in a later chapter we discuss the changing analysis given by management writers to industrial conflict, we shall indicate how both the sophistication and breadth of discussion contained within the covers of this publication compare favourably with more recent writing.[58]

A second major publication was probably the outstanding British work of the 1930s – Urwick's *Management of Tomorrow* (1933).[59] Despite its title this book as much summarized the work of the 1920s as added any new ideas. The scientific approach suggested by Taylor, his philosophy of the 'mental revolution', the founding of managerial authority upon function, the 'law of the situation', the irrelevance of ownership for the new manager who was assuming a public responsibility, foreman specialization in small group leadership, and the new theory of organization – all these ideas are contained within its pages, and all are essentially products of the previous decade or even earlier. One of the few features in this work which points ahead is Urwick's almost complete lack of concern for trade unionism as this might impinge upon the enterprise. Indeed, trade unionism is given only one reference in the book (and this is on a historical point), while human relations leadership is given several lengthy passages.[60]

Thirdly, one should mention another major work of the 1930s – Elbourne's *Fundamentals of Industrial Administration* (1934) – which also largely summarized concepts and methods derived in the 1920s. Much of this book, in fact, is given over to industrial economics and cost accounting. In its sections on management proper, Elbourne reproduced Urwick's 'principles' of 1928. He also argued strongly for the value of management education, and against the school of thought that assumed management was merely an art which could only be appreciated through extensive practical experience. Unlike Urwick, but following most of the writers of the 1920s such as Lee, Renold and Sheldon, Elbourne gave considerable attention to trade unionism, arguing that managers would do well to recognize its largely constructive nature. Indeed, the book closed with a quotation of Sheldon's, demanding that management should always heed the legitimate rights of the work force.[61]

MANAGEMENT THOUGHT DURING THE 1930S

Apart from the two works by Urwick and Elbourne just mentioned, there was little of note published in book form by British management writers during the 1930s. Most of the source material for this decade derives, in fact, from conference reports and short articles. These may largely be found in the two British management journals which came into existence during this decade – *Industry Illustrated* in 1933 and the *British Management Review* in 1936. There are two major developments to note during this decade, and we shall summarize these in turn. They are first Urwick's formulation of the 'classical' theory of formal organization, and second the incorporation of Mayoism into the British management approach to labour relations.

(1) *The theory of organization*
We have seen from Urwick's paper of 1928 how his analysis of organization drew upon both Fayol and Taylor. Fayol's delineation of managerial tasks in terms of forecasting, planning,

organization, co-ordination, command, and control provided
the framework for much of Urwick's writing on management.
Taylor's idea of functional specialization provided Urwick's
theory of organization with the conceptual means to cope with
the growing range of differentiated managerial specialisms.
Moreover, Urwick was greatly encouraged by Mooney and
Reiley's conclusion that the same principles of co-ordination,
scalarity, and functional sub-division had appeared in a range
of diverse organizations throughout history, and that these
were equally applicable to modern industry.[62] Their analysis
thus suggested to Urwick not only the necessity for industrial
management to operate on a bureaucratic rather than traditional basis (to use Weberian concepts), but also the likelihood
that a study of organizational structure *per se* would uncover
principles that had a universal applicability.

Setting off from these premises, Urwick became convinced
of the necessity to determine the organization of an enterprise
in advance of its actual operation, and that this could be done
irrespective of its production technology, market, or social
environment. There is included in a paper first given by Urwick
in 1933, a passage so fundamental to his view, and to the whole
subsequent 'management principles' school in Britain, that it
deserves quoting at length. He advanced his thesis of organization as a 'technical problem' in the following way:

'It is the general thesis of this paper that there are principles which
can be arrived at inductively from the study of human experience
of organization, which should govern arrangements for human
association of any kind. These principles can be studied as a technical question, irrespective of the purpose of the enterprise, the
personnel composing it, or any constitutional, political or social
theory underlying its creation. They are concerned with the method
of subdividing and allocating to individuals all the various activities,
duties and responsibilities essential to the purpose contemplated,
the correlation of these activities and the continuous control of the
work of individuals so as to secure the most economical and the most
effective realization of the purpose.'[63]

It is important to note that in this treatment of organization
as a purely technical matter, an abstraction from social relationships was clearly entailed and recognized:

'The art of administration demands knowledge of the human factor.
But this does not mean that it is impossible to study the structure
of enterprises anatomically, to isolate organization and treat it as
a technical problem.'[64]

This approach clearly disregarded the possibility that optimum organizational structures would vary with the nature of their environments, technology, or workflow activities. Further, it preferred to ignore the warnings of industrial psychologists such as Frisby. In a paper of 1933, Frisby came close to the modern 'self-actualization' argument of Argyris, McGregor and others when he indicated how an organization structure 'based on mechanical principles' could prove inadequate in practice through its unanticipated and deleterious effects on a human sense of responsibility, morale, and willingness to co-operate.[65] In his *Elements of Administration*, which first appeared in 1943 and which summarizes his thinking on organization, Urwick again repeated his idea of designing 'the ideal plan of organization', starting with what he called a 'clean sheet'. Structure should be laid out first and the rest would follow.[66]

The way in which Urwick treated organization principles, as optimal arrangements deriving logically from given problems of co-ordination and control, bears some similarity to Follett's assumption that a 'law of the situation' could indicate clearly an optimal and acceptable solution to problematic issues. Moreover, in his analysis of organization, Urwick accepted Follett's view that requisite managerial control should be seen to derive from the needs of the system itself. The more depersonalized, formalized, and 'technical' the operation of managerial authority, the less it stood in the way of fully co-operative industrial relationships. For instance, he suggested with reference to Taylorism that: 'the removal of much of the routine of management from detailed personal control to the operation of the system eliminated an important source of friction from industrial life.'[67]

Urwick argued that the attempt to build 'a pure theory of organization' should in the long run be 'inductive'. By this he meant that 'it must be based on a widespread study of past and existing enterprises both in business and in other walks of life'. Among non-business enterprises which were relevant, he included 'governments, churches, or armies'. These points were made in 1933, and this idea of comparative structural analysis clearly derived from the example set by Mooney and Reiley. Urwick set his comparative approach in opposition to what he later called 'empiricism'.[68] This latter referred to the ideas of what might be called the 'practical manager' school, which more recently has been represented by men such as Sir Frederic Hooper (and which will be referred to again in Chapter 5). This school argued that management was sufficiently an art to mean that good industrial administration had to rely upon a manager's own personal capabilities and upon the accumulation of his own personal industrial experience. It doubted the usefulness of attempts to formulate principles of management on these grounds, as well as on the related argument that the situation of no two organizations was similar enough to allow the comparative approach to furnish any precepts of general applicability.

Whatever Urwick's original intention to follow an 'inductive' approach, he never indicated the comparative data on which his formulations were based in such a manner that it could be scrutinized by critics. It appears that he preferred after a while to take the universality of his principles for granted. Indeed, he proceeded to issue ambitious claims for his type of administrative theory. For instance, that it would 'revolutionize human arrangements for collaboration of all kinds – for war, for peace, for government, for domestic life – for every aspect of our efforts to live together'.[69]

Emerging from Urwick's weaving of threads from Taylor, Fayol, and others, was the now well-known 'line and functional' (or in American phraseology 'line and staff') model. In Mooney and Reiley's terms, this model reconciled the scalar and functional principles with that of co-ordination. One important innovation that Urwick added to the model derived from his military experience. This was the incorporation of what he called 'staff officers'. These could enable the restrictions imposed by the span of control principle to be avoided, and thus help to maintain a closer personal contact between levels in a large organization. They would relieve senior executives of much detailed work and detailed communication, yet they would have no independent formal authority of their own.[70] The inclusion of precepts such as unity of command, limited span of control, and a clearly specified balance of authority with responsibility, meant that Urwick's organizational model approximated to the 'mechanistic' type recently conceptualized by Burns and Stalker.[71] It is also worth noting that by relying for his argument upon Graicunas' mathematical model of spans of control and consequent relationships, Urwick was not so much following the inductive and comparative method to which he aspired, as its reverse.[72]

These 'logical' management principles were among the major achievements of British management thought during the inter-war years, and probably its most original. During the course of the 1930s they received appropriate exposition in the leading journals.

(2) *The incorporation of Mayoism*
In spite of Mary Parker Follett's lectures on authority and co-ordination between 1926 and 1933 and Urwick's own apprecia-tion of her work, there was in British management thought during the 1930s relatively little discussion on the dynamics of behaviour at the level of managerial organization. Such analysis was at this time mainly confined to the motivation of operative employees. This is an interesting feature for it implied that co-ordination at managerial level was chiefly a matter of correct structural arrangement, and that there was little problem in
· securing acceptance of goals laid down by senior management. Commonly-held goals and rational behaviour were assumed to be the rule among managers. This assumption was of course made in an industrial context that did not embrace so acutely the problem of the widespread employment of 'cosmopolitan' specialists, whose integration into administrative systems is a topic of acute interest today.

Follett's theories were couched in terms of democratic social relationships, and there is every indication that she regarded the views of all the parties within an enterprise as being of the same order of logic. Nevertheless, she was soon being inter-preted by British writers to suggest that managers should try to lead other groups to their own point of view, a course which tended towards a persuasive 'domination' rather than a demo-cratic 'integration'. Early in 1934, Urwick took the view that: 'Integration is essentially a question of turning away from what people say they want and finding out what they really want. It is an act, not of conciliation or compromise, but of invention.'[73] But in an address of the same year to the Industrial Co-Partner-ship Association, Urwick argued that scientific management did not allow for the participation by workers in higher adminis-tration and policy. Referring to Follett's concepts of 'deperson-alisation of orders' and 'law of the situation' as alternative solutions he stated that: 'Identification of all employees with the higher administration of business enterprises must be by methods of indirect and remote, rather than by methods of direct and immediate, control.'[74] Northcott's interpretation of 'power with' also emphasized persuasion as a means to gaining co-operation within the enterprise. In these ways Follett's philosophy of control was applied not so much as a means to attaining the ideal of organizational democracy which she had hoped to foster, but simply as a management technique.[75]

Follett's 'law of the situation' and Urwick's logical management principles themselves implied that management could operate on the basis of a rational 'logic of efficiency'. The growing emphasis on persuasion which had been noticeable in British management thought since 1918, suggested in turn that workers operated on the basis of some other logic. This other logic had to be rendered compatible with the managerial pursuit of efficiency. Given the persistence of output restriction, resistance to change, and other signs of worker non-co-operation with managerial rationality, it was to be expected that the notion of worker 'sentiment' or non-logic developed by Elton Mayo and his colleagues should find a ready welcome in British management thought.

It was in fact the theory of industrial behaviour expounded by the Harvard 'Human Relations School', and not the practical implications which followed, that was novel to British management thought in the mid-1930s. The conceptual contributions of Mayoism centred on 'informal organization', social group influences on worker action, the importance of 'social satisfactions', the desire for 'spontaneous collaboration', the idea of contrasting managerial and employee logics of 'efficiency' and 'sentiment', and the wider social mission of management in reforging the bases for social cohesion in 'adaptive' industrial society. In Britain, the most influential book of the Mayo school during the 1930s was T. N. Whitehead's *Leadership in a Free Society*, published in 1936 on both sides of the Atlantic. This work developed the Harvard philosophy much further than had been the case with Mayo's *Human Problems of an Industrial Civilization* (1933). Moreover, Whitehead was able to make use of the later stages of the Hawthorne research as a 'scientific' support for his arguments.[76]

Earlier in this chapter we indicated how by the close of the

1920s British management writers were coming to anticipate some major features of the Mayo school's analysis; particularly the 'social' and non-logical view of worker motivation, the inattention to trade unionism, and the severely restricted view of industrial conflict. On the matter of trade unionism, it is interesting to recall that at the time of the famous experiments Hawthorne was virtually a non-union plant. Trade unions receive no discussion in Mayo's writings, while in Whitehead's it is suggested that their functions are only social, and that these can therefore be superseded by a suitably 'socially skilled' management.[77] Similarly, during most of the 1930s with a quiescent union movement, British management writers contented themselves with ignoring the role of trade unions in industry. When we come to discuss the post-1945 years, which saw a revitalized union movement present new challenges to industrial management, we shall see how those writers adhering most closely to the Mayo approach were, in Britain, also those most overtly hostile towards trade unions.

Although there is no doubt that the theory of the 'adaptive society' and the nature of the social mission posited by Mayoism for managers were both novel to British thinkers, the associated idea of managerial legitimation in terms of social responsibility was not new at all. And while in May 1937 the editor of *Industry Illustrated* received Whitehead's exposition of this social mission with great enthusiasm – calling his book 'a tract for our times all will read who have any concern for the future of democratic civilization' – the legitimatory aspects of Mayoism were not in the 1930s generally granted any of the same prominence in British management thought as in the following decade.[78] We shall suggest later that the fundamental reason for this different use of the Mayo school's ideas over time lies in the changed environment in which the management movement had subsequently to work.

At the level of practical managerial methods, an emphasis on human relations foremanship continued to be evident in British writing of the 1930s, both before and after the publication of the Harvard works. All the practical essentials of Mayoism, with the exception of systematic employee counselling, were contained in British management thought long before Hawthorne made its influence felt. During the 1930s journals and other works contained abundant reference to a foremanship which, although remaining identical in its fundamentals, was still labelled 'new' and was to be so called in the 1940s as well.[79] It was increasingly argued that the nature of worker behaviour depended primarily upon the foreman, and that he could maintain a harmony and cohesion in industry which management thinkers were coming to regard as some kind of natural state.[80] Bearing this and the developments of the 1920s in mind, one can appreciate how Mayo's conclusion in a British article of 1931, that supervision was the single most important influence on work group morale, came as no new idea.[81] And in fact neither this article, nor the address to the Oxford Management Conference in 1930 upon which it was based, appear to have aroused an undue amount of attention in the British management movement. Where Mayoism did exert some fresh influence was in directing the discussion of foremanship on to work groups. For during the 1930s British writing still showed some uncertainty whether to take the individual or the work group as the primary reference for employee orientations and behaviour.

It is thus evident that several fundamentals of Mayoist theory, and virtually all of its practical implications, are to be found in British management thought some time before the Harvard writings. This also appears to be true of the American case. For instance, Mary Gilson, a prominent member of the American personnel management movement, when reviewing Roethlisberger and Dickson's report of the Hawthorne research in *Management and the Worker*, complained that the whole experiment had wasted a great deal of time and money 'discovering the obvious', as she put it. She claimed that all the book said was already known in 1927 when the experiments first started, and was even then accepted as part of good management practice.[82] It is worth mentioning here that in her review Gilson missed a point which differentiates this particular book from other works of the Mayo School, and which was certainly ignored by management thinkers on both sides of the Atlantic – namely, that the authors warn of the inability of supervisory human relations training to have any significant influence on the kind of fundamental conflict situation found in the Bank Wiring Room.[83] Nonetheless, the emphasis on supervisory leadership contained in all the other Harvard writings was so much in line with the view already prevailing in American management thought that one wonders how much this existing current of opinion in fact influenced the final conclusions of the Hawthorne investigators themselves.

It is, we would argue, misleading to conceive of a simple and sudden revolution in management thought following the Hawthorne experiments, which replaced a crude Taylorist or behaviourist view of worker motivation by human relations, or which transformed what was recommended as good management practice. Some social scientists would seem to hold this view of events,[84] which we suggest is not true for British management thought and not entirely so even for British social science. We have already seen how, with little delay, British industrial psychologists attacked the 'engineering' view of the worker implied in Taylorism, and how in fact even they were preceded in this by Quaker employers. Further, it would not be accurate to conclude that British industrial psychologists were exclusively behaviouristic in their analysis of worker action. The work of Myers and Muscio around 1920 belies such an interpretation, while by the later 1920s prominent industrial psychologists were becoming aware of the important influence that could be exerted by the work group on an individual's values and actions.[85]

In the event, the British management movement appeared in the later 1930s to absorb the work of Mayo and Whitehead with remarkable ease, and with little sense that it was dealing with a new development of any revolutionary proportions.[86] In fact, we shall come to notice that any talk of Mayoism as a new set of ideas was more typical of the 1940s – for then, in different circumstances, the management movement had the task of selling human relations ideas to industry in general, for which this approach was new and had to be explained as such. However, back in 1937 it was possible for the editor of *Industry Illustrated* to welcome Whitehead's book because 'the leading theme is a belief we have always maintained in these columns'.[87] The reports of the Hawthorne experiments were well received because they gave apparently impeccable scientific support to ideas and methods already in favour among British management writers. It was now possible for spokesmen such as Byng to say as he did in 1936 that: 'Recent psychological research has *shown* that the most important factors affecting an operative's efficiency are his mental attitude towards his supervisor and his conditions of work'[88] (our emphasis).

This stamp of scientific authenticity provided by the impressively long and expensive Hawthorne experiments has undoubtedly played a most important part in the continued popularity of various forms of human relations up to recent years. Whatever ideological purposes may have been contained within this movement, it should not be forgotten that many writers and educators have furthered the human relations approach out of a sincere belief that they were propagating a scientifically proven viable management technique. If blame is today to be allocated for the analytical shortcomings underlying this approach, then it should first be directed towards those at Harvard who claimed to be designing experiments and interpreting their results as trained social scientists. Indeed, the authority granted to them by virtue of their academic status was acknowledged by management thinkers such as the editor we just quoted, who said of Whitehead: 'He speaks with authority, for in company with Professor Elton Mayo he has observed scientifically the behaviour of certain groups of workers over long periods of time.'[89]

Urwick soon recommended Whitehead's book to his audiences. A study group of the 36th Oxford Management Conference 'fully subscribed' to Mayo's view that (as it put it) 'the contentment of the individual is the greatest single factor in efficient production'. The Quaker employers at their 1938 Conference included a public lecture in which Howard Collier from the Birmingham University Department of Industrial Hygiene and Medicine gave a classic statement of the human relations approach to conflict in asserting that: 'men strike for higher wages, when they really "need" better human relations'.[90]

(3) *Other developments in the 1930s*
Now that effective managerial methods appeared to have been discovered for both formal and informal aspects of enterprises, it is not surprising that some authorities at the centre of the management movement should by the later 1930s feel content that 'there is before us a living "science" of management'.[91] Moreover, this confidence in the advance of techniques was paralleled by a growing assurance that the role of managers was now fully accepted and valued by society at large. Ideological challenges to management's position from the labour movement were minimal by this time, and it must have been natural to

G

conclude that the sheer passage of time was leading to a public acceptance of managers' rights to industrial authority. By the 1930s there is very little concern within British management thought for the kind of assertion of moral superiority over ownership which was to be found in the early 1920s. Instead it now did not seem to matter overmuch how managers had attained their position of control; as Northcott put it, 'Somehow or other we got there. We are the appointed leaders.'[92] The zest with which *Industry Illustrated* first opened its pages in 1933 provides some instance of this growing self-assurance: 'The future of British industry lies with its principal executives. With their technical skill and their power of leadership they represent a national asset altogether beyond price.'[93]

In spite of this self-appointed praise, it was noticeable that by the 1930s far fewer management writers gave the kind of prominence to the ethic of service than had been the case in the earlier 1920s. And during the 1930s such claims were more in evidence early in the decade. Seebohm Rowntree, who had always been one of the foremost exponents of the idea of industrial social service, when writing in 1931 on 'Some Industrial Problems of Today' came to focus almost exclusively upon the technical means to increase industry's economic performance. The overriding problem at that time, he admitted, was unemployment and the inefficiency of British industry.[94] Indeed, by the 1930s some attention was again being given to the profit motive as a legitimate measure of, and motive for, better business performance.[95]

Similarly, during the 1930s the shift within British management thought at the end of the previous decade, away from ethical claims and concessions towards a more exclusive and single-minded concentration on the technical requirements of efficiency, was continued in other ways. For instance, by the mid-1930s a member of what a few years before had been a 'welfare' movement, could write of 'getting the best out of workers' by means of the appropriate supervisory style.[96] The works committee, once a symbol of shared control, was now being discussed from a technical point of view – as a useful safety valve.[97] Even the Quaker employers at their 1938 Conference, while still conscious of the social requirements of their secular ethic, in effect admitted that they had not yet found any means of avoiding a hierarchical structure of control within companies so long as a minimum standard of performance was to be maintained.[98]

The democratic principle was by now becoming relegated to an apology for persuasion. In an article on the pursuit of higher productivity, Northcott described this 'democratic organisation of industry' as one 'that brings the manager as the leader into collaboration with the workers participant in the group'.[99] While several writers were still insisting that opportunities of promotion had to be kept open for all employees,[100] others, particularly from the mid-1930s onward, emphasized the need to restrict the range of managerial recruitment, and hence took a pessimistic view of the promotion chances available to most workers.[101] Indeed, the exercise, popular during this decade, of constructing somewhat overpowering lists of qualities desirable in managers and foremen itself strongly implied a restricted range of recruitment. In fact, some of these qualities, such as 'good appearance', 'good education', and 'powers of leadership', could in Britain readily be interpreted to exclude people of working class background.[102]

Finally, we have already commented on the greatly decreased attention given by the British management movement through much of the 1930s to relations with trade unionism. The popularity of a human relations approach did not encourage a view of trade unions as the rightful outlet of worker self-expression or as a proper means to the operation of 'constitutional' democratic procedures within the enterprise. However, compared with some writing that was to follow in the late 1940s, there was at this time little overt anti-unionism in British management thought. Indeed, at the close of the 1930s when once more both union membership and the number of industrial stoppages were rising, one or two management spokesmen again began to take more note of trade unions, and to urge managers to try and work in co-operation with them.[103] Nonetheless, while in practice a few firms such as I.C.I., Hans Renold Ltd., and those under Quaker management might continue to work in close contact with union representatives, to operate highly sophisticated consultative and judicial mechanisms in their factories, and to support industrial co-operation by means of a wide range of material benefits, these provisions could no longer be said to comprise the predominant emphasis in British management thought's approach to labour relations.

SUMMARY – AND A NOTE ON
THE LIVERPOOL UNIVERSITY STUDY OF
'THE NEW MANAGERIAL IDEOLOGY'

The broad shifts within British management thought during
the 1920s and 1930s may be summarized in the following way.
There was, first, a decrease after the late 1920s in the attention
given to social responsibility and the assertion of managerial
independence from ownership. There was a continued move
towards a solidary view of the enterprise, and a narrowing
analysis of industrial conflict. After the late 1920s trade unionism by and large received little attention in management
thought. There was a steadily increasing emphasis on the human
relations approach to high labour productivity. There was some
confusion whether to emphasize the individual or the group as
the reference point for employee action, but towards the end of
this period the writings of the Mayo school began to focus
attention on to the work group. There was a pronounced
reaction against constitutional democracy in industry or any
effective worker share in control. By the 1930s, although human
relations methods were still being labelled as democratic, these
really comprised a manipulative system of managerial control
which made only limited concessions to employee participation
in decision-making.

With the steady development of organization theory,
emphasis was being laid increasingly upon the need for bureaucratic rather than traditional modes of operation, particularly
if the latter was taken to imply that management should be
regarded as an art rather than a science. Management 'principles' were developed and it was claimed that these were
universally applicable. The human relations technique of
managing labour was also assumed by the 1930s to be of value
in all situations. Finally, discussion on the range of suitable
managerial recruitment was, even in the 1920s, tending towards
the view that limitation was inevitable so long as management
required minimum levels of ability, and so long as superior
education was limited to certain groups in society. However,
some management thinkers did express their disappointment
at the lack of promotion opportunities for the majority of
manual workers.

We have argued that if the inter-war period is taken as a

whole, then there was within British management thought a noticeable shift in emphasis from an overt expression of legitimatory values such as 'service', 'democracy', or employee welfare, towards a concentration upon the technical requirements of industrial efficiency. We suggested that this shift in attention paralleled changes in general industrial and social conditions. However, we hasten to add that it was only an underlying trend. Indeed, in management writing of the 1930s there remained ample evidence of what social scientists today would consider to be a value-laden, or at least over-simplified analysis of industrial relationships. And one is forced to conclude that in some cases this type of analysis was serving definite legitimatory functions. For instance, the attempt to label human relations techniques as democratic and the claim that managers could act as workers' leaders, speaking for their interests and reconciling these with managerial requirements, clearly possessed ideological functions. It is likely that the neglect of trade unionism, and the narrowing analysis of industrial conflict which accompanied human relations, rested in part upon similar considerations. A point to emphasize, and which is one of the most interesting features about human relations, is that this appeared to offer such an effective technique because its very mode of operation was its own legitimation. Persuasive and employee-centred managerial leadership was assumed to be effective because at the same time it was alleged to satisfy workers' deep-felt needs for social satisfactions. Hence the technical process of managing labour was in essence to effect a 'spontaneous' worker acceptance of managerial authority.

Bearing this in mind, one has also to recall that for most British management writers in the 1930s human relations stood, together with the new administrative theory, as a technical advance. Whatever distortions we may see today in the assuming away of power and conflict by both these sets of ideas, it appeared to the management thinker of the 1930s that both human relations and management principles were founded upon quite adequate scientific procedures. The former were now backed by the Hawthorne studies; the latter, it was claimed, had followed inductively from a procedure of extensive comparison between organizations. To the extent that these approaches appeared to enjoy scientific support, they would clearly have to be regarded as possessing considerable value for technical performance in industry. And an examination of the relevant literature strongly suggests that in the event British management thought at this stage welcomed them mainly for their technical purpose. Proposals along human relations lines that in 1918 would typically have been stressed as part of management's greater regard for the well-being of employees, would by 1938 typically be viewed with an eye to increased productivity. The following chapter indicates how it was only in the changed circumstances of the 1940s that the idea of a managerial social mission contained in Mayoism was given greater prominence. On the basis of considerations such as these we find it most meaningful to interpret the history of British management thought between the wars in terms of a relative movement from legitimation to technique.

The fact that British management thought was made up of many individual writings renders the process of interpreting movements within it a far from easy matter. For the same reason, it is not adequate to portray this system of thought in terms of just one or two 'representative' writers. The study into *Management in Britain* carried out by members of Liverpool University selected Sir Alfred Mond, Chairman of I.C.I., to represent what they called 'the new managerial ideology' of the inter-war years.[104] Such a narrow selection of sources tends towards an under-statement of the variety of ideas characterizing the formative stages of management thought. There is no reason why Elbourne, Lee, Rowntree, Urwick or several others should not have been singled out as well.

As can be seen with the Liverpool study, one result of equating Mond's writing with management thought as a whole has been to emphasize growing scale and capitalization as determinants behind the new ideas on labour management, at the expense of giving little or no attention to other relevant factors such as changing trade union pressures or the sources of the new concepts themselves. To concentrate on Mond (and on a single collection of papers at that) is, moreover, to overlook the nuances of emphasis between alternative concepts in management thought as these appeared *over the course of time* in response to changing industrial conditions: for instance, the shifting balance of power between organized labour and employers. By taking Mond as their only source, the Liverpool authors have also overlooked the important developments in organization theory during the inter-war years. For even the management principles carried some implication for the 'new managerial ideology' in so far as they could be used to suggest the need for hierarchical control, and also in so far as they implied a 'law of the situation' to which other interests in the enterprise should be subordinated. Complexities such as these are missed by the Liverpool study. Also absent is an analysis of manage-ment thought in terms of legitimatory and technical purposes, which we argue is a necessary means to appreciate all its facets. Certainly, to select one author, and at that not one of the most original management thinkers, is to convey a misleading simplicity to what is an intricate field of study.

Finally, there is one further qualification to a review of management thought in the inter-war period. This is that the new literature, and the activity of the management movement at the Oxford and similar conferences, continued to remain alien to the great mass of practising managers and employers. Membership of the various management institutes remained minimal, and the Institute of Industrial Administration actually collapsed for several years after 1924. In 1939 the Works Management Association had only about 900 members out of an estimated 250,000 works managers in the whole of British industry.[105] Several writers complained bitterly of industry's indifference to the development of new ideas and concepts. Bowie, for example, could in 1930 chastise the great bulk of British employers, particularly those in the coal, iron and steel, cotton, woollen, pottery, and gas industries, for their conserva-tive individualism, opposition to business education, ignorance of research findings, nepotism, and secretiveness.[106] And cer-tainly the attempts of many employers in this period to cut wage-rates and lengthen hours of work in a desperate search for lower costs were completely at variance with those elementary lessons of industrial psychology which had long been absorbed by the management intellectuals.

NOTES

1. O. Sheldon, *The Philosophy of Management*, London: Pitman 1923, pp. 26, 27.
2. Editorial, *The Accountant*, 11th Feb. 1922, reproduced in the *Journal of Industrial Administration* (*J.I.A.*), I, 10, Feb. 1922, p. 318;

O. Sheldon, *op. cit.*, pp. 7, 29, 281-282; J. Lee, *An Introduction to Industrial Administration*, London: Pitman 1925, pp. v, 89; O. Sheldon, 'Industrial Organization' in ed. J. Lee, *Dictionary of Industrial Administration*, London: Pitman 1928, p. 365.

3. Cf., G. C. Vyle, 'The Third Factor in Industry', *J.I.A.*, I, 12, May-June 1922, pp. 355-359.

4. Quotations in order: O. Sheldon, *op. cit.* 1923, p. 15; J. Lee, *The Social Implications of Christianity*, London: S.C.M. 1922, p. 114; Sir A. Mond, *Industry and Politics*, London: Macmillan 1927, p. 38; *idem*, 'Rationalisation and Industrial Problems', *Manchester Guardian, Supplement on Industrial Relations*, 30th Nov. 1927, p. 7.

5. I.I.A., *The Case for the Institute*, London 1922, reproduced in T. G. Rose, *A History of the Institute of Industrial Administration 1919-1951*, London: I.I.A. 1954, p. 27.

6. G. C. Vyle, *op. cit.*, p. 356; J. Lee, *op. cit.* 1925, p. 4; O. Sheldon, *op. cit.* 1928, p. 365; J. A. Bowie, *Education for Business Management*, London: Oxford University Press 1930, p. 23.

7. I.I.A., *op. cit.*; O. Sheldon, *op. cit.* 1928, p. 366.

8. Quotations in order: I.I.A., *op. cit.*; J. Lee, *The Principles of Industrial Welfare*, London: Pitman 1924, p. 93; J. Lee, *op. cit.* 1925, p. 155; G. C. Vyle, *op. cit.*, p. 359.

9. J. Lee, *op. cit.* 1922, pp. 114-115; O. Sheldon, *op. cit.* 1923, p. 76; C. H. Northcott, 'Moral Duty of Management' in ed. J. Lee, *op. cit.* 1928, pp. 502-505; A Briggs, *Social Thought and Social Action*, London: Longmans 1961.

10. J. Lee, *op. cit.* 1925, p. 14.

11. C. H. Northcott, *op. cit.*, p. 505; cf., W. Wallace, 'The Workers' Share of the Profit' in *Quakerism and Industry 1928*, London: Society of Friends 1928, p. 19.

12. E.g., J. McKillop, 'A Specification of a Manager', *J.I.A.*, I, 9, 10, 11, Jan., Feb., March-April 1922, pp. 282-287, 309-313, 338-342.

13. B. S. Rowntree, 'The Aims and Principles of Welfare Work – II', *Welfare Work*, I, 2, Feb. 1920, p. 19; J. McKillop, *op. cit.*, p. 340; Sir J. Stamp, reported in the *J.I.A.*, II, 14, Nov.-Dec. 1922, pp. 45-46; L. Urwick, 'University Education for Business', in ed. J. Lee, *op. cit.* 1928, pp. 1014-1019.

14. G. H. Miles, 'Promotion in Industry', in ed. J. Lee, *op. cit.* 1928, pp. 692-695.

15. F. W. Taylor, *Principles of Scientific Management*, New York: Harper 1911, pp. 6-7, 26, 83; Cf., J. Lee, *Industrial Organization: developments and prospects*, London: Pitman 1923, pp. 76-79; C. H. Northcott, *op. cit.*, p. 505.

16. E. Cadbury, address of welcome in *Quakerism and Industry 1928*, *op. cit.*, p. 1; B. S. Rowntree, 'A Constructive Policy for Capitalism', *Manchester Guardian, Supplement on Industrial Relations*, 30th Nov. 1927, p. 10; H. N. Casson, *Handbook for Foremen*, London: Efficiency Magazine 1928, p. 110. (cf., Casson, *Labour Troubles and How to Prevent Them*, London: Efficiency Magazine 1919, pp. 155-163.)

17. Sir A. Mond, *Industry and Politics*, *op. cit.*, p. 125.

18. Cf., Sir A. Mond, C. G. Renold and B. S. Rowntree in *Manchester Guardian, Supplement on Industrial Relations*, 30th Nov. 1927, pp. 7, 10, 24.

19. *Quakerism and Industry 1928*, *op. cit.*, Report of the Conference, p. 89.

20. H. N. Casson, *op. cit.* 1928, p. 143; C. H. Northcott, 'The Principles and Practice of Industrial Relations', chapter IV in C. H. Northcott, O. Sheldon, J. W. Wardropper and L. Urwick, *Factory Organization*, London: Pitman 1928, p. 146 ff; L. Urwick, papers in International Industrial Relations Association, *Rational Organization and Industrial Relations*, The Hague: I.I.R.A. 1929, pp. 7, 42-43.

21. Quotations from: Sir A. Mond, *op. cit.*, *Manchester Guardian Supplement* 1927, p. 7; cf., E. Jaques, *Equitable Payment*, London: Heinemann 1961.

22. J. Lee, *op. cit.* 1922, p. 114; *idem, op. cit.* 1925, p. 171.

23. *Quakerism and Industry 1928*, *op. cit.*, Report of the Conference, p. 90.

24. C. H. Northcott in Northcott *et al.*, *op. cit.*, p. 109.

25. O. Sheldon, *op. cit.*, 1923, pp. 35-36; eds. H. C. Metcalf and L. Urwick, *Dynamic Administration: the collected papers of Mary Parker Follett*, London: Pitman 1941, p. 123 ff.

26. In order of quotation: J. Lee, *op. cit.* 1922, p. 114; J. Lee, *op. cit.* 1923, p. 14; O. Sheldon, *op. cit.* 1923, p. 195; J. Lee, *op. cit.* 1924, p. 53; Sir A. Mond, *op. cit.*, *Manchester Guardian Supplement* 1927, p. 7; C. G. Renold, in *ibid.*, p. 24; Sir A. Mond, *Industry and Politics*, *op. cit.*, p. 38; C. H. Northcott, *op. cit.* in ed. J. Lee, 1928, p. 505; O. Sheldon, 'Distribution of Responsibility' in *ibid.*, p. 745.

27. J. Lee, *op. cit.* 1925, p. 5.

28. Cf., Sir A. Mond, *Industry and Politics*, *op. cit.*, p. 110; H. N. Casson, *op. cit.* 1928, p. 142; J. Lee, 'Discipline' in ed. J. Lee 1928, p. 180; C. H. Northcott, 'Personnel Policy and Procedure', in International Industrial Relations Association, *op. cit.*, p. 97; J. A. Bowie, *op. cit.* 1930, p. 7.

29. O. Sheldon, *op. cit.* 1923, pp. 267-268; A. G. Ikin, 'The Qualities Desirable in a Foreman', *Journal of the NIIP*, II, 1, Jan. 1924: 13-17; anon., 'Foreman-training' in ed. J. Lee, 1928, pp. 317-318; J. W. Wardropper, 'Foremanship' in *ibid.*, pp. 314-317; J. A. Bowie, *op. cit.* 1930, pp. 46-47.

30. E.g., O. Sheldon, *op. cit.* 1923, pp. 272-273.

31. E.g., J. Lee, *op. cit.* 1925, p. 54 ff.

32. E. T. Kelly, 'Welfare' in ed. J. Lee, 1928, p. 1083.

33. J. Lee, *op. cit.* 1925, pp. 157-161.

34. J. W. Wardropper, *op. cit.*, p. 315.

35. Anon., 'Foreman-training' in ed. J. Lee, 1928, p. 317; C. H. Northcott, *op cit.* in International Industrial Relations Association, 1929, p. 97; L. Urwick in *ibid.*, pp. 7, 13.

36. Cf., G. Shann, 'The Philosophy of Welfare Work', a paper read to the Conference on 'Welfare Work in Factories', Bournville 1909, reprinted in *Welfare Work*, VII, 78, June 1926, esp. p. 106.

37. B. S. Rowntree, 'The Aims and Principles of Welfare Work', *Welfare Work*, I, 1, Jan. 1920, p. 5.

38. 'What the Welfare Workers' Institute Stands For', *Welfare, Work*, I, 4, April 1920, p. 57; Editorial, *Welfare Work*, VIII, 89, May 1927, p. 81.

39. J. Lee, *op. cit.* 1925, pp. 172-173.

40. E. T. Kelly, 'The Welfare Supervisor' in ed. J. Lee, 1928, p. 1084; A. S. Cole, letter in *Welfare Work and Personnel Administration*, XIII, 135, March 1931, p. 278.

41. O. Tead, 'Methods of Increasing Output', in ed. J. Lee 1928, p. 560. (Tead was a prominent member of the American management movement.)

42. O. Sheldon, *op. cit.* 1923, chapter V, esp. p. 187 ff; J. Lee, *op. cit.* 1925, esp. p. 99; Sir A. Mond, *Industry and Politics*, *op. cit.*, *passim*; C. G. Renold, speech reported in *Towards Industrial Peace*, report of a conference held at the London School of Economics Feb. 1927, pp. 260-262; J. Lee, *Letters to an Absentee Director*, London: Pitman 1928, letters 14 and 18.

43. C. H. Northcott *et al.*, *op. cit.*, p. 146.

44. Institute of Industrial Administration, *op. cit.* 1922.

45. J. Lee, 'Discipline' in ed. J. Lee, 1928, p. 180.

46. O. Sheldon, *op. cit.* 1923, pp. 68-69.

47. C. G. Renold, 'Scientific Management' in ed. J. Lee 1928, p. 767; L. Urwick, 'Principles of Direction and Control' in *ibid.*, p. 169.

48. C. G. Renold, quoted in M. Bloomfield, *The New Labour Movement in Great Britain*, London: Fisher Unwin 1920, p. 163; numerous early articles on organization structure in the *Journal of Industrial Administration* (*J.I.A.*). E.g. that by A. H. Railing in vol. II, 14, Nov.-Dec. 1922, pp. 48-54, and the issue on organization, I, 6, Oct. 1921; O. Sheldon, *op. cit.* 1923, chapter IV; O. Sheldon, 'Function of Administration and Organization' in ed. J. Lee, 1928, pp. 10-16.

49. J. Lee, 'The Pros and Cons of Functionalization' (a paper of Sept. 1928) in eds. L. Gulick and L. Urwick, *Papers on the Science of Administration*, New York: Columbia University Press 1937, pp. 173-179.

50. J. Lee, *op. cit.* 1925, p. 7.

51. E. T. Elbourne, editorial, *J.I.A.*, I, 11, March-April 1922, p. 322.

52. H. R. Sankey, 'Training for Administration in Industry', *J.I.A.*, II, 14, Nov.-Dec. 1922, p. 36.

53. J. Lee. *op. cit.* 1925, p. 52.

54. L. Urwick, 'Principles of Direction and Control' in ed. J. Lee, 1928, pp. 161-179.

55. L. Urwick, 'Rational Organization' in International Industrial Relations Association, *op. cit.* 1929, pp. 37-38.

56. Sir A. Mond, *op. cit.*, in *Manchester Guardian Supplement* 1927, p. 7; L. Urwick, *The Meaning of Rationalisation*, London: Nisbet 1929, p. 26.

57. C. S. Myers, *Business Rationalisation*, London: Pitman 1932, chapter 2.

58. Ed. J. Lee, *Dictionary of Industrial Administration*, London: Pitman 1928.

59. L. Urwick, *Management of Tomorrow*, London: Nisbet 1933.

60. *Ibid.*, pp. 7, 145 ff, 153 ff.

61. E. T. Elbourne, *Fundamentals of Industrial Administration*, London: Macdonald & Evans 1934, esp. pp. 562-563, 570-576, 596, 606-607.

62. J. D. Mooney and A. C. Reiley, *Onward Industry! – The principles of organization and their significance to modern industry*, New York: Harper 1931.

63. L. Urwick, 'Organization as a Technical Problem' (a paper of 1933) reprinted in eds. L. Gulick and L. Urwick, *Papers on the Science of Administration*, *op. cit.*, pp. 49-88. Quotation is from p. 49.

64. L. Urwick, 'The Function of Administration, with Special Reference to the Work of Henri Fayol' (a paper of 1934), reprinted in eds. L. Gulick and L. Urwick, *op. cit.*, p. 122.

65. C. B. Frisby, 'Psychology Applied to Organization', *The Human Factor*, VII, 6th June 1933, pp. 224-231.

66. L. Urwick, *The Elements of Administration*, London: Pitman 1943, pp. 36-39.

67. L. Urwick, 'Organization as a Technical Problem', *op. cit.*, p. 52.

68. L. Urwick, *Management of Tomorrow*, *op. cit.*, pp. 51, 56; *idem, The Elements of Administration*, *op. cit.*, p. 117.

69. L. Urwick, 'Administration and Society', *British Management Review*, III, 2, April-June 1938, p. 29.

70. L. Urwick, *Management of Tomorrow*, *op. cit.*, pp. 64-66; *idem,* 'Organization as a Technical Problem', *op. cit.*, esp. p. 61 ff.

71. T. Burns and G. M. Stalker, *The Management of Innovation*, London: Tavistock 1961, chapter 6.

72. V. A. Graicunas, 'Relationship in Organization' in eds. L. Gulick and L. Urwick, *op. cit.* 1937, pp. 183-187.

73. L. Urwick, 'Mary Follett: a Philosophy of Management', *Industry Illustrated*, April 1934, p. 20.

74. L. Urwick, 'Co-partnership and Control', *The Human Factor*, VIII, 11, Nov. 1934, p. 394.

75. C. H. Northcott, summary of the 1936 Oxford Management Conference, *Industry Illustrated*, Oct. 1936, p. 7.

76. E. Mayo, *The Human Problems of an Industrial Civilization*, New York: Macmillan 1933, esp. chapter VIII; T. N. Whitehead, *Leadership in a Free Society*, London: Oxford University Press 1936.

77. T. N. Whitehead, *op. cit.*, chapter XI.

108   BRITISH MANAGEMENT THOUGHT

78. Editorial, *Industry Illustrated*, May 1937, p. 9.
79. E.g., A. H. Seymour, 'Successful Foremanship in Modern Industry', *Labour Management*, XVIII, 196, June 1936, pp. 105-106.
80. E.g., Editorial, *Labour Management*, XV, 161, May 1933, p. 77.
81. E. Mayo, 'Supervision and Morale', *Journal of the NIIP*, V, 5, Jan. 1931, pp. 248-260.
82. M. B. Gilson, review of F. J. Roethlisberger and W. J. Dickson, *Management and the Worker* 1939 in *American Journal of Sociology*, XLVI, 1, July 1940, pp. 98-101.
83. F. J. Roethlisberger and W. J. Dickson, *Management and the Worker*, Cambridge, Mass.: Harvard University Press 1939, pp. 536-537.
84. E.g., J. Woodward, 'Industrial Behaviour – is There a Science?', *New Society*, IV, 106, 8th Oct. 1964, p. 12.
85. B. Muscio, *Lectures on Industrial Psychology*, London: Routledge rev. ed. 1920, p. 266 ff; C. S. Myers, *Mind and Work*, University of London Press 1920, chapters IV and V; G. H. Miles, 'Industrial Psychology' in ed. J. Lee, *op. cit.* 1928, p. 382; J. Drever, 'The Human Factor in Industrial Relations' in ed. C. S. Myers, *Industrial Psychology*, London: Butterworth 1929, p. 33 ff.
86. E.g., 36th Oxford Management Conference, report of a study group on 'Welfare Aspects of Personnel' in the *British Management Review*, II, 2, April-June 1937, p. 209.
87. Editorial, *Industry Illustrated*, May 1937, p. 9.
88: E. S. Byng, 'Administration – a Profession', *The Human Factor*, X, 11, Nov. 1936, p. 387.
89. *Op. cit.*, p. 9.
90. L. Urwick, reported in the *British Management Review*, April-June 1937, p. 28; 36th Oxford Management Conference study group, *op. cit.*; H. E. Collier, 'The Needs of Everyman – a Study of Human Relations in Industry', in *Quakerism and Industry 1938*, London: Society of Friends 1938, p. 93.
91. Editorial, *Industry Illustrated*, Oct. 1937, p. 9.
92. C. H. Northcott, 'Planned Progress of Business, *British Management Review*, II, 1, Jan.-March 1937, p. 129.
93. Editorial, *Industry Illustrated*, Jan. 1933, p. 1.
94. B. S. Rowntree, 'Some Industrial Problems of To-day', *Journal of the NIIP*, V, 7, July 1931, pp. 370-375.
95. E.g., T. E. Hull, 'Everyday Principles of Works Management', *Industry Illustrated*, July 1933, p. 6.
96. E.g., A. H. Seymour, 'Successful Foremanship in Modern Industry', *op. cit.*, p. 106.
97. J. J. Gillespie, *Training in Foremanship and Management*, London: Pitman 1934, p. 155; 39th Oxford Management Conference discussion group, reported in the *British Management Review*, IV, 1, Jan.-March 1939, pp. 85-87.
98. *Quakerism and Industry 1938*, *op. cit.*, speeches by J. H. Guy, pp. 23, 28, 31; and by William Wallace, p. 110.

99. C. H. Northcott, 'Survey of the Conditions Necessary for Optimum Productivity', *British Management Review*, III, 3, July-Sept. 1938, p. 223.

100. E.g., A. P. M. Fleming, 'Recruitment for Industry', *British Management Review*, I, 2, April-June 1936, pp. 179, 182.

101. E.g., 37th Oxford Management Conference, reports of discussion groups on 'Recruitment and Training Managers of the Future', and 'The Works Manager, his Training and Duties' in *Industry Illustrated*, Nov. 1937, pp. 24-25 and 32.

102. E.g., F. H. Bullock, 'What the Works Manager Expects from Foremen and Supervisors', *Industry Illustrated*, March 1934, pp. 52, 55; A. P. Young, Speech reported in *Industry Illustrated*, Nov. 1934, p. 65.

103. 38th Oxford Management Conference, study group on 'Relations with Organised Labour', *British Management Review*, III, 3, July-Sept. 1938, p. 78; C. H. Northcott, 'Human Aspects of Administration', *British Management Review*, IV, 1, Jan.-March 1939, pp. 114-124.

104. I. C. McGivering, D. G. J. Matthews, and W. H. Scott, *Management In Britain*, Liverpool University Press 1960, p. 91 ff.

105. Editorial, *Industry Illustrated*, May 1939.

106. J. A. Bowie, *op. cit.* 1930, pp. 115-136; Cf. also I. C. McGivering *et al.*, *op. cit.*, pp. 89-91; L. Urwick and E. F. L. Brech, *The Making of Scientific Management*, *op. cit.*, vol. II, p. 191 ff.

CHAPTER 5

A PERIOD OF STRESS
(World War II and after)

The Setting – the Zenith of Human Relations: (1) the influence of Hawthorne and of Mary Parker Follett; (2) the supremacy of human relations in Britain; (3) human relations, repetition and analogy; (4) human relations, the function and meaning of 'participative' leadership; (5) human relations, a narrowed perspective of industrial conflict; (6) human relations, its pervading influence – The Concept of Managerial Professionalism; professionalism and recruitment to management – Principles of Management – Dissent from Human Relations: (1) alternatives to human relations in British management thought; (2) some early critiques of human relations – Summary.

THIS chapter reviews the years from 1940 to about the mid-1950s. The first part of this period saw considerable public criticism of managerial inefficiencies, and political changes which placed new strains upon those who spoke and thought for management. At the same time there was a culmination of previous developments within British management thought. Human relations and the management principles attained their greatest influence, immediately before they came to attract the critical attention of empirical social science. It was a time when, as late as January 1954, the editor of *The Manager* still felt able to claim that management enjoyed 'a well-established structure' of knowledge which possessed 'only minor gaps'.[1]

This chapter divides into five main sections. The first briefly summarizes the environment of management thought during this period. The second and longest section is concerned with the human relations approach at the height of its influence. The third considers the progress of the idea of managerial professionalism, and the fourth refers to further writing on management principles. Finally, the fifth section describes some early examples of dissent from human relations which may be found in the management literature. These foreshadow more recent critiques at the hands of social scientists, which are to be discussed in Chapter 6.

I. THE SETTING

The national emergency in the summer of 1940 brought out both the vital necessity for competent industrial management, and the way in which the majority of British employers had ignored even the most elementary technical advances made by the management movement. The 17th Report of the Select Committee on National Expenditure issued late in 1940, and the Chief Inspector of Factories' Report for the same year, together clearly indicated how most employers were oblivious of the lessons deriving from research into fatigue and working conditions during the First World War. The gravity of this situation, concurrent with Bevin's appointment to the Ministry of Labour, led to direct governmental action enforcing the appointment of personnel officers in all but small factories and the compulsory provision of minimum 'welfare amenities. Shortly after, the government strongly encouraged the widespread establishment of joint production committees following the Essential Work Orders of 1941.[2]

Sir Walter Puckey writing in 1944 commented that this extensive introduction of joint committees meant that 'the theory of the "infallibility of management" was severely shaken'.[3] In fact, the whole process of admonition from the State was a stigma on British management. As the war proceeded, a number of publications fanned the flames of criticism by their indictment of managerial inefficiencies, and by reporting how hostile managers frequently were to new methods of accommodation with labour.[4] Following these events and continuing some time after the war, British management was faced with a relatively hostile press, a fact which led some management spokesmen to comment bitterly on the low public esteem of their colleagues in industry at large.[5] Altogether, after the lacuna of the 1930s the management movement once more faced the need not only to excuse those it stood for, but also to impart to them concepts and methods which it had already come to take for granted.

This need by no means relaxed once the war was over. If the 1945 election result was in part a condemnation of the 1930s, then correspondingly the rough managerial methods associated with an easier labour market shared in the blame. Moreover, full employment and the greatly strengthened trade union movement presented powerful inducements for managers to find a more effective philosophy towards labour than domination or indifference. We shall see shortly how this changed balance of power in industry was widely recognized by management thinkers, and how they most strenuously urged an alternative human relations approach on to managers out in the factories. With renewed bargaining strength, trade union expectations increased regarding rights of consultation and negotiation. Nationalization was in fact granting union officials access to boards of control, and enshrining by statute a form of joint consultation which specifically endorsed the right to criticize managerial inefficiencies.

However, it is important to notice that under the nationalization statutes the rights of worker representatives were confined to criticism, rather than including any control over or participation in managerial decisions. These rights were directed at performance rather than policy. Further, the trade union movement by now had little intention of using nationalization as a means to 'workers' control'. Indeed, it took great care to avoid the creation of 'dual responsibility' for its officials. If union officers were appointed to the boards of nationalized industries they were relieved from their union duties.

The situation facing the British management movement after 1945 was thus fundamentally different from that following the First World War. Both situations found the movement in a defensive position, but what they had to defend was not the same. The previous situation was one in which an important part of the labour movement and many intellectuals were questioning managerial authority at its very roots; many were at that time attacking the very principle of management. However, at the close of the Second World War, the necessity of a managerial function was generally accepted, and criticism was now directed mainly at the performance managers were offering and the methods they were using. We shall suggest in this chapter that this difference in setting had some bearing on the fact that the renewed attempt at social legitimation to be found in management thought during the 1940s and early 1950s was part and parcel of the human relations techniques upon which it relied. There was a profound difference between this kind of legitimation, which in essence followed from what was considered to be effective technique, and the notions formulated around 1918 of renunciation, shared control and the like, which in a sense had been advanced prior to 'technical' considerations. It would not be too far wrong to simplify and conclude that the earlier type of legitimation was aimed at securing the right of managers to perform at all, while the later type was much more a justification of the methods that were chosen to obtain effective performance.

Certainly, the economic crises of the post-war years, the balance of payments gap, and the notion of a planned economy, all focused attention on to managerial performance. This in fact continued to attract severe criticism,[6] and it remains today among the more popular public references for national economic ills. Members of the management movement, the intellectual apologists, were during this period themselves moved to complain that so many British employers failed to share their concern for new concepts and methods, particularly in the field of labour management.[7]

This last fact serves as a reminder that after the Second World War, as before it, there was an important distinction between the activities of the management movement and British managers at large. This gap was narrowed somewhat after the beginning of the war by the remarkable development of new writers, the steady growth of membership among the various management institutes, and recently by the rising interest in management education. For instance, the membership of the Institute of Industrial Administration rose from 517 at the end of 1939 to 2,508 by the end of 1945. The British Institute of Management with which it merged in 1951 had 19,000 members at the end of January 1968. The membership of the Institute of Personnel Management (formerly the Institute of Labour Management) rose from 760 in 1939 to 5,730 by 1963, despite a new constitution in 1955 which made entry to the Institute more difficult. The 1960s appear to have witnessed a particularly rapid rise in this Institute's membership – for the figure was still only 2,993 in June 1960.

On the other hand, these rising membership figures still did not account for the great majority of practising managers. The I.P.M. proportion has been unusually high, accounting in recent years for perhaps a third of all personnel officers. However, in 1948 the British Institute of Management estimated that there were upwards of 400,000 persons exercising managerial responsibilities in manufacturing industry alone, and the figure today is certainly higher. In the same year the B.I.M. estimated that, making no allowances for duplications, the membership of all existing management institutes taken together was no more than 20,000. One can now see what a small proportion of British managers are covered by the central management institute with its recent membership figure of 19,000; similarly in June 1963 the Institution of Works Managers had only 5,164 members.[8] During the post-war period the proportion of managers experiencing management training courses remained minute,[9] and even recently (1966-67) the total number of students enrolled for the major effort in management education, the national Diploma in Management Studies, was only 3,700 in England and Wales. While the extreme lack of sympathy for management thought and education found among practising managers during the inter-war years was by now on the wane, it remained formidable. Puckey, for instance, has recently reminded us of the hostility which many managers showed during the war towards even the introduction of joint consultation.[10] In short, management thought remained the product of relatively few intellectuals.

II. THE ZENITH OF HUMAN RELATIONS

(1) *The influence of Hawthorne and of Mary Parker Follett*
During the 1940s, the writings of the Mayo school, and to a lesser extent those of Mary Parker Follett, were taken up and expounded by the British management movement on a considerably wider scale and with more force than during the 1930s. The war had only too clearly indicated the painful divergence between management thought and managerial practice. It had shown management thinkers that their educative task had to start almost at the beginning. For instance, it was found that in the early 1940s the vast majority of personnel managers, let along other managers, had not even heard of the various publications on the Hawthorne experiments.[11] It is this awakening to the task of 'selling' their ideas to industry at large which explains why it was only in the 1940s that manage-

ment writers began so insistently to advertise their human relations teaching as a 'new' step forward for industry. One is faced at this time with a number of works bearing titles such as *The New Foremanship* and *New Times, New Methods and New Men*.[12] The human relations approach was now given an unprecedented level of propaganda, although it will become abundantly clear that the managerial methods expounded were by no means novel to British management thought.

During the war years, exposition of the Mayo school's work remained in the hands of a relatively small band of writers – E. F. L. Brech, F. J. Burns Morton, C. H. Northcott, and L. Urwick being chief among them. After 1945 the human relations approach was carried forward by a wave of new spokesmen, prominent among these being J. A. C. Brown, V. M. Clarke R. P. Lynton, J. Munro Fraser, J. F. Scott, G. R. Taylor, and R. F Tredgold. Mayo himself came over to address the 1947 National Conference of the Institute of Personnel Management. Undoubtedly the most influential of these early British publications on the Hawthorne researches was Urwick and Brech's long series of articles in *Industry Illustrated* from November 1944 to July 1946, later incorporated into the third volume of their *The Making of Scientific Management*.[13] More recently, J. A. C. Brown's review in the Penguin *Social Psychology of Industry* has probably had most impact; it has certainly enjoyed great popularity among management teachers.[14] In the work referred to, Urwick and Brech summarized their reason for reproducing the Harvard School's writings, and gave an interpretation of the Hawthorne experiments which came to be widely accepted within the British management movement:

'These investigations have not yet attracted in this country, especially among the ranks of sociologists and industrial managers, the degree of interest that their quality deserves or the appreciation and attention that their importance demands. Yet they are in themselves a handbook of all that is implied in the modern approach to management, which sees it as in essence a leadership of people and a social task of human beings among other human beings.'[15]

Mary Parker Follett's formulations on human relations also received a sustained, and even growing, attention during the 1940s and 1950s, largely on the assumption that they implied much the same *practice* of management as did the Mayoist writings. In fact, these writings were seen as a further stage in developing that science of human relations for which Follett had worked. The Mayo emphasis on 'social skills', oriented towards both the maintenance of social integration in the factory and the acceptance of managerial goals, was regarded as implying much the same type of managerial procedure as Follett's notions of 'integration' and 'power with'. Both Follett and the Mayo school implied that the 'human' side of management involved in essence a process of personal persuasive leadership. This was intended to release the enthusiasm for co-operation with management which, according to Mayo, work groups possessed as the result of their deep-felt needs for 'belonging'. Management had to adopt a participative procedure which on the one hand allowed workers to feel some emotional involvement in the activities of the enterprise, while on the other hand retaining initiative and final authority firmly in managerial hands. The methods of persuasive leadership indicated by Follett, and even more by Chester Barnard and the Mayo school, were expected in these ways to add a carefully regulated dynamic aspect to the static organizational framework already outlined by the management principles.[16]

Hence both informal and formal relationships now appeared to be open to managerial control. Strictly speaking this would be the case at any level of the enterprise (following Follett and Barnard), but in the event the greater part of discussion in British management thought along human relations lines was confined to the question of securing the co-operation of lower level employees. Speaking at the 47th Oxford Management Conference in 1944, Urwick discussed this synthesis of ideas from Follett and Mayo:

'We are back at the same point as was emphasized by Mary Follett and by Elton Mayo. Our practical war experience issues in the same conclusion as their scientific studies. Industrial relations are primarily a matter of psychology. They must be an integral part of all management, not a segregated function. And the key to them is effective leadership at all levels.'[17]

Urwick, in fact, edited two volumes of Follett's papers in 1941 and 1949, which made her work considerably more accessible.

This synthesis of Follett and Mayo was chiefly one of managerial method, in which the theoretical inconsistencies between the two pioneers were largely overlooked. For instance, the very significant divergence between Follett's concept of 'constructive conflict' and Mayo's deep abhorrence of conflict in any form appears to have received little attention among British management writers. Nor was much notice given to the difference between Follett's belief that all levels in the enterprise could come rationally to accept the 'law of the situation', and the Mayoist assumption that worker action was largely governed by a 'sentiment' which was of a different order to managers' rational appraisal of the situation in terms of costs and efficiency. Thus in Follett's theory, integration within the enterprise was expected to derive from a sharing in decision-making on the basis of functional knowledge. In Mayo's theory, integration had to be achieved by the calculated social manipulation of one party by the other. We have mentioned in Chapter 4 how, regardless of her theoretical standpoint, British management writers were in the 1930s already coming to interpret Follett in practical terms not at all dissimilar to the recommendations of the Mayo school. Indeed, the whole continuity of human relations in British management thought is expressed far more in terms of recommended managerial methods than in the finer points of conceptual analysis. This continuity at the level of technique helps to explain how management thought was able so readily to absorb sources expressing such diverse values as did the Quaker employers, Mary Follett, and Elton Mayo.

(2) The supremacy of human relations in Britain

Human relations occupied a pre-eminent position in British management thought until about the mid-1950s. Not only did it dominate discussion on the 'human' side of management, but it also caused this for a while to overshadow the study of other branches of management. Its salient points are well known to all students of management. Indeed they are so familiar that there is some danger of overlooking alternative schools of thought present among management spokesmen during this period. We discuss these alternatives shortly.

Human relations, in the form it took by this time, incorporated several assumptions deriving from a combination of previous British writing and from ideas set out by Follett and the Mayo school. In the first place, the industrial enterprise was regarded in an extremely solidary light – as an 'organic' unity possessing a single, commonly-held 'culture'.[18] Earlier British thinking, as expressed in Northcott's favourite phrase – 'a venture in co-operation' – joined with Follett's 'integration' and Mayo's 'spontaneous collaboration' to support this view of the factory as a natural unity.

Secondly, following Mayo, the problem of labour management was seen as the removal of barriers to collaboration and the reconciliation of both efficiency and social satisfaction within the ambit of common purpose provided by the goals of the enterprise. The worker's 'whole person' had to be enlisted in pursuit of this common purpose during his hours of work. Moreover, the Hawthorne experiments and various attitude surveys were taken as evidence to show that the primary source of worker motivation lay with non-monetary, 'social' rewards from work.[19] Further, the Relay Assembly Room at Hawthorne (which received considerably more attention in Britain than the very different story in the Bank Wiring Room) had suggested that worker productivity depended primarily not on physical working conditions but on contentment and social satisfaction. This in turn seemed to relate chiefly to the structuring of the work group and the style of first-line supervision.

Thirdly, this reasoning placed the onus for securing worker performance squarely upon management, and in particular on the foreman. It was assumed that worker attitudes and efforts were largely determined by the quality of supervision. The foreman had 'probably more influence than any other on workroom atmosphere, efficiency and morale', an assumption which in fact we have met with already, back in the early 1920s.[20] However, in the 1940s a combination of publicly exposed mis-management early in the war, and of the callousness popularly associated with the depression years, turned foremanship into an issue of some urgency for the management movement. The burden placed on the foreman reached unbearable proportions, and indeed there is a case for suggesting that much of this development was legitimatory as well as technical in purpose; that in fact the blame for the mis-management of labour was being shifted on to the foreman's shoulders.

In the event, pages of exhortation appeared in the 1940s and early 1950s, warning foremen that they should secure results by concentrating on the human leadership aspects of their task, listing the qualities necessary for men who wished to be selected as supervisors, and backed by a continuous repetition of slogans such as 'morale', 'teamwork' and other elements in the

human relations philosophy. There was scarcely any appreciation of the practical difficulties likely to face foremen in their
efforts to motivate industrial workers who now enjoyed the
relative security of a full employment economy. Instead the
supervisor was presented with instructions by writers such as
F. J. Burns Morton to the effect that:

'The foreman is expected to be the father of the flock, to be the natural
as well as the appointed leader to whom people may turn with
confidence for advice and guidance. On the foreman will depend
the degree of enthusiasm for the job. . . . As a leader in the workshop
the foreman should: (a) weld the group together as a harmonious
whole, (b) maintain authority in the democratic group, (c) encourage
spontaneous discipline, (d) accept full responsibility for the group, (e)
establish firm, fair, friendly treatment of employees, (f) raise morale,
and create enthusiasm, (g) inspire security, certainty and confidence.'[21]

It was again stressed that foremen formed an integral part of
management, and managers were urged to follow policies which
made this a reality in practice.[22]

Fourthly, the human relations emphasis on common interests
led to discussion on methods of communication aimed at making
this common purpose clearly known to all employees. Downward rather than upward communication received most
attention. It was felt that communication should be informal
and via the medium of supervisory leadership, rather than
channelled through joint consultation.[23] For this last procedure
was thought to involve considerable problems of reporting
back, while the presence of trade unionists as employee representatives might carry the risk of 'distorted' information passing
back to the shop floor. The irony in having to make known to
employees what was supposed to be a shared purpose, and of
having in effect to create a co-operation which was supposed
to be spontaneous and eagerly desired, indicates the manipulative features in what was put forward as a democratic and participative system of industrial control. This inconsistency appears
to have been excused by the assumption that 'misunderstandings'
could easily arise in large organizations, and that communications were merely an attempt to minimize these. In other words,
the sheer hierarchical distance in such organizations between
top management and workers meant that the former had to take
special care in communicating their interpretation of the common interest down to workshop level.

Not surprisingly, little satisfactory explanation was found for trade unionism in this scheme of things. Some writers, Northcott for instance, were prepared to admit that union membership should be encouraged. Other exponents of human relations, G. R. Taylor and Urwick for example, did not see the need for unionism with the type of management they were advocating. Taylor was particularly forthright on this matter: '. . . the unions have a vested interest in maintaining a management-worker conflict, because it is their function to organise such conflict. In the sort of factory organisation which I have attempted to describe there would be no function for the unions as they now exist.'[24] This second type of writer favoured an attempt to win back the loyalty of factory workers from their trade unions. For not only were unions external to the individual enterprise and its special interests, but it was assumed (following T. N. Whitehead) that a socially skilled management could now satisfy workers' needs for belonging in a far more direct way than unions could ever do.[25]

That management should now make an attempt to satisfy workers' 'social' needs was a fundamental assumption among all those favouring the human relations approach. Spokesmen both within and outside the British management movement took the view that something was amiss if the factory was not a socially satisfying environment for employees, and if these satisfactions had to be found elsewhere.[26] This analysis was limited to a social-psychological frame of reference, and indeed many professional psychologists added their authority to it.[27] It focused on the small group level of inter-personal interaction, and did not encourage a necessary and complementary appreciation of how institutions external to the enterprise, including organized interest associations, could influence worker action. For, after all, such considerations did not fit easily into the new type of personnel policy whose 'keynote . . . must be the removal of the old anomaly of divided loyalties'.[28]

Finally, although the greater part of the human relations emphasis on worker contentment was directed at the increase of co-operation and productivity within factories, there was also some attempt to incorporate Mayo's ideas on the wider social purpose of the administrator. This was especially true of the 1940s, and as we note in the later section on professionalism, it formed part of a revival in social legitimation put out by the management movement, chiefly to meet the tide of social criticism it faced at the time. There was some repetition of the old denial that profitability was management's primary goal. An attempt was made to emphasize instead the notion of co-operation for a common goal and to stress the social goodwill which was presumed to follow from this approach. Lloyd Roberts, who for a while after 1938 became President of the Institute of Labour Management, among others gave out this message. A speech of his in 1943 to an audience of foremen was reported in *Labour Management*:

'Mr Lloyd Roberts built his address round the naval phrase "A Happy Ship". He said that the old conception in industry was based on the amount of money to be made out of it, and he suggested that the proper outlook was how much happiness sprang from it; happiness resulting from the efficiency of its human relations and bred of a sense of security and self-respect in all the members of the team. The development of this outlook depended to a great extent on the foremen in whose hands rested the responsibility for communicating the spirit of this policy to the workers.'[29]

The chairman of the National Coal Board, opening the 1951 I.P.M. National Conference, expected the 'new' foremanship to create what he called 'a happy industrial family'.[30] Some writers went further in accepting a Mayoist view of the industrial manager as an agent of social rehabilitation. A. P. Young in 1947 was of 'the view that the world of industry can become the most powerful generator of this spiritual energy of goodwill for which the people everywhere are hungering in their hearts'.[31] As recently as 1957 the editor of *Personnel Management* (as the journal was now called) took the view that managers should pay more heed to their 'great responsibility' regarding drunkenness and sexual licence among the young.[32]

Even though they may seem extreme, these views were by no means exceptional among human relations spokesmen in this period. It is not difficult to recognize the neo-paternalism that lurked close behind them. Interestingly, the idea of the managerial social mission received additional support during the 1940s from some prominent members of both the clergy and judiciary.[33] We shall note later how human relations concepts came to find acceptance even among senior members of the labour movement, a most extraordinary situation considering their implications for trade unionism and constitutional procedures within the enterprise. There was also some reference in management thought during this period to the older theory of 'holding the balance' between the various parties to production. However, this was now subordinated to the newer concept of social cohesion, which of course avoided any implication of conflicting interests. For, as will become clear, the view of industrial conflict which was by now accompanying human relations did not include a willingness to recognize the existence of divergent interests within the industrial enterprise.

These social legitimations were complemented by a set of apologies for the manipulative methods that were now being urged so openly upon British employers. It was claimed that the participative style of managerial leadership could translate 'the vision of a true industrial democracy into a living dynamic reality'. Or as Northcott put it in 1951, 'sound administration is democratic'.[34] In this way a combination of Follett's ideal of organizational democracy – the 'power with' – and the social psychologist's more technical 'democratic leadership' style was assimilated into management thought. Nevertheless, while some writers might as a result proclaim a twofold responsibility for management – A. R. Cooper, for instance, echoed John Lee's words of 1925 in writing of 'producing both men and materials'[35] – the former and idealistic task, however convenient it was from the legitimatory point of view, was now definitely being viewed as a by-product of the latter.

In short, Lord Piercy has perhaps supplied us with one of the best summaries of the human relations theme in management thought during this period, when as recently as 1959 he stated:

'To be efficient, so runs the newer thinking, the industrial enterprise must constitute a social group; a social group which is harmonious, confident in its leadership, aware of and interested in the common aim of the undertaking.'[36]

We hope now, in the following pages, to illustrate further the nature of human relations during the 1940s and 1950s by picking out a few of its more distinctive features.

(3) *Human relations – repetition and analogy*
It has already become apparent that human relations possessed several less appealing features. It tended to rely upon exhortation, and was prone to sweeping pronouncements. Its language was often vague. Moreover, it was repetitive, both in the way

that one writer closely followed what others had said and in the sense that many features of what Piercy called 'the newer thinking' were in reality far from new. We have seen that the 'new foremanship' was far from original. And while writers such as Burns Morton and G. R. Taylor now felt that employees had to be led away from their 'wrong views on economic matters', so equally had Casson in 1919.[37] If in 1948, M. A. Cameron could argue that Communism derived support from a managerial failure to understand industrial relations, Casson again had made a similar point back in the 1920s.[38] Mrs V. M. Clarke's view, that 'what most enlightened businesses realise is that industry is not merely concerned with production but with the "making of men" ', had not only been put in identical terms 25 years beforehand, but came very near to Edward Cadbury's opinion of 1912 which we quoted in Chapter 2.[39]

This repetition of ideas indicates the historical continuity enjoyed by British management thought. It illustrates how it derived many of its concepts from ideas which had already been formulated by previous management writers. It would also seem to suggest that many of the problems facing the management movement over the years had changed not so much in kind as in relative urgency. To contrast this historical continuity in management thought with the extreme criticism it has recently received from many social scientists, is to appreciate the revolution in outlook which they are attempting to effect in management education.

The analogies employed by writers in this period to support the human relations approach showed a similar lack of novelty. The First World War had encouraged thinkers such as Deeley and Hichens to hold out military leadership and 'the comradeship of the trenches' as models for management to emulate. In much the same way, the careful attention given by Montgomery and Slim to the preservation of morale in adverse circumstances, through close communication and personal leadership, was put forward as a model for management. Slim's list of charismatic leadership qualities closely matched those which management spokesmen were urging foremen to adopt. And these were equally vague – courage, willpower, flexibility of mind, knowledge, and integrity. His definition of leadership as 'the projection of personality' fitted well into the human relations scheme. As late as 1961, Slim was to be found giving perhaps the most

senior lecture in the British management world, using the kind
of analogy we have mentioned. Particularly enlightening was
his universalistic type of claim that 'all leadership, civilian or
military, and at all levels whether of ten men or ten million
men, is essentially the same and calls for the same qualities'.[40]
Urwick, who felt that a certain amount of managerial charisma
had to supplement a sound organization as the basis for effective
industrial operation, also readily employed the army analogy.
For he insisted, as he had always done, on his equally universalistic belief that principles of organization and leadership were
the same in any institutional context.[41] Among others who have
employed the military analogy, we may single out Tredgold
mainly to illustrate the quality of reasoning behind the comparison: 'I cannot help feeling that the Army has something
still to teach industry (it has been going a long time).'[42]

Another popular analogy was that of the 'football team'.
Sir Frederic Hooper, for instance, described 'a good climate of
work' as one in which the worker 'speaks and thinks of the
whole business unit he works in as "we", in the same way as a
man at cricket or football says "we" when he talks of his team'.[43]
While, of course, an analogy is intended only as an approximate
illustration, one has to take its implications seriously, particularly when these are spelt out for us. To take a last example,
there is a sociological naïvety (or a cynicism) somewhat difficult
to credit, when a senior industrialist tries to compare management to the leadership of a children's 'gang', enthusiastic and
co-operative in the building of a 'den' or the pursuit of a game.
However, in this case Sir Ernest Lever used his analogy openly
to illustrate the essentially manipulative system of industrial
control he was advocating: 'The managed and the led should
be able to see manager and leader clearly and not too far ahead,
knowing the way, showing the way – they will then follow
willingly.'[44]

(4) *Human relations – the function and meaning of 'participative'
leadership*
We have seen how in much human relations writing a form of
neo-paternalism stood together with slogans of 'participation'
and even of 'democracy'. Similarly, how 'common purpose'
was typically defined so as to exclude the representation of
employees' purposes by their own chosen trade union officers.

Inconsistencies such as these require closer examination. It is necessary, first, to ascertain what motivated this kind of 'double-talk', and second, what these management writers really meant by their concepts.

To take the first question, human relations spokesmen were in fact often quite frank in admitting the purpose that lay behind their doctrines. For such openness was imperative if they in turn were to convince the mass of British management that it was worth attending to what they taught. We noted earlier in this chapter that the greater part of the labour movement at this time was no longer committed to a policy of 'workers' control', in the sense of workers actively assuming the managerial role itself. Indeed, the Trade Union Congress had in 1944 explicitly rejected this type of demand.[45] Nonetheless, we also noted that British management in this period was burdened with a reputation of poor performance and of using incompetent, anti-social and old-fashioned methods of labour management. Simultaneously the maintenance of full employment was making it difficult to motivate labour by the traditional, material means of 'carrot and stick'. There was unquestionably a major shift in the balance of factory power towards manual employees. Whatever the acquiescent attitudes of trade union leadership, unofficial activity at shop floor level was from a managerial point of view coming to present a serious nuisance. In short, a major task now facing the management movement was the propagation of a human relations technique, which it believed would procure discipline and encourage greater co-operation towards the pursuit of productivity.

Thus British management thinkers argued that in this new situation industry had of necessity to adopt a new set of workshop tactics. As early as 1943, Burns Morton wrote that any continuation of older authoritarian methods of supervision 'is completely to misunderstand the character of the social forces so obviously in full spate'.[46] Hooper wrote in 1948 of the 'swing in the balance of power' in industry, concluding that 'the implications for management are clearly tremendous'. Managers, he felt, had to adopt Follett's method of 'power with' in order to retain any effective control over the situation at all.[47] Management's 'dwindling powers of coercion' was a starting point for Munro Fraser's fairly recent exposition of the human relations approach.[48]

These writers and others clearly recognized how full employment had presented industrial management with twin difficulties. First, the loss of sales from a buoyant market which any local labour dispute would bring and, second, the impracticability of imposing discipline and inducing effort by means of traditional managerial methods. Some commentators also believed that managerial powers were further limited by the rise in general standards of education, which appeared to encourage a new critical awareness among manual workers.[49] What is particularly important and revealing is how the very human relations thinkers who gave little emphasis to factors such as power and conflicting interests in their analyses of industrial relationships, were in this way the first to admit them when explaining the underlying purpose of their writing. Whether we allow that this inconsistency was accidental or not, it serves as an indication of how ideological values could lead to the presentation of a distorted analysis of industrial life.

This paradox is partially explained by the fact that human relations methods, including the propaganda which accompanied them, appeared to afford the best method of maintaining, and even extending, managerial control in the new situation. Despite the influence held by Mayo, for whom at the close of his life the managerial social mission of saving the world from social chaos became a prime concern, British management thought preferred to treat notions such as 'participation' and 'social satisfaction' as derivations of what now seemed the most effective method of managing labour. In fact, an examination of the second point we raised – namely what management writers really meant by their labour relations precepts – will serve to illustrate how the values they presented were essentially designed to justify managerial techniques.

It is perhaps easier to begin by showing what 'participative' or 'democratic' leadership did not mean. For most writers it did not imply any advanced form of plant-level 'constitutionalism' allowing for a close working with employee representatives over an unlimited range of problems. As recently as 1960, many personnel management spokesmen were apprehensive at the idea of factory wage bargaining because they feared it would afford greater power to shop stewards. They continued at the time to prefer purely consultative techniques at factory level, and to draw a sharp distinction between these and negotiating procedures. In reality this policy was an attempt to limit the day-to-day challenge to managerial policies which might come from those who strictly speaking were the 'democratically' elected leaders of the workforce.[50] W. H. Scott has quite justly analysed this approach as one of managerial neopaternalism, in fact labelling it 'constitutional paternalism'.[51] Roger Falk in a Penguin book on management took up this label with some enthusiasm, writing that this policy hoped to create 'a sense of responsible participation' and 'a spirit of sharing'. He added, with honesty, that this system of management 'stems from the new controllers of businesses, the managers themselves'.[52] In other words, it was not democratic.

Thus 'democratic leadership' on this interpretation did not mean that workers or their representatives were to hold any sanction over final policy-making or over the actual process of managerial decision. The editor of *Industry Illustrated* was in 1946 quite clear about this:

'Giving the employee freedom or scope does not mean he must have a licence to break into the manager's office. The pertinent question for the worker, as for the manager, is how far the system encourages and enables him to exercise initiative on his own job.'[53]

A long line of writers supported this blunt assertion, reminding readers that managers possessed a right to authority which derived from their specialized training or their personal expertise. They alone could therefore offer an adequate interpretation of the 'law of the situation'.[54] For example, in an article entitled 'Aspects of Democracy in the Organisation', W. H. Dunkley persisted in writing of 'conferring on the men a sense of "power with"', while at the same time arguing that 'democratically-elected management is impracticable. This has been proved by experiment.'[55] Hooper pointed out with respect to works councils that their purpose was 'not to demonstrate democracy, still less to ensure that the workers run the business'. Their criterion was, on the contrary, 'that they add to, and never detract from, the power wielded by management'.[56] For human relations, the term 'democratic' indicated a leadership style that was quite simply a means for the imposition of managerial command upon those who were led. And, to be fair, one has to admit that not all writers held back this fact. For instance, J. A. C. Brown acknowledged that the term 'democratic leadership' should be given a strictly qualified meaning – as a

particular technique, not as the fulfilment of an ideal. Also
Burns Morton, who used the phrase sparingly, thought 'it is
not so much that he (the worker) should be consulted as that
he should be advised of the change' upon which management
had decided in advance. In other words, for human relations
thinkers, 'participation' and 'democracy' referred to techniques
of communication and motivation.[57]

We thus return to our earlier point; namely, that much of
the allusion to ethical principle in human relations at this time
was concerned with adding a gloss to what was believed to
be the most scientific way of getting workers to perform as
managers required. Even someone such as Mrs V. M. Clarke,
with all her exposition of 'the making of men', was in little
doubt that managers' fundamental aim in adopting human
relations had to be the motivation of men and women to
produce more at lower cost.[58] Oubridge insisted that it was
management's task to 'correlate' the common purpose of the
work group with the operative purpose of the whole industrial
unit.[59] Burns Morton was more forthright. In his opinion,

'The test of true leadership is whether the supervisor, day in and day
out, can get a first-class job in minimum time per unit with his
workers taking pride in their accomplishment and admiring their
"boss".'[60]

Perhaps the type of analysis associated at the time with
claims of 'participation' and 'democracy' can best be illustrated
by following in more detail two sources which both appeared
in 1950, around the high point of this human relations phase.
They are, first, a series of lectures delivered by Urwick to
students at the Industrial Administration Department of the
then Birmingham Central Technical College and, second, G. R.
Taylor's monograph *Are Workers Human?*[61]

Urwick began by asserting his approval of 'a more democratic spirit in industry', but he quickly added that this had to
be reconciled with a managerial attempt to win back from trade
union officials 'a greater proportion of the effective leadership
of those who work in those (industrial) units'. Taylor devoted a
chapter of his book to what he called 'the self-governing group'
but, as we have seen in an earlier quotation (page 120 supra),
he joined Urwick in excluding trade unionism from the scope
of this democracy. For both writers, what really lay behind
unionism and its demands was the failure of factories to satisfy

workers' emotional needs. Taylor believed that the 'hopeless repetition' of wage demands was, along with childishness and apathy, a symptom of this failure. He concluded that 'employees want much more than justice from management, they want love'. For his part, Urwick thought in similar terms that 'workers are apt to develop sentiments of antagonism to developments which threaten their social living'. Worker motivation was primarily emotional:

'. . . the feeling of participation, of belonging to an institution which is doing something worth while, the narrower sensation of belonging to a team . . . they are the tap-roots of (worker) enthusiasm. . . . We are all of us to some degree and in some respects children. We need someone to play the father to us.'

It was the manager who could fill this paternalistic role. At the same time these worker sentiments and needs conveniently afforded the manager an opportunity of making sure that employees followed the company line:

'It is peculiarly the function of the leader to make its objective explicit to all who share in the undertaking, to see that they not only know what it is and understand what it is, but are enthusiastic about what they know and pleased to be partners in what they understand.'

However, in Urwick's view it was not sufficient to present the purposes of an enterprise to its workers in purely rational terms. This in turn implied that workers were not capable of fully appreciating where their own best interests lay:

'. . . leadership is primarily concerned with morale, a psychological condition. . . . Men do not really respond to reason, to arguments expressed in words . . . their full emotional resources can only be mobilised if there is an appeal to their emotions as well as to their reason.'

Taylor and Urwick were well aware that industrialists were not simply concerned to fulfil the emotional needs of their employees. Fundamentally, their interest was in securing greater motivation to production. Taylor went on to claim that 'the industrialist must make his employees happy if he is to get maximum production'. Taking as evidence Mayo and Lombard's wartime study in the Southern California aircraft industry, Taylor argued that the securing of production through happiness depended upon managerial social skill in developing 'well-knit groups'.[62] He agreed with Urwick that 'people feel safer and happier in a group than they do on their own'. He thus recommended the modification of those factory layouts which hindered the formation of employee groups.

Finally, both writers made it clear that worker 'participation' was by no means to entail any real share in control. Urwick dismissed the idea of a 'self-governing workshop' as 'lunatic'. Such notions, he commented, 'fail to realise . . . that the purpose of a workshop is to work, to get production'. Although Taylor wrote of 'the self-governing group', he was also in no doubt that this was a means to increase, not to relinquish, managerial control. He recommended that managers should deliberately set out to change workers' attitudes by means of what he called 'free discussion'. Through this type of participation, workers would be shown how their attitudes were formed and the disadvantageous consequences these might be having for company goals.

In the light of these manipulatory doctrines, it is understandable to find a reviewer of a later but similar set of lectures by Urwick commenting that 'he believes, like most people, in benevolent autocracy in industry. He wants leadership to be, not more democratic, but more enlightened.'[63] These later lectures were in fact delivered at the end of 1955. One can notice from other publications that by the mid-1950s Urwick was prepared to be even more forthright about his antagonism to the idea of 'industrial democracy'. By this time he argued openly that much of the talk on this concept was loose and based upon a 'dangerous' and 'misleading' analogy. He was at the same time prepared to discard some of his earlier legitimations in terms of the managerial servicing of workers' emotional needs. In 1956 he stated quite bluntly that:

'. . . the primary purpose of a business undertaking is not to do good to its employees. It is to supply consumers with needed goods or services as economically as possible. There is some danger that . . . care for employees will become an activity pursued for its own sake. . . and divert attention from the true purpose of business.'[64]

This admission provides an apposite comment on the function and meaning of 'participative' leadership.

(5) *Human relations – a narrowed perspective of industrial conflict*
Previous chapters have shown how a number of human relations ideas had their origins in the earliest stages of British manage-

ment thought. They also indicated that, at these early stages, there was some tension between the focus of human relations concepts upon the communal or solidary aspect of industrial relationships, and an appreciation of the contractual nature of the industrial enterprise. We suggested that, in accordance with changes in the socio-industrial environment, management intellectuals were able to resolve this analytical tension by increasingly ignoring features of industrial relationships which were not amenable to managerial control and a managerial outlook. These features, such as workers' different economic interests, were precisely those which militated against a solidary view of the enterprise. This trend is a complex one, and was also associated with the desire of the management movement to concentrate its energies on developing a 'science' of managerial control. This for the same reason encouraged the growing emphasis on solidary aspects of the enterprise. In the following discussion, we shall attempt to illustrate how this trend resulted in a severely restricted analysis of industrial conflict. We do so by referring back to earlier managerial writings, with which the human relations approach of the post-Second World War period may be compared.

In Chapter 3, we indicated the remarkably broad and sophisticated analysis of industrial conflict which several managerial writers put forward during the Reconstruction era. Equally noteworthy was the analysis contained in the Liberal Party's 1928 report on *Britain's Industrial Future*. This devoted chapters to 'industrial discontent and its causes' and 'collective bargaining', respectively. Among its authors were Seebohm Rowntree, Lawrence Cadbury, C. G. Renold, and interestingly enough L. Urwick. It analysed five main causes of industrial conflict: low income levels, lack of worker security, lack of worker status commensurate with democratic citizenship, lack of information on company finances, and belief in the existence of an unfair division of rewards from production. It is important to notice how this analysis recognized both the presence of conflicting material interests, and the link between members' orientations within enterprises and their roles in the wider society. Among its recommendations, this committee stipulated that employers should be compelled to set up works councils possessing considerable rights both of consultation and of receiving company information.[65]

In general, the view of the industrial enterprise as an all-embracing solidary monolith, as a cohesive system directed emotively by paternalistic managers, was far less evident among management thinkers during the 1920s, or even the 1930s. For instance, back in 1923 Sheldon admitted that labour had other legitimate objectives of its own choosing, and that the be-all and end-all of worker aspirations were not confined to the factory precincts. In his opinion: 'The worker in industry is seeking a living, that it may provide for him the means to a life outside industry.'[66] In addition, Sheldon believed that one of the major causes of industrial conflict derived from beyond the factory gates, and had its roots in the wider social structure. For society was divided: 'into those who give orders and those who receive them. It is a distribution of power, advantages, and opportunities, based upon no acceptable code of ethics, to which the spirit of the mass of Labour is opposed.'[67]

It is true that Mayoism also associated a failure of co-operation within enterprises with a wider social phenomenon – inadequate social cohesion in the so-called 'adaptive' society. However, the Mayoist view, and that of the latter-day human relations approach, is distinguished from earlier British argument by its belief that managers could themselves eliminate the effects of wider social structure by deliberately fostering social cohesion within industry. In other words, as the Mayoist view ascribed industrial conflict almost exclusively to socio-emotional deprivation, it was thought possible for managers to solve it through suitable action at the small group or interpersonal level. We can, at this point, begin to appreciate the greatly reduced analytical perspective of these more recent views in comparison with those of Sheldon and his period. Clearly, the practical success of human relations methods would tend to depend upon which of these two schools of analysis came nearer to the realities of industrial life.

Other writers during the 1920s pointed out the likelihood that large scale organization and the routinization of tasks would give rise to employee monotony and to a serious degree of 'alienation' from factory activities.[68] The *Dictionary of Industrial Administration*, edited by John Lee, contained a particularly comprehensive set of discussions on problematic aspects of industrial relationships. Unlike most other works of the management movement, it invited and received quite outspoken contributions from trade union leaders. In fact, we have already commented how in this period management thinkers generally displayed a greater willingness to appreciate trade union objectives than was to be the case during the 1940s and 1950s. In short, it would be difficult in recent years to find many members of the management movement prepared to admit what Bowie, a management educationalist, stated in Lee's *Dictionary* of 1928:

'The modern growth of large-scale production and the development of horizontal and vertical consolidations have dwarfed the importance of the individual worker, and tended to tie him for a lifetime to his bench. Industry has become dehumanized, the ladder of promotion broken, and the workers segregated in a separate class out of which present conditions make it impossible for the vast majority to climb, and within which they reach their highest remuneration at a comparatively early age.'[69]

This may be sweeping generalization, but recent sociological research is indicating how in essence it remains true for many manual workers today.[70]

Finally, another instance of the narrowed perspective of industrial conflict within British management thought may be seen in comparing our recent quotations of Urwick's views on worker motivation and supervisory style with the analysis he put forward back in 1933. For example, at that time he also commented on relations between foremen and manual workers but in very different terms: 'The quality and kind of relations which should subsist between the workers and those immediately in contact with them are undefinable. Because working relations must depend on the nature of the work.'[71] Moreover, it has been the regret of many social scientists that Urwick did not apply his next caution to the human relations literature coming over the Atlantic during the 1940s, and which he then took a leading role in promoting. For, writing in 1933 of the different social environments of the United States and Britain, he continued:

'The difference is never clearer than in this question of foremanship. A foreman in the United States is a man who does a particular job. A foreman in Europe is still a man of a particular social class. That is why the American literature on foremanship is inapplicable to European conditions. What is more, it is apt to have a narcotic effect – to inhibit European employers from thinking through the situation honestly.'[72]

We have at several points during this study suggested developments in the environment of British management thought which encouraged this narrowing of perspective in the analysis of industrial relationships. In particular, the sheer levels of unrest and challenge to managerial control evident in the earlier 1920s, the struggle of many employers to cut wage-rates, the unemployment and poverty which prevailed – all these provided keen reminders of how divergent economic interests, savage industrial discipline, insecurity, and other components of class differentiation formed a real basis for sustained conflict. Moreover, the young management movement was at this time engaged in securing the manager's right to authority both against labour, and in opposition to legal ownership. In order to win social approval for its assumption of industrial control, management had to commit itself to socially approved policies and to express recognition of the interests and aspirations of other parties to industry.

These are extremely general points. However, they would seem to go some way towards explaining the broader perspectives contained within management thought in the early stages of its development. Certainly, these environmental circumstances had changed considerably by the 1940s – indeed, we noted how they began to alter even by the late 1920s. For instance, trade union ideology softened. Attention to 'workers' control' gave way to a focus on the centralization of union activities. The right of managers to final authority in industry was slowly being conceded, albeit grudgingly. And while the factors promoting a sense of social cleavage in industry have even today by no means disappeared, their manifestations in terms of poverty, insecurity, and the like were, by the 1940s, becoming less extreme. In other words, there was now some superficial plausibility in assuming those features of the wider social structure which had occupied the attention of earlier writers to be of little relevance from a managerial point of view. In addition, the practical success of some features in human relations, particularly when these accompanied superior working conditions, and entailed a less harsh type of management than was customary elsewhere, lent encouragement to the growing view that conflict within the enterprise could be eliminated.

We are in this way relating the increasing predominance of

human relations up to the 1950s with changes in the environment of the management movement. This is not to deny the encouragement which American social psychology, particularly the Mayo and Lewinian schools, undoubtedly gave to this process. However, it is to emphasize again that the process itself was already long under way by the time that the first reports of the Hawthorne experiments came across the Atlantic. For its roots we have to look at the peculiarities of British events.

(6) Human relations – its pervading influence
Although the analytical limitations of human relations may appear reasonably clear to us today, we can begin to appreciate how this approach was able to dominate British management thought when we notice the extent to which it also came to influence British academic social science. Indeed, the social researchers who, following Mayo, proposed human relations methods and accepted the theory behind them represented a kind of 'guiding light of science' for management thinkers.

British social psychologists, in particular, tended to support a human relations interpretation of motivation, behaviour and relationships in industry.[73] Perhaps more surprising is the extent to which the human relations frame of reference came to influence British industrial sociology during the 1940s and early 1950s. An exclusive focus on the plant, an evaluative assumption regarding the necessity of eliminating industrial conflict, and an overriding bias towards managerial points of view, were all to some degree accepted by several prominent sociologists, as a number of their critics have indicated.[74] For a while, industrial sociology leaned towards the assumption that employees necessarily desired to participate in and identify with firms as social institutions. At the same time it omitted an adequate review of factors external to the enterprise which might influence behaviour within it. By adopting a policy-recommending role these studies tended to become aligned with an exclusively managerial point of view and this contributed to their restricted analytical perspective.[75]

Also deserving notice, and quite surprising in view of the open anti-unionism of much human relations writing, is the extent to which trade union leaders and members of the Labour Party came to subscribe to its precepts. This presumably is a further indication of the respect which was granted to the learning of social scientists who put forward human relations ideas. Back in 1942 Austen Albu, who was both a practising works manager and a member of the Labour Party, welcomed the Hawthorne experiments as a sign that 'science is beginning to catch up with common sense' in recognizing the importance of the 'human factor'. However, he also warned that there was a danger of manipulation behind the notion of managerial leadership.[76] In 1945 Sir Stafford Cripps was also content merely to point out to personnel managers their need to focus attention on to the human aspects of management as the most important industrial problem facing post-war Britain.[77]

Nevertheless, by the 1950s some Labour Party intellectuals appeared ready to accept the spirit of Mayo's thesis to a remarkable degree.[78] Speaking at a 1964 conference, a member of the T.U.C. General Council specifically recommended Mayo's writings – to an audience of management studies teachers. He emphasized to them the importance of good communications, concluding that 'the clearer the vision, the better the understanding'. It is thus not surprising that he also suggested as a lesson for management the analogy of Montgomery's style of leadership before El Alamein, a comparison we have discussed earlier.[79] Similarly, at another recent conference trade union speakers were at pains to stress that 'co-operation' would derive from good communication within firms; they used among other illustrative expressions that of 'the family spirit'.[80] It was left to Frank Cousins to speak out against these assumptions of his colleagues. Addressing an audience of personnel managers, he argued that the trade unions still retained an independent role in modern industry with the corollary that: 'We will not resolve our problems if we think we have a common purpose: we have two different purposes.'[81]

III. THE CONCEPT OF MANAGERIAL PROFESSIONALISM

The censure of managerial performance during the 1940s brought some response from the management movement in terms of an increasing discussion of professionalism and social responsibility. Old phrases such as 'reconstruction' and a 'new order' reappeared in management journals. We have already noted the revival of social legitimations in Mayoist terms which occurred in management thought during this period (page 120).

One novelty was the haste with which some writers strove to identify themselves with the 'planned society' which was expected to continue at the end of the war.[82] This move might have had some affinity with the rationalization concept of the late 1920s, but there can be little doubt that it also represented some attempt to support management's social image. The new industrial order in which the management movement was again proclaiming its good faith was in the words of the editor of *Labour Management* one 'in which not individual gain, but the good of the whole, is to be the ruling passion and the guiding principle'.[83] Wilfred Brown at this time spoke of a 'personal humility and readiness to serve others rather than . . . the arrogance and selfishness of the past'.[84] There is evidence, even in the management literature itself, to suggest that some British employers were suddenly taking to public utterance of these sentiments in order to forestall any challenge from the political Left at the end of the war.[85]

However, although management spokesmen were definitely more sensitive to outside criticism during the 1940s, they did not consider the managerial role to lie in any fundamental jeopardy. In fact, the message contained in Burnham's *Managerial Revolution* was not ignored. Among those who drew on Burnham's thesis was James Bowie, who had for a long time taken the extreme view that management should adopt a professional closed shop.[86] 'The managers,' he stated, 'are to be the dominant class of the future.' Indeed, his chief concern was whether British 'managers are ready for their exalted function'.[87] This question he posed together with other members of the management movement, who were unquestionably disheartened by evidence that the general run of managers was often far from enthusiastic towards the new concepts and methods being formulated. We shall in fact shortly return to this point when we observe how an increasing number of management spokesmen were coming to admit the difficulties involved in any idea of management as a full 'profession'. These doubts were themselves an indication that intellectual apologists felt sufficiently confident that there was a public acceptance of the principle of managerial authority to enable them to engage in this kind of open admission. And, so far as one can judge, values serving purely legitimatory functions – 'service' perhaps being the prime example – did not secure the same relative prominence in management thought during the 1940s as had been the case in the period just after 1918.

The attempts to claim a professional standing for industrial management during the 1950s were sporadic,[88] and although they have not entirely ceased even today, they increasingly took on the air of an academic exercise. Indeed, during the 1950s it was as often social scientists who attempted to erect philosophies of managerial professionalism. For instance, in 1956 Bamforth attempted to construct what he called 'a generally acceptable philosophy for management *and therefore for all who work*, which will be fitted to the realities of the times and provide a common purpose laid on deeper foundations than those of current party politics'. The emphasis is our own, for the paternalistic assumption should not be overlooked. In the event, Bamforth fell back upon the far from original notion of service to the community![89]

Similarly, in the same year, Paterson claimed that faced with full employment and enjoying freedom from ownership, managers were 'becoming industrial humanitarians' and learning 'to conduct the enterprise for the total good'. Moreover, Paterson was prepared to go much further and to endorse an argument which paralleled Mayo's concept of a social mission at its most extreme: 'It is not the quantity or value of the work produced that ought to form the main object of management's care, but the effect which producing of that work naturally creates on the mind and body of the workmen.' However, one should not take this expression of social idealism wholly at its face value – it also contains an ulterior motive. For Paterson argued that, if managers were prepared to accept this standard of professional morality, they could then feel that their authority was perfectly legitimate: '. . . if a manager is perfectly clear about the morality of his right to command, then he need have no doubts about his right to expect and to enforce obedience.'[90]

Thus Paterson's authority turns out to be a system far more of the manager's own personal definition, and far less open to challenge in principle by those subject to it, than was Follett's 'law of the situation'. As the head of a management studies department said of Paterson's argument, it approached a 'divine rights' theory for managers, and was utterly out of touch with industrial realities.[91] It is not surprising to find that Paterson's view of joint consultation was equally autocratic.

Joint consultation for him merely represented a device which 'if properly used' would promote the identification of workers with the enterprise.[92] These, one should remember, were the expositions of an academic social scientist only a decade ago.

We may recall (from page 130 *supra*) how in the very same year Urwick had felt obliged to warn managers against a vague 'do-goodism' which could detract from economic performance. Brech joined him in this view, and we shall see later on that even the personnel management movement was coming to accept this warning.[93] In fact, it would appear that this less sentimental view of managerial responsibility was becoming more prominent among British management writers by the mid-1950s than the one held by social scientists Bamforth and Paterson. For example, Urwick's 1954 monograph, *Is Management a Profession?*, was concerned to promote the idea of professionalism for different and more technically-oriented reasons. In Urwick's eyes, professionalism was no longer valuable so much for providing an ethical basis on which to secure social legitimation, but rather as a means of stressing the technical importance of the existing body of management principles and techniques which he felt must be taught to managers and management trainees. He bitterly attacked those business men whose argument, that successful management could only derive from 'learning by experience', cast doubt upon the value of management studies. For Urwick, professionalism now meant primarily that management should turn its back on this 'amateur' approach, which he thought in many cases merely represented social prejudice against trained managers on the part of company directors, and devote far more attention to systematic study.[94]

It is at this point that Urwick touched upon one of the principal debates which persisted throughout the development of British management thought – the extent to which good management depended upon art or science, upon experience and personal flair or upon systematic training and careful investigation. Among those taking the former view was Sir Frederic Hooper, who insisted that the canons of successful management 'come from the wisdom of experience, from an alert imagination, from a receptive and enquiring mind'. These spokesmen represented a somewhat anti-intellectualist tradition, hostile to the recommendations of social scientists, which Hooper called 'the theories of observers'.[95] They searched in particular for a definition of the personal qualities believed necessary for good management.

Urwick himself indulged in this exercise, and devoted a book largely to the subject. But he insisted that this was an inadequate foundation on which to build management education. Some specialist management functions, he pointed out, required little leadership of men at all. He reserved a special scorn for those who argued that successful managers were born as such. It was not that practical experience was considered inessential as an accompaniment to formal training and adequate academic background – Urwick, and men such as Elbourne, had long agreed that such experience was vital. It was simply that the Hooper type of view could readily imply that formal study was itself superfluous.[96] To the extent that this formal study of management was in the 1950s based upon Urwick and Brech's formulation of 'management principles', many industrialists appear to have felt more sympathy for the Hooper argument. A managing director wrote in 1949 that the discussion of management problems to be found in the literature was becoming academic and divorced from the realities of industry. In particular, he attacked the attempt to enshrine 'one-best ways' of management in the so-called 'principles'.[97] Since for Urwick and Brech the claim of professionalism was linked with the idea that the 'principles' gave management an underlying systematic body of knowledge, it is not altogether surprising that the notion of professionalism itself came to be received with less enthusiasm by other management writers.

We commented earlier in this section that, during the 1940s and after, an increasing number of management spokesmen were in fact coming to challenge openly the claim that industrial management was a profession in any full sense of the term. For instance, in 1943 the editor of *Industry Illustrated* warned his readers that 'it is by no means to be taken for granted that management can be professionalized'. A body of literature, first principles, an ethical code of practice, and a disciplinary system to enforce such a code, all these, he felt, were lacking.[98] Ten years later, H. E. Roff then the Director of the Institute of Personnel Management, admitted much the same lack of professional attributes.[99] A sub-committee of the Institute of

Industrial Administration concluded in 1954 that during the thirty years of its existence the Institute had made little progress towards its goal of professionalizing management. Even if the I.I.A. had with its examinations become a recognized qualifying association, the committee was forced to admit that with a tiny membership of 2,700 it hardly represented British management as a whole.[100] One of those commenting on the report believed, as we suggested just now, that the practising manager's lack of interest in the professional issue was linked to his mistrust of the whole idea of management education, at least in the way it was then presented:

'. . . there are thousands who are indifferent or lukewarm, among the hundreds of thousands engaged in management, whose attitude is "we couldn't care less". It is not that industry generally is merely indifferent to management as a profession, it does not believe in the need for specific education and training in management.'[101]

Similarly, in 1956 the editor of *Personnel Management* treated very cautiously the question of to what extent personnel management had become professional.[102] This was despite the fact that the Institute of Personnel Management administered a quite rigorous examination scheme, and that in recent years its membership covered around a third of the estimated total of personnel officers. Finally, to take an example from the 1960s, Sir Walter Puckey has recently written that in his opinion it is too soon to consider industrial management a true profession. However, he has urged instead that managers should endeavour to adopt a professional outlook in terms of higher standards of training and performance.[103]

In recent years, when management writers have referred to professionalism, they have almost always confined their attention to managerial training and competence.[104] The notion of rendering service to specific claimants, which formerly was closely associated with the claim of managerial professionalism, has correspondingly given place to a much less definite idea of 'social responsibility'.[105] This very general affirmation of good intentions is one which *any* occupational group would find it difficult to avoid. Professionalism in its full sense implies clearly stated obligations to client groups, whereas social responsibility looks out much less formally to an amorphous society at large. Thus while professionalism implied that the management movement collectively would need to maintain standards.

social responsibility does not imply any rigorous regulation of managerial activities. As well as entailing a less arduous ethical commitment, social responsibility is in fact often put forward as a policy in terms of its technical benefits for managers themselves. For instance, it is suggested as a means to secure goodwill and co-operation *for* management as often as an implicit sacrifice to be tendered *by* management.

In short, after reviving to meet the criticisms and uncertainties of the 1940s, discussion of professionalism within British management thought has since considerably lessened. Apart from the contributions of one or two social scientists (who as educators might have felt they possessed some vested interest in the issue?), remaining discussion on managerial professionalism is now concerned with its technical rather than its legitimatory aspects. A general expression of social responsibility is quite willingly made, but this is relatively non-committal. The available evidence suggests that most management writers today would agree with the replies received on this issue from the great majority of management teachers interviewed in a study by the author.[106] Namely, that much previous writing about managerial professionalism amounted to irrelevant status seeking, and that priority had now to be given to finding better technical methods of management – to 'getting on with the job'. We have argued that this shift in thinking can be related to changes in the environment of the British management movement since the war. This has seen a focusing of 'informed public opinion' on to the quality of managerial performance, and we outlined these developments earlier in this chapter. This movement in management thought represents a decline in the weight given to purely legitimatory elements – it is in one sense a decline of 'ideology'. We shall note in the following chapter how this trend has recently affected other approaches to the study of industrial relationships, at the level of labour relations and administrative organizations.

Professionalism and recruitment to management
One of the arguments of the 'management is an art' school against the concept of professionalism was that it implied a restriction on the range of managerial recruits who were prima facie to be considered suitable. This restriction derived from the insistence of Urwick and others that a training in the 'science'

of management was necessary for adequate performance in the modern and complex conditions of industry. This need for training in turn implied that only those with a minimum level of general education could be taken on as recruits. An extreme advocate of this latter approach was James Bowie with his hopes that management would develop into a 'closed shop'. On the other hand, men such as Sir Frederic Hooper, who felt that good management came primarily from the application of an alert mind to practical experience and not from any paper qualifications, argued that opportunities of promotion had to be kept open for all employees. Indeed, he went further and, in a perhaps rather disingenuous challenge to labour critics, implied that promotion in British industry *was* in fact open to anyone: 'If the rank and file of a business or of a cricket team can do the job of management or captaincy better than those who hold those offices, then let them come to the top and do the job better.'[107]

This, however, was not the predominant view in management thought during this period. Many writers stressed that as educational selection grew more efficient so inevitably managerial posts could be filled only by those with higher academic qualifications. Urwick, in his work on management as a profession, put this argument very succinctly:

'It is doubtful if the old promoted-ranker type of manager can continue to measure up to what British business will require, even if there are enough of him. And with the democratization of educational opportunity which has occurred over the last decade it is obvious that there will be less first-class ability starting on the shop-floor.'[108]

Similarly, a British Institute of Management study group reporting in 1955 (under Hooper's chairmanship!) placed highest value on the university graduate for managerial recruitment, and concluded: 'that school-leavers, as such, cannot be considered a direct source of recruitment for managerial training in the same sense as the university graduate or man of similar maturity and calibre'.[109]

It is therefore understandable that two industrial consultants should find cause to censure severely those employers who promised their workers opportunities for promotion when these were in fact becoming less and less available. The result, they argued, would only be to heighten industrial unrest.[110] It may

tentatively be suggested that in so far as the management movement was prepared to acknowledge a restriction in the range of
recruitment, it gave point both to the neo-paternalist philosophy
implicit in human relations (for workers were seen to be intel-
lectually less developed than managers), and to the search for
alternative human relations techniques for enlisting worker
co-operation.

IV. PRINCIPLES OF MANAGEMENT

During this period the development of 'management principles'
advanced little further than Urwick's exposition in *The
Elements of Administration* (1943), to which we referred in the
previous chapter. In fact, apart from the writings of Urwick
and his colleague Brech, British management thought gave
relatively little attention to the further refinement of organizational principles. One exception was an issue of the *British
Management Review* in 1948, which was devoted to the subject.
Nevertheless, a great deal of the discussion within its pages
extended little further than a prolonged debate over definitions.[111] Indeed, even today the problem of variations in terminology continues to trouble not only the study of organization
but many other aspects of management as well.

In the course of the 1950s both Urwick and Brech began to
adopt an increasingly flexible formulation of management
principles. For instance, both writers now agreed that the
essentially 'static' and formal principles had to be supplemented
by a study of the 'dynamics' of motivation and behaviour at all
levels of the enterprise. The implications arising from Follett's
work on co-ordination, and from that of Mayo and Barnard
on communication and persuasion, had to be added to the
anatomical framework which followed from the principles.[112]
These principles remained as before – a combination of precepts for optimum organizational structure and an abstract
characterization of the tasks performed by an ideal-typical
manager. However, there was also during this period a greater
willingness to qualify the claim of universal applicability which
had previously been applied in a dogmatic manner to the principles.

For example, Urwick by the mid-1950s was prepared to

admit the inherent limitations of the controversial 'span of control' principle. He emphasized that the principle had in any case only applied to cases where there was interlocking between the tasks of subordinates, so as to give cross-relationships between them important enough to warrant their superior's active attention. If the organization were of such a size that this principle conflicted with the need to limit the number of hierarchical levels – and both considerations were aimed at maintaining reasonable communications within the organization – then Urwick's solution remained as it had always been, a use of the 'staff assistant'.[113]

Brech's version of the span of control principle was even more flexible. The span of control, he wrote, should be limited to 'a reasonable number of *executive or supervisory* subordinates, if their activities are interrelated'.[114] The emphasis is ours, for it is important to notice that span of control problems of the same magnitude did not normally arise with the supervision of operatives or clerical workers. At these levels there was usually not the same extent of cross-relationship between subordinates' activities, and the very nature of their work also meant that cross-relations which did arise tended to involve a relatively low level of discretionary content requiring regular review from above. However, while Brech in this way paid homage to caution, the consequent imprecision in his definition rendered the principle itself of little positive value other than as a very general point for managers to bear in mind.

While Urwick in most cases still appeared to abide by his earlier opinion that management principles were, or should be, universally applicable in all organizations, industrial and other,[115] Brech once again preferred to maintain greater caution albeit at the expense of clarity. In 1953 he concluded that: 'there would appear to be certain basic maxims of organisation structure commonly applicable, but with considerable differences in actual application'.[116] Similarly, in an article of 1954 on the question of decentralization or centralization, Brech concluded that as between these principles 'the balance . . . is not determined by a formula which can be applied indiscriminately to each and every organization. It is a matter individual to each organization specifically.'[117] Earlier he had gone so far as to attack one of his own textbooks for conveying the impression that there was a 'one best way' of designing an organization.[118]

K

Expositions of the management principles were never distinguished for their clarity. The added confusion resulting from the pirouetting of these thinkers during the 1950s, in face of the lack of respect shown for their work by a number of other management writers, must have been substantial among the few who took the trouble to read their publications. The extent of this confusion is well illustrated by the following extract from a manager's essay which in 1957 gained a British Institute of Management medal:

'Although the same management principles hold good for any kind of organization, the application of those principles will vary according to the type of activity in which it is engaged. Such variations are, however, more apparent than real.'[119]

Presumably his examiners thought they knew how to interpret this in practical terms, though it is doubtful if many managers did!

In short, during this period management principles were the concern of few management thinkers. Most of these principles suffered from an excessive vagueness which, among other reasons, impaired any practical utility they might possess. In particular, there was considerable indecision as to how far the principles were universal rather than situational in nature, and even their exponents came to acknowledge their incapacity to account for the dynamic aspects of social relationships within the enterprise. Moreover, and related to this last point, they failed completely to account for structured conflicts within organizations, or to appreciate that some principles could themselves promote symptoms of frustration, aggression, or other forms of non-cooperation if taken to an extreme – for instance, the principles of task specialization. Indeed, as with the human relations approach, the principles represented a marked tendency within the management thought of this period to assume away conflicts in industrial relationships.

V. DISSENT FROM HUMAN RELATIONS

(1) *Alternatives to human relations in British management thought*
Human relations was only the most popular of three distinguishable schools of management thought on employee relations during this period. There were also those who advocated the use of more formal procedural machinery with respect to relations between managements and employees, a standpoint

which in turn provided the two alternatives to human relations. First was the belief that 'joint consultation' by stressing matters of common interest (and avoiding those where interests diverged) would itself lead to an atmosphere of greater co-operation within factories. The second derived from a far more sophisticated analysis, and indeed was the product of only one or two thinkers. This latter approach envisaged formal committees as the basis of some form of 'constitutionalism' at plant level, through which a wide range of issues could be discussed *and* bargained over with worker representatives. In other words this last method did not attempt to avoid matters of divergent interest. It will become clear that the difference between these two approaches to the use of formal machinery came close to that between joint consultation as normally interpreted and the older Whitley scheme of works committees. We shall in fact confine the term 'joint consultation' to the first variety.

During the war, joint consultation was quite widely welcomed by management writers. In the form of 'joint production committees' it also had the full support of the government. There was the expected spate of papers in the journals, especially in *Personnel Management*, welcoming the idea as the start of a new era in industrial relations, while Walpole, one of its foremost exponents in 1943, went so far as to claim that 'this one stroke would do more for British industry than any other one single act of statesmanship that I can think of'.[120]

Some writers who had taken up the human relations approach also attached considerable importance to formal joint consultation – Northcott for example.[121] However, it would appear rather more of them felt that informal consultation and methods of personal leadership actually operative *within* workshops and departments would be far more effective in motivating workers towards managerial goals. Brech, J. A. C. Brown, G. R. Taylor, and Urwick provided instances of this view. Brown, for example, thought that without the prior creation of a co-operative atmosphere in the factory, joint committees were 'likely to prove dreary sessions' and to accomplish little in the way of raising 'morale' or even of exchanging views on serious matters.[122]

On the whole, the human relations writers who showed least enthusiasm for joint consultation were also those who evinced the greatest hostility or indifference towards trade unionism and towards any idea of formal worker representation at all. On the other hand, those expounding joint consultation were generally at pains to insist that it should not in any way be used to subvert the activities of union officials over matters such as wage negotiations.[123] And writers such as Northcott, who absorbed many human relations concepts yet (probably because of his experience at Rowntree's) also saw considerable possibilities in formal consultation, tended again to be in favour of respecting the authority of union officers.[124] When we have discussed the third, 'constitutional', approach to labour relations in this period, it will become apparent that most management thinkers could be fitted consistently along a continuum between 'manipulative' and 'constitutional' methods of managerial control, according to their various recommendations. As we emphasized earlier in this chapter, the dominant trend of management thought during the 1940s and early 1950s approached the manipulative end of this continuum.

Joint consultation may be placed somewhere around the middle. In the way it was normally interpreted in management thought, it excluded any negotiation over wages and conditions of employment together with any other matters not under the heading of purely production issues and problems of 'common interest'. For as Walpole said regarding wage matters and the like: 'We do not even discuss such things more than we can possibly help, because they contain a hint of antagonised viewpoints which is unpleasant.'[125] Advocates of joint consultation might speak in terms of 'full partnership' or 'a belated extension of democracy into the field of industry',[126] but it was also praised as a management technique which could render managerial authority more effective by allowing it to rest upon 'the force of fact', or in other words upon Follett's 'law of the situation'.[127] In short, joint consultation was not regarded as a mechanism for full constitutionalism within the enterprise.

It is this last point which makes the third approach to labour relations during this period so interesting and important. Among the few who adopted it, Wilfred Brown and Sir Charles Renold (C. G. Renold) deserve particular mention. The policies which they described as operating within their companies come close to the model of plant level constitutionalism which the Liverpool University study of *Management in Britain* strongly recommended, yet found to be little used in British industrial practice.[128]

The system in operation at the Renold and Coventry Chain

Company in many respects continued to bear the stamp of the early 1920s, when indeed most of the present arrangements were already in force. This system, like that at Brown's Glacier Metal Company, did not signify a weak managerial executive system. On the contrary, both writers have stressed that any scheme of constitutional negotiation at factory level could only deal satisfactorily with important matters if the managerial as well as the workers' side was well organized, united, and sure of its mind.[129] In the opinions of Brown and his consultant Elliott Jaques, it was only possible to establish adequate executive authority if the 'roles' in which it resided and the sanctions which other groups held over it were first openly acknowledged and clearly defined. It was therefore essential to set up a formal and constitutional system in the factory, and to forego the imprecision associated with human relations techniques. Brown and Jaques felt that human relations, when it implied a vague 'groupism' and 'get-togetherness', was technically ineffective because it blurred the boundaries of executive authority, and so enabled managers to avoid unpleasant but necessary responsibilities.[130] Renold also held strongly to the view that a sound organization was far more important than any notions of 'a new spirit in industry'. Taken by themselves, such notions would remain 'mere evanescent stunts'.[131]

The schemes expounded by Brown and Renold had the following common features: a representative system based on shop stewards; the provision of substantial information to representatives; a set of mutually agreed rules which clearly defined the rights of all parties within the formal system; the combination of negotiation with consultation; and a deliberate attempt to reinforce the status and responsibility of foremen. Renold went so far as to urge trade unions to adapt their structure so as to allow themselves to take a more active part in workshop bargaining. The chief shop steward of the Glacier Metal Company, who has a wide knowledge of the engineering industry, stated in a personal conversation with the author that he believed trade union representatives in that company had a greater freedom to raise issues and to get action taken than in any other firm he knew.[132] A number of the above provisions bear a close similarity to practice at York under Seebohm Rowntree, which also appears to have operated with considerable effect.[133]

Perhaps the most significant dissent which these thinkers made from both the human relations and the joint consultation approaches was in their analysis of industrial conflict. Here again they adopted a broader view, which if anything had its roots in a much earlier school of British management thought. Wilfred Brown, for instance, recognized that an enterprise did contain some conflict of economic interests, that an employee could well be subject to a 'dual loyalty' between his trade union and his firm, and above all that a lack of co-operation derived fundamentally from a prevailing system of relationships and attitudes structured by forces which were not accounted for in a human relations analysis.[134] Renold, commenting on his own system, in turn put forward a comparable view of conflict:

' "Negotiation" implies that there are divergent interests to be reconciled. "Consultation" implies a basis of common interest in the prosecution of a common enterprise.

'In industry both propositions are true. There is a basic community of interest in a common enterprise, and also divergence of interest in the pursuit of it. To ignore the latter is to be unreal.

'It may well be that it was the acceptance of this duality of relationships, as signified by the recognition of the Shop Stewards as representing the workers for all purposes, that has given the schemes described their undoubted vitality.'[135]

Renold on occasion also wrote in imprecise terms about an employee sense of belonging, and Brown also saw value in an employee-centred supervisory style.[136] However, the point of importance is that these men were at the time among the few who did not believe that foremanship styles or an attempt to foster 'belonging' would *of themselves* do more than a limited amount to alter the system of relationships prevailing in any given factory. It is at points such as these that their analyses differed so fundamentally from the pure human relations approach. They might, and did, for instance, talk in terms of furthering workers' loyalty to the enterprise, but in contrast to the view of Urwick and others such participation was to involve trade unionism.[137] Again, both writers were concerned to enhance executive authority, but unlike human relations, or even the normal type of joint consultation, they admitted this quite openly and did not attempt to disguise their motive through slogans about 'democracy'. Brown had, indeed, quite early in his career admitted the incongruity between the employee's civil democratic rights and his lack of ability to challenge the

arbitrary decisions of managers in the industrial sphere. It was
this kind of thinking which led to the development of the elaborate set of formal arrangements now in force at the Glacier
Metal Company.[138]

We have accorded some attention to these writers for several
reasons. Their practical provisions refer back to those envisaged
by the Whitley Report, and their analysis of conflict and worker
aspirations also recalls the tenor of some writing in the 1920s.
Yet, on the other hand, this approach to labour relations
heralds one the merits of which are perhaps receiving wider
recognition today, now that the analytical weaknesses of human
relations are, through the influence of academic social science,
coming to be more widely appreciated (we give a few examples
in the following chapter). Finally, the work of these writers
suggests quite correctly that human relations was by no means
universally accepted without criticism in British management
thought, even at the time of its greatest ascendancy up to the
mid-1950s. In fact, we now continue with a brief mention of
cases where a more overt hostility was shown towards human
relations at a time before it reached more widespread disrepute
in the British management movement. Both this sub-section
we are now concluding and the next serve as important qualifications to the tendency of some commentators to assume that
human relations and post-war British management thought
are virtually synonymous.

(2) *Some early critiques of human relations*
The early criticisms of human relations from members of the
management movement fall into three broad categories. There
was, first, a charge that it was not realistically oriented to the
fundamentally economic function of industry. Second was the
charge of a rather more ethical nature that human relations was
merely a euphemism for undesirable manipulative procedures.
Third was a more technical charge that British management
writers had accepted the Hawthorne research and its applicability to the British industrial scene too uncritically.

First, a few spokesmen had by the mid-1940s already come to
reach the same conclusion that we have seen Urwick to arrive
at ten years later: that the economic efficiency of enterprises
could be jeopardized if overmuch attention were paid to the
social contentment of employees. These early critics maintained

that to overstress a social-psychological approach to productivity held the danger, and perhaps insincerity, of implying that a factory's primary purpose was to function as some kind of psycho-therapeutic clinic rather than as a producer of economic goods at economic costs. This attack came initially from one or two practising managers who met senior intellectuals of the management movement on their own ground – in the journals. For instance, 'John Blunt' wrote the following to *Industry Illustrated* in March 1947, which deserves an extensive quotation:

'It seems to me that the time has come to call a halt to the claptrap that we read so much, especially in journals like Industry Illustrated about the purpose of industry being to produce better men and women. It is sheer nonsense . . . the purpose of industry is to produce commodities and services – in other words, what the textbooks call "economic goods". An industrial unit or enterprise stands or falls by its success in attaining these objectives. If in pursuing these ends the factory or workshop can provide the situation in which its members can develop their personalities and individual purposes then it will be making a further social contribution. My plea is simply for a little more intellectual integrity in management literature. Some of the difficulties we are labouring under in industry today, with the unrealistic attitude to work, and to the function of a factory, are due to the false prophets of the past few years.'[139]

This attack was supported in subsequent issues of the journal by further letters, none of which was signed openly! Another manager, for example, agreed that, 'It is time some practical managers who read your journal rose in revolt against all this molly-coddling claptrap about "committees", "employee satis-factions", and Hawthorne experiments.'[140]

A further critic, writing to the editor of *Personnel Management* in 1949 put a similar point when he attacked the use of what we called 'the army analogy' to support human relations. The services, he argued, did not have to pay regard to costs in the same way as industry; in any case the greatly different social situations of the two institutions rendered this a false analogy.[141] These critiques derived from men who called themselves practising managers, but it would be misleading to dismiss them merely as members of the 'unenlightened' mass – for after all they were subscribers to the leading management journals. And as an additional instance, Chelioti, who was certainly not far from the centre of the British management movement, also struck a note of caution when in 1946 he pointed out that in

modern industry an appreciation of technology was essential
for good management – leadership abilities were insufficient
by themselves. Ten years later, the suggestion of social scientist
Paterson that the business enterprise existed for its member
employees rather than for production, brought a rebuke as
sharp as those just quoted.[142]

Perhaps the most powerful of these early charges of insincerity
and unreality came from R. Appleby, now Chairman of Black
and Decker Ltd., writing in a 1952 issue of the *British Management Review*. His attack was in fact directed at management
thought as a whole. He was concerned at the claim that managers could be disinterested professionals, at the suggestion in
Follett's 'law of the situation' that personal authority in the
enterprise could be avoided, and that this together with the
notion of service to the community could lead to the idea of a
'common purpose' throughout the whole enterprise:

'Quite naturally, these ideas, being out of accord with the facts, and
expressing, as they did, a pious sentimentalism, could not command
the respect of labour. But not only did they lower the respect of
labour for management, they also lowered the respect of executive
management for those who propounded such ideas. How was it
possible for a manager at the heart of affairs to attach much consequence to a "management movement" capable of such utter-
ances?'[143]

Appleby thought that the 'profession of disinterestedness'
and 'the implied paternalism' contained in management
thought resulted from a lack both of certainty and of a sense of
direction. He did not argue, as we have done and as the second
school of critics did, that such claims were also designed to
justify motivational techniques. His main thesis in fact was to
emphasize that management 'is the servant of its employers,
whether they be public or private employers. . . . Still less does
society look to management to erect a philosophy towards
humanity'.[144]

The second charge against human relations reinforced the
suspicion of insincerity held by the first set of critics. This
complaint was on the grounds of its manipulative bias and the
air of deception surrounding its shibboleths. For example, Sir
George Schuster in the 1951 Beckley Social Service Lecture was
quite in agreement with an emphasis on the type of treatment
accorded to employees in industry, and he urged that this should

endeavour to follow Christian principles. But, he specifically attacked Mayo and his school for emphasizing a type of 'social skill' which held very real dangers of manipulation. He pointed out that 'Hitler and Stalin have given examples of consummate skill in the manipulation of mass psychology'.[145] Similarly, Gillespie, in a remarkable book, criticized the fact that manipulative control was being advocated under the misleading participative slogan of 'democratic co-operation':

'Sometimes management is deliberately using the attractive symbols of democracy, participation, co-operation, man-to-man discussion, group decision, etc., to create the desired atmosphere within which it can smoothly manipulate the attitudes of its employees, retain their loyalty, and still run the business "as it should be run", without irritating interferences from below.'[146]

It may be mentioned that in this particular book, *Free Expression in Industry* (1948) Gillespie advocated a system of industrial control which incorporated some advanced democratic features. In this, workers elected their own leaders who would then deal directly with higher management. Foremen were to become technical experts acting in an advisory capacity to workers and management. Variants of this 'free group expression' system have been adopted with apparent success in a number of small firms.[147]

Finally, the third charge was that British management thought had been too eager and incautious in building on the results of the Hawthorne research which had taken place in an American social environment. In 1948 the P.E.P. (an organization interested in, but perhaps not strictly part of the 'management movement') gave clear warning against the wholesale acceptance of experimental findings which, it pointed out, were already many years dated and pertained to an industrial and cultural environment very different from the British. In its opinion, 'There has been a great deal of uninformed talk about its (Hawthorne's) importance, which has led to unsafe generalisations about the application of its findings to this country.'[148]

Gillespie also criticized the way human relations writers relied upon the Relay Assembly Test Room experiment, with its peculiarly structured situation of a small selected group of female operatives separated from their department as a whole. Again, Guy Hunter in 1951 criticized the claim that management had found 'laws of group behaviour'. In his paper he was

Aberconway Library

Due Date: 25/04/2007 23:59

Title: British management thought
                 : a critical analysis / by
                 John Child.
Author: Child, John.
Classmark: 658 C

Item number: 2002291344

concerned to place himself squarely in the Hooper 'management as an art' school of thought, and to dispel what he called 'the illusion of scientific management'. He therefore went on to attack the so-called 'science' of organization, pointing out the doubts that surrounded its formulations such as the span of control principle.[149]

SUMMARY

The 1940s brought an increase in public criticism of British management. This was directed primarily at the quality of its performance, and secondly at the way in which labour had been treated before the war. It did not, however, amount to any demand for the radical restructuring of industrial control. We suggested that this development in effect modified the environment of the management movement. It would appear that the changed situation can explain a great deal of the revived protestation that management would further democratic relationships, participation, social happiness, goodwill, and similar socially approved values. In other words, under the pressure of circumstances there was some renewed attention in management thought to the question of legitimation.

In this period, it is far from simple to separate out the legitimatory from the technical content in management thought. There was now not so much need for management apologists to justify independence from legal ownership or the exclusion of labour from industrial control, as the technical use to which managerial authority was being put. Thus in human relations, a dominant theme during and after the Second World War, values such as those we have mentioned were closely associated with a technique of labour management. In the human relations approach it is possible to find subtle combinations of legitimatory and technical elements – it is this which lends it an air of deliberate deception. For instance, the scientific study of workers' socio-emotive needs, deriving from Hawthorne and other small group research, was taken as the basis for *both* a technique to promote higher worker productivity and an attempt to dismiss trade unionism as irrelevant for modern factory life.

It is its apparent scientific backing which helps to explain why human relations held so much influence not only over British management thought but over some labour leaders as well. Indeed, one may suggest that it is in the work of social scientists themselves, such as Mayo, that one can find a source of the ideological mixture of fact and value which was used to serve management's technical and legitimatory purposes at one and the same time. In human relations technical performance was assumed to derive from the pursuit of what at first sight appeared to be an acceptable social goal – the increase of employee contentment. Only a more critical appraisal indicated how readily this system might entail the manipulation of employees at the expense of those who were chosen representatives of their material interests. In this way human relations could be, and was, used to support a philosophy hostile to the organized labour movement. This placed it in contrast to the accommodating attitudes expressed in the Reconstruction period after 1918, and during the early 1920s.

At the time of its greatest influence, human relations led much of British management thought towards an extreme analysis in terms of organizational solidarity, an almost exclusive emphasis on social motivations, and on the role of personal leadership. It completely discounted the likely technological, financial, and socio-environmental constraints bearing upon any viable managerial policy. As with the management principles, it was assumed that human relations precepts were universally applicable. It is again possible to discern in this last assumption both a genuine belief that universality had been indicated by the results of scientific, comparative research, and an overstatement of available managerial knowledge associated with the somewhat legitimatory attempt to enhance management's 'professional' status.

We also noted the presence within the management movement of some dissent from these dominant themes. This stemmed from the feeling that such themes were not practical (particularly in financial terms), and that they were unduly dogmatic and inflexible. A few commentators were even prepared to question the assumption that they rested upon an adequate scientific foundation. There is, moreover, some evidence that by the early 1950s many British managers were already aware of the shortcomings in the 'human' side of management thought, and that they were beginning to pay more attention to clear-cut and concrete techniques in fields such as accounting and marketing.[150]

Finally, in this period several management writers began

openly to admit the unrealistic nature of managerial claims to professional status. Others came to use the term 'professional' sporadically, and then mainly to indicate technical competence only. We suggested that this general increase of open critical self-awareness within the management movement was a product of its growing assurance that managerial authority rights were in principle now socially accepted, and that what 'public opinion' required was a more effective technical contribution by managers towards an easing of the nation's economic ills.

In the next chapter we shall note the growth during the 1950s of social science research into industrial behaviour. Much of this research was in Britain sponsored by governmental agencies themselves interested in the improvement of industrial performance. This work was in large part paralleled by similar studies in the United States. It came to indicate many theoretical and practical inadequacies within Britain management thought. Some of its main conclusions were also recorded in British management journals, and we shall try to illustrate its subsequent influence upon informed opinion in the management movement. In particular, this social science research has shown how past efforts to establish a generally applicable body of management knowledge foundered upon their neglect of the great variety in the different industrial situations which exist in practice. These efforts had tended to ignore the constraints placed upon managerial action by a range of technological, market, and social parameters. They had overlooked how these parameters might give rise to intra- as well as inter-organizational conflicts, and they had failed to realize how such parameters would present themselves in different combinations in different enterprises. The influx of this recent research has served to reduce the ideological element in the discussion of management problems, to the extent that management thought had previously ignored such complicating factors for legitimatory purposes – first, in an attempt to claim for management an established body of expert knowledge it did not possess, and second in an attempt to claim a total community of interest within industry between managers and other groups.

NOTES

1. Editorial 'Commentary', *The Manager*, Jan. 1954, p. 9.
2. L. Urwick and E. F. L. Brech, *The Making of Scientific Management*, vol. II, London: Management Publications 1947, esp. pp. 207-215.
3. W. Puckey, *What is this Management?*, London: Chapman & Hall 1944, p. 4.
4. Mass Observation, *People in Production*, London: Murray 1942; M. Benny, *Over to Bombers*, London: Allen & Unwin 1943; cf., A. Albu, *Management in Transition*, London: Fabian Society Nov. 1942, p. 3.
5. E.g., G. Chelioti, broadcast reported in *Industry*, July 1947, p. 11.
6. Cf., R. P. Lynton, *Incentives and Management in British Industry*, London: Routledge & Kegan Paul 1949, chapters IV-IX.
7. E.g., E. F. L. Brech, 'The Management Lessons of the War – Industrial Relationships', *British Management Review*, V, 3, 1945, pp. 26-58; Editorial, *Personnel Management*, XXXIV, 322, Dec. 1952, p. 195; E. Meigh, 'The Implications of Membership of a Professional Body', *British Management Review*, XII, 3, April 1954, p. 132.
8. Hon. L. Russell, 'Management and Productivity', *British Management Review*, VII, 4, 1948, p. 66; A. Crichton, 'The I.P.M. in 1950 and 1960', *Personnel Management*, XLIII, 358, Dec. 1961, pp. 253-270; G. Millerson, *The Qualifying Associations*, London: Routledge & Kegan Paul 1964, appendix I; M. M. Niven, *Personnel Management 1913-63*, London: Institute of Personnel Management 1967.
9. E. Sidney, 'Evaluating Management Training', *Industrial Welfare*, XXXVIII, 6, Nov.-Dec. 1956, p. 164.
10. Sir W. Puckey, *Organization in Business Management*, London: Hutchinson 1963, 'A Personal Introduction', p. 11.
11. L. Urwick and E. F. L. Brech, 'The Pioneers of Scientific Management, Third Series. I – The Hawthorne Investigations', *Industry Illustrated*, Nov. 1944, p. 12.
12. E.g., F. J. Burns Morton, *The New Foremanship*, London: Chapman & Hall, vol. I 1943, vol. II 1949; V. M. Clarke, *New Times, New Methods and New Men*, London: Allen & Unwin 1950.
13. L. Urwick and E. F. L. Brech, *The Making of Scientific Management*, vol. III, 'The Hawthorne Investigations', London: Management Publications 1948; chapter 5 of the author's Ph.D. thesis referred to in the preface has a bibliographical appendix giving a comprehensive list of British writings from 1940 onwards which adopted a human relations approach.
14. J. A. C. Brown, *The Social Psychology of Industry*, Harmondsworth: Penguin 1954, and personal investigation by the author covering 126 management teachers in 46 colleges of technology 1964 – reported in part II of his Ph.D. thesis.
15. *Op. cit.*, p. 2.

16. C. I. Barnard, *The Functions of the Executive*, Cambridge, Mass.: Harvard University Press 1938, esp. chapter XVII.

17. L. Urwick, 'Industrial Relations – Retrospect and Prospect', *British Management Review*, V, 2, 1944, pp. 66-67.

18. E.g., E. F. L. Brech, 'The Personnel Function: the Nervous System of Management', in Institute of Industrial Administration, *Management in Action*, London: I.I.A. 1943, p. 49; F. C. Hooper, *Management Survey*, London: Pitman 1948, pp. 75, 89 (Penguin printing); R. M. Aldrich, 'Personnel' in ed. E. F. L. Brech, *The Principles and Practice of Management*, London: Longmans 1953 and 1963, p. 515, 2nd ed.; W. H. Dunkley, 'The Culture of Large Organizations' in ed. D. C. Thomson, *Management, Labour and Community*, London: Pitman 1957, esp. pp. 6-7.

19. On enlisting 'the whole person' cf., J. Munro Fraser, *Human Relations in a Fully Employed Democracy*, London: Pitman 1960, p. 17; On the primacy of non-monetary rewards cf., J. A. C. Brown, *op. cit.*, chapter 7. Also *idem*, 'Surveying the British Scene' in The Polytechnic, Dept. of Management Studies, *New Developments in Industrial Leadership*, London 1955, p. 15.

20. H. W. Locke, 'An Approach to the Problem of Foreman Training', *Labour Management*, XXIV, 259, April 1942, p. 57.

21. F. J. Burns Morton, *Foremanship – a Textbook*, London: Chapman & Hall 1951, p. 281.

22. F. J. Burns Morton, 'General Principles of Foremanship and Supervision', in ed. H. McFarland Davis, *Introduction to Foremanship*, London: MacDonald & Evans 1942, p. 22. Also all Burns Morton's other writings; A. Sanders, 'Training Supervisory Staffs for Industrial Management', in Institute of Industrial Administration, *Training for Industrial Management*, London 1943.

23. E.g., G. R. Taylor, *Are Workers Human?*, London: Falcon Press 1950, p. 120.

24. G. R. Taylor, *op. cit.*, p. 171. See also pp. 172-3; C. H. Northcott, *Personnel Management: its scope and practice*, London: Pitman 1945, p. 250; L. Urwick, *Urwick Management Lectures*, Birmingham, Central Technical College Students' Union Industrial Administration Group 1950, esp. p. 46.

25. Cf., T. N. Whitehead, *Leadership in a Free Society*, London: Oxford University Press 1936, chapter XI; F. J. Burns Morton, *Teamwork in Industry*, London: Chapman & Hall 1948, p. 221; *idem*, *op. cit.* 1949, pp. 163-164; L. Urwick, 'The Obstetrics of Leadership', *British Management Review*, XIII, 2, April 1955, p. 79.

26. Editorial, *Labour Management*, XXVIII, 284, Feb.-March 1946, pp. 1-2; E. F. L. Brech, *Management – Its Nature and Significance*, London: Pitman 1948, esp. p. 58; Sir G. Ince (Ministry of Labour), 'Industrial Relations and Human Relations', *Personnel Management*, XXXVI, 327, March 1954, p. 17.

27. E.g., P. H. Cook, *The Psychology of Management-Worker Relations*, London and Melbourne: Oxford University Press 1943.

28. A. H. Merrie, 'Factory Discipline', *Labour Management*, XXVI, 273, April-May 1944, p. 38.

29. R. Lloyd Roberts, speech reported by D. S. A. E. Jessop, 'Foremen in Conference', *Labour Management*, XXV, 271, Dec.-Jan. 1943-44, p. 132.

30. Sir H. Houldsworth: opening address to the 1951 I.P.M. National Conference, *Personnel Management*, XXXIII, 318, Nov.-Dec. 1951, p. 263.

31. A. P. Young, 'Industry as an Educational Force', *British Management Review*, VI, 2, 1947, p. 78.

32. Editorial, *Personnel Management*, XXXIX, 339, March 1957, pp. 1-2.

33. E.g., The Archbishop of Canterbury, 'Management and the Nation' in Institute of Industrial Administration, *Training for Management, op. cit.*, esp. 351-352; Lord Justice Evershed, 'Some Reflections on Industrial Relations', *Personnel Management*, XXIX, 294, Nov.-Dec. 1947, pp. 259-264.

34. Sir E. Lever, 'The Place of Management in the Economy of the Country', *British Management Review*, XIII, 3, July 1955, p. 192; C. H. Northcott, review in *The Manager*, Sept. 1951, p. 514.

35. A. R. Cooper, 'The Human Relations Aspect of Management' in ed. D. C. Thomson, *op. cit.* 1957, p. 16.

36. Rt. Hon. Lord Piercy, 'The Management Viewpoint', *The Manager*, April 1959, p. 252.

37. F. J. Burns Morton, *op. cit.* 1948, p. 67; G. R. Taylor, *op. cit.*, chapter VI; cf., H. N. Casson, *Labour Troubles and How to Prevent Them*, London: Efficiency Magazine 1919, chapter VII.

38. M. A. Cameron, Principles of Management', *British Management Review*, VII, 3, 1948, pp. 58-59; cf., H. N. Casson, *Handbook for Foremen*, London: Efficiency Magazine 1928, p. 114.

39. V. M. Clarke, *op. cit.*, p. 22.

40. Viscount Slim, 'Leadership in Management', *Journal of the British Institute of Management*, I, 4, April 1958, pp. 231-239; Viscount Slim, 'Leadership' (the 7th Elbourne Memorial Lecture, Nov. 1961), *The Manager*, Jan. 1962, p. 37.

41. L. Urwick, 'Administration and Leadership', *British Management Review*, V, 4, 1945, p. 91; *idem, Leadership in the Twentieth Century*, London: Pitman 1957, esp. chapter 4.

42. R. F. Tredgold, *Human Relations in Modern Industry*, London: Duckworth, 2nd ed. 1963, p. 5.

43. F. C. Hooper, *op. cit.*, p. 84; also G. R. Taylor, *op. cit.*, p. 87.

44. Sir E. Lever, 'The Place of Management in the Economy of the Country', *op. cit., British Management Review*, July 1955, p. 188.

45. Trade Union Congress, *Interim Report on Post-War Reconstruction* 1944, paras. 90-104.

46. F. J. Burns Morton, *op. cit.* 1943, p. 10.

47. F. C. Hooper, *op. cit.*, p. 87.

48. J. Munro Fraser, *op. cit.* 1960, p. 13.

49. E.g., a managing director, quoted in Mass Observation, *People in Production, op. cit.*, pp. 345-346; Sir C. Bartlett (then managing director of Vauxhall Motors) quoted in W. B. D. Brown and W. Raphael, *Managers, Men and Morale*, London: Macdonald & Evans 1948, p. 117.

50. Cf., Editorial, *Personnel Management*, XLI, 347, March 1959, pp. 1-4; Editorial, *Personnel Management*, XLII, 354, Dec. 1960, p. 216; G. R. Moxon, 'Collective Bargaining: National and Local', *Personnel Management*, XLII, 354, Dec. 1960, pp. 228-233.

51. W. H. Scott, 'Management in Great Britain', chapter 16 in F. Harbison and C. A. Myers, *Management in the Industrial World*, New York: McGraw-Hill 1959, esp. pp. 312-313.

52. R. Falk, *The Business of Management*, Harmondsworth: Penguin 1961, pp. 168-169.

53. Editorial, *Industry Illustrated*, Dec. 1946, p. 11.

54. E.g., N. F. T. Saunders, *Factory Organization and Management*, London: Pitman 1946, 2nd ed., p. 108; 'Argus', 'Management Commentary', *Industry*, July 1947, p. 13; Sir R. Sinclair, 'Industry and Management', *The Manager*, Dec. 1950, p. 593; Sir E. Lever, 'The Place of Management in the Economy of the Country', *op. cit.*, *British Management Review*, July 1955, pp. 190-191.

55. W. H. Dunkley, 'Culture and Personality in the Organisation – 2: Aspects of Democracy in the Organisation', *The Manager*, Jan. 1955, pp. 40-41.

56. F. C. Hooper, *Management Survey, op. cit.*, p. 104.

57. J. A. C. Brown, *The Social Psychology of Industry, op. cit.*, p. 236; F. J. Burns Morton, *op. cit.* 1948, p. 188.

58. V. M. Clarke, *op. cit.*, pp. 18-19, 88.

59. V. W. Oubridge in *Industry Illustrated*, April 1945, pp. 24-26.

60. F. J. Burns Morton, *op. cit.* 1943, p. 72.

61. L. Urwick, *Urwick Management Lectures*, Birmingham, Central Technical College Students' Union Industrial Administration Group 1950, references from pp. 44-52; G. R. Taylor, *Are Workers Human?*, London: Falcon Press 1950, references from pp. 28-37, 40, 66-68, 79, 84, 171-172 and chapter XI in general. Another summary of Urwick's views which indicates the influence of Mayoism is his 'The Importance of Management' in ed. D. C. Thomson, *op. cit.* 1957, pp. xi-xix.

62. Cf., E. Mayo and G. F. F. Lombard, *Teamwork and Labor Turnover in the Aircraft Industry of Southern California*, Cambridge, Mass.: Harvard University Press 1944.

63. Review of *Leadership in the Twentieth Century, op. cit.* in *The Manager*, Jan. 1958, p. 51.

64. L. Urwick, 'Management as an Intellectual Discipline', *British Management Review*, XIV, 4, Oct. 1956, pp. 222-240, quotation from p. 232.

65. *Britain's Industrial Future: The Report of the Liberal Party Industrial Inquiry*, London: Benn 1928, Book 3: 'Industrial Relations', esp. pp. 140, 148-150, and chapter XIV.

L

66. O. Sheldon, *The Philosophy of Management*, London: Pitman 1923, p. 83.

67. *Ibid.*, p. 18.

68. M. Atkinson, 'Industrial Unrest' in ed. J. Lee, *Dictionary of Industrial Administration*, London: Pitman 1928, p. 397; E. T. Kelly, 'Welfare' in *ibid.*, p. 1081; O. Sheldon, 'Industrial Organization' in *ibid.*, p. 367.

69. J. A. Bowie, 'Co-partnership' in ed. J. Lee, *op. cit.*, p. 122.

70. E.g., R. Blauner, *Alienation and Freedom*, University of Chicago Press 1964; W. W. Daniel, 'Bakers' Boredom', *New Society*, IV, 112, 19th Nov. 1964, pp. 14-16.

71. L. Urwick, *Management of Tomorrow*, London: Nisbet 1933, p. 141.

72. *Ibid.*, p. 149.

73. E.g., J. A. C. Brown, *op. cit.* 1954, and *op. cit.* 1955; C. A. Mace, 'The Functions of the Manager: an Operational Analysis' in ed. D. C. Thomson, *op. cit.*, pp. 49-63.

74. V. L. Allen, 'A Failure of Method: the Inadequacy of Present Research as a Basis for Understanding the Nature of Management', *Technology*, Jan. 1963, pp. 14, 23; D. Arram, 'A Critical Examination of the Assumptions in Some Post-war British Industrial Sociology', unpublished M.A. thesis, University of Leeds, June 1961; A. H. Richmond, 'Conflict and Authority in Industry', *Occupational Psychology*, 28, 1, Jan. 1954, p. 24; J. P. Worms, 'La Sociologie Industrielle à l'Université de Liverpool', Notes Critiques, *Sociologie du Travail*, II, 4, Oct.-Dec. 1960, pp. 367-377.

75. Cf., E. Jaques, *The Changing Culture of a Factory*, London: Tavistock 1951; J. F. Scott and R. P. Lynton, *The Community Factor in Modern Technology*, Paris: U.N.E.S.C.O. 1952; W. H. Scott, *Industrial Leadership and Joint Consultation*, Liverpool University Press 1952; W. H. Scott, 'The Scientific Study of Human Relations in Industry – II', *Personnel Management*, XXXIV, 321, Sept. 1952, esp. pp. 148-149.

76. A. Albu, *Management in Transition*, London: Fabian Society, Nov. 1942, p. 8.

77. Sir S. Cripps, 'Post-war Aims and Opportunities', *Labour Management*, XXVII, 279, April-May 1945, pp. 27-29.

78. Ed. R. H. S. Crossman, *New Fabian Essays*, London: Turnstile Press 1952, pp. 129-132.

79. L. T. Wright, 'Management Education and Industrial Relations', paper given at the Department of Education and Science Conference on 'Management Studies – Current Issues and Developments', Cambridge, 7th July 1964.

80. Conference on 'The Role of Communications in Industry', organized by Pressure for Economic and Social Toryism, Cambridge, 5th March 1964, personal notes of the author.

81. F. Cousins, 'Industrial Relations – a Forward Look', *Personnel Management*, XLIV, 362, Dec. 1962, p. 252.

82. J. A. Bowie, 'The Future of Management', *Journal of the Institute of Industrial Administration* (*J.I.I.A.*), III, 4 (new series), Sept. 1942, p. 11; G. S. Masson, paper reported in *J.I.I.A.*, III, 4, Sept. 1942, p. 18.

83. Editorial, *Labour Management*, XXVII, 279, April-May 1945, p. 26.

84. W. B. D. Brown, 'Inter-management Relationships', *Labour Management*, XXVII, 283, Dec.-Jan. 1945-46, p. 127.

85. Cf., G. C. Longdon, 'Labour Management', *J.I.I.A.*, IV, 6, March 1943, p. 16; G. S. Walpole, 'Joint Consultation at All Levels', *British Management Review*, IV, 4, 1943, p. 69.

86. J. Burnham, *The Managerial Revolution*, New York: Day 1941; J. A. Bowie, 'Education for Management', *Industry*, June 1947, p. 30; J. A. Bowie, 'Management and the Closed Shop', *Industry*, Jan. 1949, pp. 15-17.

87. J. A. Bowie, 'The Future of Management', *op. cit.*, *J.I.I.A.*, Sept. 1942, pp. 10-12.

88. Examples of professional and similar claims during the 1950s are: V. M. Clarke, *op. cit.*, pp. 41, 49, 127; L. Urwick, *Urwick Management Lectures*, *op. cit.*, pp. 11, 12; L. Urwick, 'The American Challenge in Industrial Management', *British Management Review*, XII, 3, April 1954, pp. 172-173; Sir C. Renold, 'Some Thoughts on Industrial Conflict', *The Manager*, Sept. 1955, p. 654; E. F. L. Brech, *Organisation: the Framework of Management*, London: Longmans 1957, p.v.

89. N. Bamforth, 'Towards a Philosophy for Management: an Attempt to Clear the Ground', *Times Review of Industry*, X, 108, Jan. 1956, pp. 13, 15.

90. T. T. Paterson, 'The New Profession of Management', *The Listener*, LVI, 1445, 6th Dec. 1956, pp. 921-922, quotations from p. 921.

91. F. A. Heller, letter to *The Listener*, 13th Dec. 1956, p. 999.

92. Paterson, *op. cit.*, p. 921.

93. E. F. L. Brech, *The Principles and Practice of Management*, London: Longmans 1953, p. 730; Cf., G. Hunter, *The Role of the Personnel Officer: A Group Review*, London: I.P.M. Occasional Paper no. 12, 1957, and similar writings discussed in the following chapter.

94. L. Urwick, *Is Management a Profession?*, London: Urwick, Orr & Partners 1954, esp. pp. 4-5, 8-16, 18-19.

95. F. C. Hooper, 'Management in Theory and Practice: Human Element in Business', *The Times*, 3rd Oct. 1955, p. 9; cf. also J. Marsh, *People at Work*, London: Industrial Welfare Society 1957, esp. pp. 47-48.

96. L. Urwick, *Leadership in the Twentieth Century*, *op. cit.* 1957, pp. 47-48; E. T. Elbourne, *Fundamentals of Industrial Administration*, London: Macdonald & Evans 1934, pp. 562-563.

97. A. G. Cruft, 'Scientific Management or Sterile Authority', *British Management Review*, VIII, 3, Nov. 1949, pp. 72-86; cf., 'Has British Management a Philosophy?', report of a discussion, *The*

Manager, Sept. 1953, p. 536 and the reception of Sir Arnold Plant's comments.

98. Editorial, *Industry Illustrated*, July 1943, p. 11.

99. H. E. Roff, 'Management Ethics', *Personnel Management*, XXXIV, 319, March 1952, pp. 7-8.

100. Policy Sub-committee of the Institute of Industrial Administration, reported in the *British Management Review*, XII, 3, April 1954, p. 126.

101. E. Meigh, 'The Implications of Membership of a Professional Body', *British Management Review*, XII, 3, April 1954, p. 132; cf. also the articles by F. T. Chapman and A. Roberts in the same issue of the *B.M.R.* which discussed the above report.

102. Editorial, *Personnel Management*, XXXVIII, 336, June 1956, p. 73.

103. Sir W. Puckey, *Management Principles*, London: Hutchinson 1962, pp. 19-20, 180; *idem, Organization in Business Management*, London: Hutchinson 1963, pp. 11-14.

104. E.g., L. Stephens, 'The Institute and the Personnel Manager: a Stocktaking', *Personnel Management*, XLV, 363, March 1963, p. 30; E. F. L. Brech, 'The Theory of Management', *Scientific Business*, I, 3, Nov. 1963, pp. 279-286; H. Parker, 'What Makes the True Professional?', *The Manager*, Dec. 1964, pp. 32-34.

105. Cf., J. Gloag, *Management on the Factory Floor*, London: Pitman 1961, chapter III; Sir W. Robson Brown, *Management and Society*, London: Pitman 1961, chapter I; Sir W. Puckey, *Organization in Business Management*, London: Hutchinson 1963, pp. 10, 14, 17; Dr R. Beeching, 'Can Management Afford to be Christian Today?', lecture delivered at Cambridge, 19th Feb. 1964. Although some commentators, such as George Goyder, have attempted to specify precise interpretations of business social responsibility, they appear to have had little influence on British management thought. E.g. G. Goyder, *The Future of Private Enterprise*, Oxford: Blackwell 1951.

106. Sample of 35 senior management teachers in 27 English Colleges of Technology 1964. See part II of the author's Ph.D. thesis referred to in the Preface.

107. F. C. Hooper, *Management Survey*, op. cit. 1948, p. 104; cf. also pp. 56, 130-131.

108. L. Urwick, *Is Management a Profession?*, op. cit., pp. 21-22.

109. British Institute of Management, *The Recruitment and Training of Men Intended for Management Positions*, London: B.I.M. 1955, p. 18.

110. J. Sandford Smith and A. I. G. Hewitt, 'Rising from the Ranks in Industry', *British Management Review*, VIII, 1, 1949, pp. 55-61.

111. *British Management Review*, VII, 3, 1948, articles by J. A. Bowie, E. F. L. Brech, M. A. Cameron, W. Puckey, T. G. Rose, and L. Urwick.

112. E. F. L. Brech, 'Summary and Review', *British Management Review*, VII, 3, 1948, pp. 102-103; L. Urwick, 'Management as an

Intellectual Discipline', *British Management Review*, XIV, 4, Oct. 1956, p. 237.

113. L. Urwick, 'The Manager's Span of Control', *Harvard Business Review*, 34, 3, May-June 1956, pp. 39-47.

114. E. F. L. Brech, 'Introduction' in ed. Brech, *The Principles and Practice of Management*, London: Longmans 1953, 1963, p. 69 in 1963 edition. The same definition occurs in the 1953 edition.

115. L. Urwick, *A Short Survey of Industrial Management*, B.I.M. Occasional Paper no. 1, London 1950; L. Urwick, 'Foreword' to *The Golden Book of Management*, ed. Urwick, London: Newman Neame 1956, p. ix. *But* cf. the greater flexibility admitted in L. Urwick, 'Management and the Administrator' in ed. A. Dunsire, *The Making of an Administrator*, Manchester University Press 1956, p. 47.

116. E. F. L. Brech, *op. cit.* 1953, 1963 – in both editions; p. 46 in 1963 ed.

117. E. F. L. Brech, 'The Balance between Centralization and Decentralization in Managerial Control', *British Management Review*, XII, 4, July 1954, p. 198.

118. E. F. L. Brech, 'Summary and Review' to an issue on 'Organisation', *British Management Review*, VIII, 2, July 1949, pp. 87-88.

119. E. G. Robinson, 'Management Principles and Practice', *Journal of the British Institute of Management*, I, 3, Jan. 1958, p. 212.

120. G. S. Walpole, *Methods of Stimulating Interest in Production*, reprint of an address to the Institute of Labour Management Annual Conference, Oct. 1943, p. 9.

121. C. H. Northcott, *Personnel Management*, London: Pitman 1945, chapter 12.

122. J. A. C. Brown, *The Social Psychology of Industry, op. cit.*, p. 101.

123. E.g., G. S. Walpole, 'Joint Consultation at All Levels', *British Management Review*, IV, 4, 1943, p. 71; R. Watson, 'Company Employment Policy', *Labour Management*, XXVII, 279, April-May 1945, pp. 56-58.

124. C. H. Northcott, *op. cit.*, p. 250.

125. G. S. Walpole, *op. cit.* (address of 1943), p. 8.

126. E.g., C. H. Northcott, 'Joint Production Committees: Their Place in Modern Industrial Management', *Labour Management*, XXIV, 261, July 1942, p. 86; G. S. Walpole, *Management and Men: a study of the theory and practice of joint consultation at all levels*, London: Cape 1944, p. 169.

127. A production manager, reported in Mass Observation, *People in Production, op. cit.* 1942, p. 348; Sir G. Cunningham, 'Joint Consultation', *British Management Review*, IX, 2, July 1950, pp. 60-65; R. D. V. Roberts, 'Joint Consultation' in ed. D. C. Thomson, *Management, Labour and Community, op. cit.*, pp. 130-131 (quoted).

128. I. C. McGivering, D. G. J. Matthews and W. H. Scott, *Management in Britain*, Liverpool University Press 1960, chapter 3, and Conclusion.

129. C. G. Renold, *Joint Consultation over Thirty Years*, London: Allen & Unwin 1950, Preface: pp. vii-viii, chapter 4, and pp. 107-108, 118; E. Jaques, *The Changing Culture of a Factory*, London: Tavistock 1951, chapters 7 and 8, and pp. 271-272; W. Brown, *Exploration in Management*, London: Heinemann 1960, *passim*, and 'Foreword' by E. L. Trist, esp. pp. xviii ff.

130. E. Jaques, *op. cit.*, esp. pp. 316-318. Also cf. pp. 279-280, 293-297, 300-301; W. Brown, *op. cit.*, chapter XIV, and introduction by E. L. Trist, p. xvii; W. Brown and E. Jaques, 'Consent or Command in Committee', *The Manager*, Jan. 1965, p. 18.

131. Sir C. Renold, 'Managers and Men', *British Management Review*, VII, 2, 1948, pp. 7, 9.

132. Sir C. Renold, 'Some Thoughts on Industrial Conflict', *The Manager*, Sept. 1955, p. 695; Personal conversation between the author and W. Morton, 4th March 1964.

133. B. S. Rowntree, *The Human Factor in Business*, London: Longmans, 3rd ed. 1938; W. Wallace, *Prescription for Partnership*, London: Pitman 1959, Part II.

134. W. B. D. Brown and W. Raphael, *Managers, Men and Morale*, London: Macdonald & Evans 1948, pp. 9, 10, 11-12, 93, 116; *idem*, *op. cit.* 1960, p. 279.

135. C. G. Renold, *op. cit.* 1950, p. 111; also *idem*, 'Some Thoughts on Industrial Conflict', *op. cit.*, pp. 651-654, 693-696.

136. Sir C. Renold, *The Nature of Management*, B. I. M. Occasional Paper no. 2, London 1950, pp. 10-11; *idem*, 'Some Thoughts on Industrial Conflict', *op. cit.*, p. 653; W. B. D. Brown and W. Raphael, *op. cit.*, pp. 76-79.

137. C. G. Renold, *op. cit.* 1950, *passim*; W. B. D. Brown and W. Raphael, *op. cit.*, p. 116; W. Brown, *op. cit.* 1960, esp. chapters XVI, XVII, and p. 307.

138. W. Brown, 'Some Basic Problems of Industrial Relationships', *British Management Review*, VI, 2, 1947, pp. 52-64.

139. Letter to *Industry Illustrated*, March 1947, p. 34.

140. Letter from 'W. S. H.' to *Industry*, Nov. 1947, p. 31; cf. also letter from 'J.G.' to *Industry*, Aug. 1947, p. 28.

141. Letter to *Personnel Management*, XXXI, 305, Sept.-Oct. 1949, p. 252.

142. G. Chelioti, 'The Middlemen of Industry – 2', *Industry Illustrated*, May 1946, p. 24; O. G. S. Crawford, letter to *The Listener*, 20th Dec. 1956; cf. also *Financial Times*, 'Is Management a Science?', 24th Nov. 1958, p. 10.

143. R. Appleby, 'Management and Work', *British Management Review*, X, 4, March 1952, p. 19.

144. *Ibid.*, pp. 23, 24.

145. Sir G. Schuster, *Christianity and Human Relations in Industry*, London: Epworth Press 1951, chapter 8, quotation p. 118.

146. J. J. Gillespie, *Free Expression in Industry*, London: Pilot Press 1948, p. 98.

147. N. I. Bond-Williams, 'Informal Workers' Groups: an Interim Report on an Industrial Experiment', *British Management Review*, XI, 4, July 1953, pp. 37-56; R. D. Best, 'Free Expression in a Birmingham Factory', *The Manager*, Aug. 1953, pp. 460-462, 464.

148. Political and Economic Planning, *The Human Factor in Industry*, London: P.E.P. 1948, p. 10.

149. J. J. Gillespie, *op. cit.*, p. 40; G. Hunter, 'The Illusion of Scientific Management', *Personnel Management*, XXXIII, 315, May-June 1951, pp. 118-123.

150. E.g., Editorial, *Personnel Management*, XXXV, 325, Sept. 1953, pp. 121-122.

CHAPTER 6

THE CHALLENGE OF SOCIAL SCIENCE

The Trend of Industrial Social Science: (1) the analysis of employee behaviour; (2) the analysis of administrative organization; (3) frames of reference in current industrial social science – The Reporting of Social Science Research to Management, Some Examples – Recent British Management Thought: (1) personnel management and human relations; (2) management thought on the study of organization; (3) the Glacier Project – Summary and Discussion.

IN 1950 human relations, and to a lesser extent management principles, were the predominating themes of British management thought. They appeared to be complementary and to provide managers with a comprehensive, practical means to structure and regulate behaviour within an enterprise. The principles afforded a design for formal structure. Human relations offered an approach to the dynamics of administration whereby 'informal' activities were reconciled with the formally stated purposes of the organization.

These management precepts were assumed to be universally applicable to all enterprises, including non-industrial ones. They shared the additional assumption that such enterprises could be analysed meaningfully as closed systems. These main props of management thought abstracted their analyses of organizational life from the economic, technological, social and political factors which might influence behaviour, and which therefore linked organizations as open systems with their particular environments. This kind of abstraction allowed for the assumption prevailing in management thought that it was largely within managers' own powers to fashion behaviour and relationships as might best suit their own purposes. Even the discussion of managerial professionalism, where this touched on social relationships, was now tending to focus on a solidaristic human relations notion of forging harmony and unity within the enterprise, rather than on the older idea of holding the balance between different membership groups whose interests could conflict.

Nevertheless, both the human relations and management principles approaches had their critics within the management movement, as we have noted. From the early 1950s, these initial critiques were amplified and extended by a growing fund of social science analysis and research. Indeed the point has been reached today where most writing on organizational behaviour, even for managerial consumption, appears to derive from professional social scientists. This raises incidentally the interesting question of in what sense we can speak any more of 'management thought' in this field. Certainly the impact of social science has been profound and revolutionary in its implications. For it has served to reverse a number of previously active trends within British management thought – trends towards a simplified, solidary and closed view of enterprises, towards the construction of universal precepts, and towards the unqualified recommendation of human relations methods in respect of employee productivity. Social science has called into question the practical effectiveness, let alone morality, of a manipulative system of managerial control which attempts to deny the role of conflict in industry.

There is now sufficient evidence to indicate that organizational behaviour is generally the product of a complex system of interaction between a wide variety of determinants. Thus the analysis of behaviour requires frames of reference extending from personality features, through the role and organization, to the wider socio-economic forces external to individual enterprises. The work of social scientists has clearly shown that any sufficient prediction of behaviour in industry must be advanced in respect of the conditions prevailing in a given situation. Furthermore, it has also indicated that the ability of managers to influence behaviour and to avoid the presence of conflict within their organizations may be severely limited by determinants over which they have little control. In fact some social scientists have recently come to stress not only that conflict is a normal concomitant of organizational life, but that it can in some respects possess positive functions for effective operation, particularly regarding adaptation to change.[1]

The present chapter is divided into four main sections. The

first outlines features in the recent development of industrial social science which have borne closely upon management thought. It is of necessity a selective review, and it leans towards sociological work in so far as this has probably had the greatest impact on management thought. The second section illustrates how the findings of social science were passed on to the British management movement. The third examines recent British management writing, noting particularly the impact which sociological findings may have had on this. This section includes a special review of the Glacier Project. The final section is a short summary and discussion. The implications of social science for approaches adopted in management education is discussed later, in Chapter 8.

I. THE TREND OF INDUSTRIAL SOCIAL SCIENCE

The accumulation of research findings since the last war has resulted in steadily widening theoretical perspectives among most industrial social scientists. Several authors, particularly Tréanton and Reynaud in their trend report for *Current Sociology*, have recorded these developments in detail.[2] Our present review is confined to the selection of findings which have been most directly relevant to management thought. We shall start with the analysis of employee behaviour, and then continue with the analysis of administrative organization.

(1) *The analysis of employee behaviour*
American and French sociologists from the later 1940s, and British sociologists from the early 1950s, joined in a sharp reaction against the Mayo school.[3] The earliest critiques of human relations came in advance of detailed research findings in support of their case, which rested on the combination of an outraged sociological perspective and an alarmed liberal philosophy. As Landsberger has indicated, the strength of this attack derived from a recognition of the ideological elements contained in Mayoism. First, its peculiar 'world-view' of social disorganization and anomie in the so-called 'adaptive' modern industrial society. Second, its managerial orientation which led it to justify a manipulation of workers for managerial ends, on the grounds that workers found in the industrial enterprise a necessary security, belonging, and personal leadership which they had been denied in the wider society. Third, its unwilling-

ness to recognize the existence of features which did not accord with this analytical scheme. For instance, the role of conflict as a manifestation of differences in power, economic interests, class position and ideology; the role of trade unionism; and the availability of institutionalized means to regulate collective bargaining and to accommodate conflict.[4]

Subsequently, a series of research findings confirmed the analytical deficiencies of too restricted a social-psychological view of employee behaviour, especially when this adopted an exclusively managerial point of view. Fundamental assumptions of human relations were put to question by evidence that supervisory training programmes in 'social skills' could fail to have any substantial practical effect back in the factory,[5] that neither permissive nor employee-centred supervision bore a necessary relationship to high productivity,[6] and by instances where there was no apparent relation between high employee morale and high productivity, and where even low morale was associated with high productivity.[7] Similarly, the human relations emphasis on structuring cohesive work groups was found on occasion to go against managerial interests. For while such groups might exhibit lower anxiety than less cohesive ones, it was discovered that they could also turn out persistently below average rates of productivity.[8] Furthermore, instances were found where apparently high employee satisfaction (which should also be regarded as a constituent of high 'morale') accompanied output restriction and various unofficial practices in defiance of formal managerial rules.[9]

These last findings suggested additional qualifications to a purely human relations view of employee behaviour. Human relations had contrasted formal managerial rules with informal employee practices subverting these rules, in terms of a logic of 'efficiency' and a non-logic of 'sentiment'. This distinction did not allow for cases where the informal practices served to compensate for inadequacies in formal procedures, with a result beneficial for the operation of the organization.[10] Moreover, the human relations explanation for employee output restriction, in terms of a shared practice designed to sustain informal shop floor social networks, was often found to be inadequate. A prime motive for output restriction could after all be a materialistic one, in the form of a careful and quite rational calculation of the optimum 'effort-bargain' available.

Further, this practice could possess other positive functions for employees in terms of increasing their satisfaction in the work place. For instance, it could accord with their prevailing notions of 'fairness' by giving those on inferior equipment, or with 'tight' piece-rates, the chance to earn the same as their workmates. Or it enabled employees to retain a minimum area of control over their own activities in face of the continual extension of managerial regulation by means of techniques such as work-study and inspection.[11] In fact, the Mayo school's own interpretation of output restriction has been challenged by evidence that the Western Electric Company *did* after all employ a subtle method of rate-cutting and that the experiment in the Bank Wiring Room had itself to be discontinued because several of the wiremen were laid off during the Depression.[12]

Two other sets of research findings have also seriously questioned the human relations view of employee behaviour. First, evidence that under certain work conditions, particularly those where technological and other features do not conduce to high levels of intrinsic task satisfaction, the majority of workers *do not seek* high levels of personal involvement with management, supervisors, or even work-mates, and indeed do not take up this kind of employment primarily for 'social' rewards such as these. In these cases, their central life interests are not based upon the place of work and, *pace* human relations, they do not look to the enterprise to fulfil any needs for 'belonging' which they might have.[13] Second, and running counter to what is more of an implicit assumption in human relations, some researches have indicated that workers could combine approving attitudes towards their company with a continuing loyalty to their trade union, even in situations where there was considerable conflict between the two sides.[14]

Finally, some commentators have cast quite serious doubts not just on the broader interpretations which the human relations school gave to the Hawthorne experiments, but on the scientific validity of the experiments themselves and the reporting of their results. One of these re-appraisals concluded that the results of the first three experiments, far from supporting a human relations view, were 'surprisingly consistent with a rather old-world view about the value of monetary incentives, driving leadership, and discipline'.[15] Another concluded of the Bank Wiring Room study that there was nothing in the evidence to disprove the accepted view that employees restrict their levels of output because they believe it to be in their economic interests to do so.[16]

Thus it became clear that worker behaviour could not be fully explained by a limited human relations perspective. And, in the event, additional findings have shown the determinants of this behaviour to reside not merely in the social life of the primary group, but first in the structure of the enterprise as a whole and second in the interaction between the enterprise as a social system and elements in the wider society.

We may start with the former group of factors. Pelz's study of the conditions under which supervisory action evoked a positive response from employees indicated how relations at this level were in part a function of the total power structure in an enterprise.[17] In 1950 Worthy reported experience in Sears, Roebuck which strongly suggested that organizational features such as advanced specialization and restricted spans of control could reduce employee morale through limiting the scope for employee responsibility and initiative.[18] This finding added weight to the case which Frisby had put forward in 1933 (see Chapter 4). It also looked forward to the more recent analyses of McGregor and other organizational psychologists which we shall consider shortly.[19] In addition, Worthy found that employee morale decreased with an increase in size of plant. Others have supported this finding, together with a comparable relation between morale and size of work group.[20]

Among other behavioural determinants which pertain to the enterprise, technology has been found to be among the most important. Indeed, it is likely to have some bearing upon the prevailing structure of organization.[21] It has been found to influence job satisfaction, worker behaviour, and the structure of supervisor-worker relations.[22] And technological systems where workers do not directly control the pace of output are likely to provide further instances where morale is not closely related to productivity. In such cases a greater increase in productivity may derive from an attention to engineering rather than psychological variables, a fact that also runs counter to a tenet of human relations.[23] Some factors associated with technology - such as level of skill, length of task cycle, variety of tasks performed, level of responsibility - have been found to influence worker attitudes and behaviour.[24]

These last factors may lie open to managerial adjustment. This is also true of a further device, wage payment systems, the influence of which on worker behaviour remains open to some dispute. However, different systems appear to have a bearing on workers' willingness to accept shop floor changes, and on their relationships with supervisors.[25] Despite the immense difficulties of separating out the effects of financial incentives from accompanying measures such as work-study, there is some evidence that they may on their own account be instrumental in raising the level of worker effort.[26] Another plant variable open to some managerial control, which a limited amount of American research suggests might affect employee attitudes and even behaviour, is the prevailing structure of promotion opportunities up from the shop floor.[27] The influence of this variable is difficult to isolate from other managerial policies which might have a compensatory effect – such as seniority and long service payments. It would also have to be taken in conjunction with workers' expectations of promotion, and with prevailing company ideology on this matter.

In the second place, social scientists have indicated that factors external to an enterprise may influence the behaviour of its members. These factors include the stability of its product market, the state of its labour market, and the strength of union organization among its employees.[28] Sainsaulieu has recently presented interesting French data suggesting a link between the power enjoyed by worker groups within factories and the policies adopted by their unions vis-à-vis management.[29]

In addition, a whole range of variables may combine to determine 'culturally' the needs and expectations of workers. There is evidence to include among these the degree of workers' urbanization, the isolation of their communities from the wider society, their region, their family and other domestic circumstances, their ethnic and religious backgrounds, their age group, and what may loosely be termed their 'class images'.[30] Moreover, there is reason to assume that, regarding worker expectations and aspirations, a considerable cultural specificity exists between different countries – for instance between Britain and the United States.[31] This calls for the duplication of much American research before one can be certain that its findings apply to the British scene. Finally, investigations into international patterns of strike activity have suggested that, in this area as well, features specific to particular countries are important determining factors. Among such features are the unity of the particular labour movement, the extent and development of institutional arrangements in industrial relations, the strength of labour representation in the political field, and various socio-cultural factors.[32] All these features, of course, are 'external' to the individual industrial enterprise.

In the light of this accumulating body of research, it is not surprising that social scientists today have rejected as inadequate the human relations analysis of industrial behaviour, and its accompanying prescriptions for managerial policy. Few would deny that, in its time, this analysis provided valuable new insights. Indeed, in discarding the ideological aspects of human relations and in passing beyond its narrow perspectives, we should take care not to overlook the relevance which its analysis of sentiment may still possess for the study of industrial life. Likewise, some allowance should always be made for the likely independent influence of individual personality (as Levinson has argued), or of factors such as sex differences.[33] What, however, sociologists at least would emphasize is that psychological and biological variables of this nature are, in turn, qualified by the wider structuring forces which their research had delineated.

An accurate picture of organizational life is thus complex and contains great variety. This is one of the lessons emphasized by Etzioni's *Comparative Analysis of Complex Organizations*, which is among the most important and brilliant of recent analyses in the sociology of work.[34] Etzioni has in fact launched a devastating attack on the idea that organizations can be analysed in universalistic terms. Not only does his focus upon 'compliance' add a dimension which had previously been neglected in the analysis of organizational behaviour, but in tracing its correlates Etzioni opens up the whole question of how far both structure and behaviour have to be explained in terms of extra-organizational variables. In fact, it is the growing recognition that employee behaviour will be influenced by a matrix of variables relevant to particular situations which has led social scientists to take refuge in non-prescriptive concepts such as 'reality-centred' supervision, and to react against sweeping and a prioristic assumptions about worker orientations.[35]

(2) *The analysis of administrative organization*

Probably the earliest, and certainly the classic critique of management principles was put forward by Herbert A. Simon. Looking back on it in 1957, he saw no reason to restrict his original, uncompromising stand: '. . . organizational problems are not likely to be solved by slogans, but only by painstaking analysis; and I see no reason, therefore, to depart from my original evaluation of the "principles" as essentially useless.'[36] Simon showed how the principles tended to come in pairs – 'like proverbs' which when taken together were mutually contradictory: specialization – unity of command; span of control – limited number of hierarchical levels; centralization – decentralization. The presentation of dichotomies like these provided little practical guidance. In fact, all too frequently writing on administrative organization had proceeded arbitrarily by selecting one or two of these precepts, and then illegitimately positing them as 'one-best ways'. Moreover, the principles had concerned themselves only with the allocation of functions and the formal structure of authority. In Simon's opinion this anatomical approach had failed to consider some of the most significant features in the operation of organizations; particularly the processes of reaching decisions, communicating these, and translating them into action.

Following on from Simon, one set of studies has indicated the misleading nature of management principles as a guide to optimum organization structure. The principles had defined administrative roles in a formal manner, and had been taken to imply a standardized model of organization structure. Woodward, in an influential study, suggested that in practice the most effective organization structure varied according to the technology of an enterprise. This finding has received some support from a recent investigation by Blain. Recent research by the Industrial Administration Research Unit at Aston University has found organizational size, technology and dependence on other organizations to be the most powerful predictors of structural features. Different types of organization structure were identified by means of factor analysis.[37]

Another important research project under Burns and Stalker indicated that a 'mechanistic' structure with clearly prescribed formal roles and hierarchical authority might perform effectively in stable technical and market conditions, but that a less formally structured 'organismic' model proved more successful in dealing with changing and evolving conditions.[38] Using American research, Litwak suggested similarly that formal and hierarchical relationships would be most effective when dealing with routine, uniform tasks; and horizontal, informal relationships with non-uniform tasks.[39] Morse and Reimer in a study of supervision over routine clerical tasks found that 'hierarchical' non-participative supervision gave higher productivity, though lower employee morale, than did 'autonomous' participative styles.[40] Hall concluded a recent empirical study with the observation that the 'degree of bureaucratization' in structure appeared to relate to the type of current organizational activity.[41] Other research has indicated that there is no necessary correlation between operational effectiveness and individual management principles such as span of control.[42] This whole body of findings clearly implied that in the analysis of administrative organization, as in the study of employee behaviour, the universalistic assumptions contained in management thought had to give way to a situation-oriented approach.

Burns and Stalker found that a 'mechanistic' management system, which is comparable to the type implied by the management principles, placed fewer demands and strains upon individual managers.[43] Nevertheless, a number of American social scientists have recently argued that this type of organization structure is in general over-restrictive and too directive, and that in fact it is based upon mistaken assumptions about human motivation. On these grounds they have put forward a further case against the 'classical organization theory' of which management principles formed the main support. They claim that principles such as unity of command, task specialization, and limited span of control may restrict individuals' responsibility and require them to experience submissiveness. This, it is argued, is detrimental to their personal fulfilment at work (which Argyris terms 'self-actualization'), and correspondingly impairs their willingness to contribute fully to the operation of the organization as a whole.

This school is in sympathy with early leads given by Frisby and Worthy. Its members include Argyris, Bakke, Haire, Likert, McGregor, Roethlisberger, and Zaleznik.[44] It is worth while to consider their approach at this stage in so far as it follows on from human relations and since it enjoys a consider-

M

able popularity in current British management education. This may be referred to as the 'neo-human relations' approach. It shares with human relations a solidary view of the enterprise and a stress upon employees' social needs. Its orientation remains primarily social psychological. Moreover, the aim of neo-human relations continues to be the further integration of employees with the goals and social network of the enterprise, and the reconciliation of individual motivation with organizational purpose. It rarely makes any clear distinction between managerial and operative level employees, except to state that the lack of self-actualization opportunities is normally most acute at the lower end of the industrial hierarchy. As with human relations, it accords little attention to technology, economic interests, or organizational environment as factors influencing employee orientations and hence behaviour. (Argyris in a recent work has begun to show a limited awareness of the role of technology, social class and national 'culture' in this respect.)[45] Phenomena such as output restriction and loyalty to trade unions still tend to be seen mainly as indications of employees' desires to reduce a psychological feeling of submissiveness.[46]

On the other hand, the neo-human relations writers no longer believe that employees' co-operation can be won simply through supervisory social skills or by a managerial policy of mock participation. Instead, they feel it is necessary to reshape organization structure in a fundamental way. Rigid hierarchical levels should be softened into a system of interlocking groups, so that purely formal and vertical authority is replaced by wider-ranging and less formal patterns of participation and influence. Job enlargement, it is also argued, would allow greater responsibility and initiative to those lower down in the enterprise.

The structure thus proposed bears a certain similarity to Burns and Stalker's organismic model, although the latter was only applied to the level of managerial organization. However, the neo-human relations analysis remains far more narrowly conceived than that of these British authors. For instance, it does not allow for the probability that in stable and routine conditions the older mechanistic model may remain operationally the more effective. Moreover, it ignores two other features brought out by Burns and Stalker's study. First, the 'political' and 'status' systems operating within administrative organization. It was the stable status system of the mechanistic model which increased its members' sense of security. This fact, together with the reduced commitment to the total organization allowed by a mechanistic formal differentiation of roles, was found to impose less strain on managers. A finding of this nature serves as a further important qualification to the neo-human relations assumption that managers (let alone workers) necessarily desire a large degree of involvement in the enterprise as a whole.

Secondly, Burns and Stalker illustrated problems of co-operation and understanding between 'line' administrators and technical specialists deriving in part from the 'cosmopolitan', professional orientation of the latter group beyond the values and needs of the individual firm, and towards their colleagues in the wider society.[47] Cleavage between administrators and staff specialists therefore does not necessarily result only from faulty organization, as McGregor would appear to assume.[48] Some of the major weaknesses in the neo-human relations approach have recently been reviewed by George Strauss and other writers.[49] These critiques deserve attention in view of the popularity enjoyed by this school today.

A final major criticism against the management principles derives from one of Simon's points, and is also supported by findings such as those of Burns and Stalker just mentioned. Namely, that the principles, by treating administration in a formal and 'logical' manner and by abstracting from its social realities, failed to convey any significant information about the actual processes of managing. These processes include decision-making, communication, allocation of time, co-ordination of activities, control, and conflict-accommodation. Merely to set out abstract principles told managers nothing of the actual difficulties such processes were likely to bring. For instance, the principles took managerial authority as given, whereas sociological research has indicated how this must be treated as an operational problem – in Etzioni's terms it is one of securing 'compliance'.[50] Likewise, the principles failed to account for influences on managerial and employee behaviour which derive from features external to the enterprise, and which define their attachments to and expectations of the work situation. (This is a criticism which applies equally to neo-human relations.) Thus the principles, by presenting an over-simplified

definition of tasks and structure in an abstract 'ideal' organization, lent to managerial operation an ease, rationality, and
uniformity which it rarely possessed in reality. While there is
as yet rather little sociological research on actual managerial
activities, studies do exist of informal managerial systems of
influence, power, and conflict,[51] of managerial tasks and the
time allocated to them,[52] and of other managerial behaviour.[53]

(3) *Frames of reference in current industrial social science*
Social science has today discredited some of the most important
assumptions in management thought. It has not, however,
provided as yet any comprehensive and integrated alternative
scheme of analysis. This hiatus presents serious difficulties for
management education, which will be discussed in Chapter 8.
For the moment, it is appropriate to close our brief review of
trends in industrial social science with some consideration of the
analytic frames of reference within which those trends have been
contained.

Some social psychologists still prefer to treat processes of
group behaviour in relative isolation from associated organizational roles and from the overall organizational social system
of which they form part. This approach, which is manifest in
much group dynamics training, enjoys a considerable following
in the field of management education although there is some
evidence that the desired effects of this training can be jeopardized by constraints and pressures imposed by the organizational system to which trainees subsequently return. Despite
these problems and self-imposed analytical limitations, such
training undoubtedly attracts support because it appears to
relate to phenomena such as modes of inter-personal interaction
over which managers, on the face of it, would expect to be able
to exercise most control.[54]

Other social psychologists have attempted to broaden the
scope of their analysis. Thus some are giving attention to the
operation of variables such as power and conflict in respect of
role analysis.[55] 'Organizational psychologists' are endeavouring
to take account of organizational structure, technology, and
even features in the wider social environment.[56] The 'neo-human
relations' approach represents an extended frame of reference
specifically accounting for possible relationships between
organizational structure and behaviour. However, neo-human

relations also possesses analytical limitations, as we have seen. It focuses on features of organizational structure which are ostensibly open to managerial adjustment with the intention of designing these so as to encourage maximum employee involvement in, and contribution towards, effective organizational functioning. There are two critical but dubious assumptions in this analysis. First, that managers have freedom of action to design organizational structure according to an *a priori* ideal plan. Second, that there is a necessary and direct relationship between this structure and employee behaviour – in other words, a structural determinism.

More than a suggestion of determinism has accompanied the work of some 'technology theorists', as Pugh has labelled them.[57] There has been a tendency for some writers to assume a necessary and direct relationship between technological features and organizational structure or employee behaviour, with the last two as the dependent variables. As a reaction primarily to both the determinism implicit in neo-human relations and in certain writing on technology, some sociologists have revitalized the 'action frame of reference' to account for the independent behavioural consequences of orientations held by organizational members.[58] These orientations to work and to the organization are seen as deriving primarily from characteristics of members' extra-organizational social roles. Such characteristics include their domestic circumstances, previous occupational experience, labour market position and so on. Those advocating the action frame of reference regard employees' own definitions of their work situation as an important mediating variable between structure, technology and environment in the explanation of employees' subsequent identities and behaviour. This frame of reference also serves to indicate the plurality of identities which is likely to be found among different membership groups within an organization. It encourages a view of enterprises as 'plural societies', the internal differentiation of which is related to environmental as well as intra-organizational factors.

The time is probably ripe today for an attempt at assessing, by means of empirical research, the relative degrees of influence over behaviour held by the various factors which social scientists have identified. The model to be used for such research would almost certainly involve a complex system of interdependent relationships including feedback processes. As a systems model it would be allied to a viewpoint which is enjoying increasing favour at present. The systems frame of reference is particularly conducive to inter-disciplinary thinking, since it stresses the contribution to operational processes of variables upon which individual academic disciplines concentrate their attention. Inter-disciplinary analysis is particularly appropriate for management, and indeed management thought represents an early attempt to draw practical conclusions from the statements of various academic disciplines.

Several important lines of research share a broad systems viewpoint. These include the analysis of decision-making processes as a key organizational activity, and the processes of adjustment between technology, organizational structure and work social relations. This latter area of study is particularly associated with members of the Tavistock Institute and derives from their earlier concept of the socio-technical system, which takes account of the interdependence of prevailing task technology and the system of social relations in the organizational segment concerned.[59]

There is still considerable progress to be made in utilizing the systems approach. The open system model which has been used to explain relations between organizations and their economic environments needs to be broadened to allow for relations with the technical, social and political areas of environment. There has been a tendency to rely heavily upon an analogy of the business enterprise as a social 'organism' in the use of open system analysis by the Tavistock Institute. This is neither necessary nor particularly satisfactory. It presents the danger of reifying what is only an analytical construct – the 'system'.[60] Similarly, there has been an equally unnecessary and misleading tendency for the systems frame of reference to be used to cloak a kind of latter-day structural determinism. That is, the functional requirements of the business enterprise as a system are presumed to be inviolate, and are assumed to be behavioural determinants to the exclusion of other influencing factors.

II. THE REPORTING OF SOCIAL SCIENCE RESEARCH
TO MANAGEMENT: SOME EXAMPLES

Many of the research findings reviewed above were passed on to the British management movement. In the case of the management principles, we noted that by the 1950s exponents such as Brech were already modifying their universalistic claims, admitting that the principles required some adaptation to suit the situational needs of particular firms. However, the results of research on organizational structure by Woodward and Burns, both readily available to management thinkers by 1958, showed that it was not sufficient merely to adapt existing principles.[61] For they clearly indicated how the principles, by commencing their analysis from an *a priori* position as opposed to a consideration of the needs and resources of particular enterprises in particular environments, had made a fundamental error which could have serious effects upon operational effectiveness. Professor Norman Hunt expressed this point to his management readers in May 1960:

'There is little doubt that we have often been guilty of over-simplification and, in teaching what we are pleased to call "principles of management", we have perhaps hindered rather than helped our students to grapple with the complex and difficult problems of modern business.'[62]

In the same article, Hunt urged a re-evaluation of courses in human relations in the light of evidence that those attending them did not always improve their performance or relations with others once they were back in the factory. In fact, during the 1950s the management journals had also begun to carry articles by social scientists recording research that indicated the analytical weaknesses in human relations.

For example, as early as September 1952, Scott discussed findings demonstrating both the absence of any necessary relation between employee satisfaction and efficiency, and how the human relations emphasis on foreman leadership ignored the fact that, in Britain at least, many foremen identified with workers and other foremen rather than with higher management.[63] Goubitz in 1954 reported among other American studies those by Fleishman, which had indicated how the 'leadership climate' set by higher management could nullify the practical effects of training in human relations.[64] In 1956 Handyside writing for *Personnel Management* reviewed British and American studies on human relations training for supervisors, and concluded similarly that the attitudes and practices of higher managers were crucial to the influence this training had back in the factory. Moreover, he urged caution in accepting the sweeping conclusion, deriving largely from the University of Michigan studies, that different supervisory styles were a direct influence on the productivity of workers.[65]

The director of these studies, Rensis Likert, reviewed their results in the following issue of the same journal. He admitted that cases had been found where greater productivity (but lower morale) had derived from supervisory pressure than from the more participative supervisory style recommended by human relations. However, the 'hierarchical' supervision had in these experiments been accompanied by work study. Moreover, Likert argued that the low morale which had resulted from this supervisory style would in the long run impair productivity. Thus, while prepared to admit that the most effective way of supervising depended upon the specific situation, he concluded that the human relations style, backed up by scientific management techniques, would probably yield the highest long-term production.[66] Finally, in 1958 Bamforth was led to conclude that the training courses in human relations run by the Roffey Park Institute had shown little apparent effect in changing relationships back in the work situation.[67]

Social scientists who were prepared to adopt a more sociological perspective indicated in these ways to the British management movement that 'social skills' could command at most only an uncertain influence over the behaviour of employees. In addition, they were able to show that the determinants of this behaviour were far more complex and imperfectly assessed than had been assumed by the apparently straightforward reasoning and directives of human relations. For example, while A. T. M. Wilson argued in 1955 that managers might be able to create satisfying and probably more productive work relationships if they reorganized the structure of work-tasks in the plant, he also made it clear that human relations was at fault in discussing the formation of work groups while neglecting the way in which relations were structured by the job and its technology.[68] Revans, writing for *Personnel Management* in 1958, reported studies of his which had shown how plant size was a further factor influencing employee morale.[69] Both Wilson's and Revans' reports implied that management had in the last resort to weigh up economies of scale and technology against possible losses due to poor employee morale. The human relations aspect of productivity was but one of a range of con-

siderations entering into the final assessment of managerial policies in financial terms. In any case, it was extremely difficult to
translate human relations considerations into quantitative terms,
for as Revans pointed out in the same article, the influences
on behaviour at work were still largely unexplored. Marriott,
also writing in *Personnel Management*, was another social
scientist who took care to stress the lack of knowledge on motivation in work situations. Chiefly for this reason, he explained,
there was no conclusive evidence as to the net effects of financial
incentive schemes on productivity.[70]

Through these channels British management writers were
given some idea of the practical failings which might attend
the precepts upon which many of them had relied. Until the
publication of Rosemary Stewart's *The Reality of Management*
in 1963, relatively little social science research had been
incorporated into British textbooks designed to be readily
intelligible to a managerial readership. And even Stewart's
book does not pretend to report by any means all the relevant
research findings on management and organizational behaviour.[71] Previous to this book, conferences had, in addition to the
journals, occasionally passed on information about the new
body of research and the concepts associated with it. One
example was that arranged by the British Institute of Management and recorded in *New Concepts in Management* (1963), at
which papers were delivered by W. H. Whyte, A. T. M. Wilson,
D. McGregor and others.[72]

In the next section we turn to examine some recent British
management thought, particularly to note the effect which
developments in social science may have had on its formulations.

III. RECENT BRITISH MANAGEMENT THOUGHT

(1) *Personnel management and human relations*
A few managerial authorities had, even in the late 1940s,
recognized how the human relations analysis of worker behaviour ignored the relevance of conflicting interests and the
exercise of authority. Wilfred Brown and J. J. Gillespie were
two outstanding examples. Both were at the time in close
contact with members of the Tavistock Institute, whose own
research took an early lead in illustrating how human relations

had not accounted for the influence of work technology on social relationships.[73] As the 1950s proceeded, an increasing number of management writers felt obliged to modify human relations perspectives. As we list some examples, it will become noticeable that spokesmen associated with the personnel management movement took a lead in this process of re-thinking.

As early as 1953, the editor of *Personnel Management* warned his readers that they should design their personnel policies to suit the conditions of their own particular organizations rather than basing these too slavishly on research findings which were themselves specific to given situations. We assume that he had Hawthorne at least partly in mind.[74] In the same year Hutton reviewed the reports of the Anglo-American productivity teams. He took care to go beyond human relations and to emphasize the relevance of trade union policies to the search for higher productivity. He found it meaningful to analyse the conservative attitude shown in this respect by British labour in terms of a class mentality foreign to the United States.[75] In 1955, an academic psychologist writing in *Personnel Management* recorded how some of his professional colleagues had felt it necessary to warn managers that if they did not attend more to their own managerial tasks and 'stop worrying overmuch about "the psychology" of it all', they would soon go bankrupt.[76]

In 1956 the Institute of Personnel Management sponsored an important study group which concluded that the role of industry in society had to be primarily an economic one. Moreover, the group which was composed of social scientists, consultants, and senior general managers, as well as personnel officers, pointed out the dangers of manipulation which accompanied the human relations notion of a managerial social mission. 'The Group unanimously deplored any attempt to absorb the whole man in the hours of work.'[77] Its discussion was remarkably frank in recognizing the uncertainties posed for the 'human' side of management by recent research; and also in admitting that the personnel officer could not justly be called a 'professional'. Although the new views expressed by the group were presumably attributable mainly to its social scientist members, the important point to notice is that these were also gaining acceptance among members of the management movement proper. Shortly after the report was published in 1957, the editor of *Personnel Management* adopted its realistic outlook. He went on to stress that personnel managers had to remain cost-conscious (this had also been a main point of the group's report), and concluded with the warning that 'dealing with people is no excuse for woolly administration'.[78] Other regular contributors to the journal were by this time coming to admit for instance that, contrary to the implication of human relations, the weekly wage packet was still for a great many workers their main interest in industrial life.[79]

Furthermore, during the 1950s a number of writers expressed an increasingly accommodating attitude towards the trade union movement and its aspirations for its members. It is not clear how far this marked another trend away from human relations analysis, nor whether it applied to shop steward as well as 'official' union activity. For even during the 1940s many management spokesmen had insisted that schemes such as joint consultation should not be used as an attempt to undermine the authority of trade union representatives over their constituents. And we noted earlier (on page 126) how some members of the personnel management movement were concerned even in 1960 that schemes for local wage bargaining would place too much power into the hands of shop stewards. Nevertheless, the extent to which other writers were by the later 1950s prepared to argue the merits of regular negotiation and contact with trade unions, and even to see an extension in the scope of that negotiation, suggests some movement of opinion within British management thought.[80]

The personnel management movement has continued to feel quite acutely the uncertainty consequent upon the rejection of its former human relations orthodoxy and the current lack of an equally definitive replacement. It faces a number of fundamental questions. If, for instance, one of the lessons of sociological research has been that the structure of organizational relations is influenced by the decisions of engineers on the design of task systems, or by the type of organization structure which higher managers design, then should personnel management remain a specialized, often low status, function or should it be integrated into senior line management which decides on some of the crucial features influencing employee behaviour?[81] Moreover, social scientists have cast doubt on the effectiveness of personnel techniques such as communications or joint consultation which, in their restricted scope, might fail to take account of the full meaning behind employee behaviour. Thus Hunter writing for *Personnel Management* in 1961 argued that personnel managers had to realize that the workers' 'ethic' could diverge from that of management, especially on economic matters:

'In consequence, two sets of ethical judgements, each valid by its own premises, are in constant conflict. There is certainly a lesson for the personnel man here – to enter into and understand the genuine ethical drive behind the workers' attitude, never so to identify with the management premises that the opposition is seen as merely perverse.'[82]

Hunter remained closely associated with the personnel management field. In the same year he published a widely ranging work – *Studies in Management* – which serves as an excellent illustration of the difficulties posed by the largely iconoclastic nature of social science findings for those management thinkers alert enough to recognize their importance. In this book Hunter appears far more at ease with his critical analysis of previous management thought than he is when he tries to formulate some practical alternatives for managerial action.

He was induced in the first place to undertake his study by a dissatisfaction with the remoteness from the actual practice of management shown by most management textbooks. Particularly their 'failure, in discussing policies and principles, to stick closely enough to the real tensions and pressures within which actual managing has to take place'.[83] Although Hunter does not refer in detail to sociological work, he appears to be familiar with many of its implications. For he provides an analysis of the managerial problems posed by industrial behaviour which in its breadth and sensitivity probably stands alone in recent British management thought. For instance, he is aware that factors such as social class, region, level of skill, and market conditions, can have a bearing on employee behaviour. He appreciates the problematic nature of the supervisory role, the fallacy in any blind managerial attempt to foster worker 'contentment', and the part played by trade unions as an effective means for workers to pursue their best interests. He recognizes that managerial authority involves bargaining with other groups and that compliance with managerial command is by no means automatic. He also argues that a direct comparison of industrial enterprises with other organizations may be misleading, that it is unfruitful to be concerned with communications while at the same time ignoring how their content is interpreted by employees in the light of their own images, expectations, and perceived interests, and that there is no conclusive evidence to show whether management training courses have any lasting practical effect on their participants.

Yet having recognized these complications and uncertainties surrounding the human side of management, Hunter's subsequent attempts at generalization are at best imprecise and at worst go against the whole tenor of his previous analysis. For instance, he appears to claim that industrial conflict is largely a hangover from the past. He prefers to reject any institutional approach towards the accommodation of this conflict, and suggests instead that diverging interests within firms can be 'buried and forgotten under a sense of growing unity, fair treatment and common effort'. He adds a number of sweeping assertions to these cases of vague generalization. An example is his almost polemical attack on financial incentives which compares most unfavourably with Marriott's balanced and carefully documented study revised in the same year – 1961.[84] In addition, one can find Hunter from time to time falling prey to the tension which in recent years has existed between the empirical non-prescriptive approach of social science and the normative outlook which remains natural to management spokesmen. For instance, he admits the contractual nature of labour relations. Yet at the same time he expects something more; that there is something wrong with industry if it thinks in terms of contract. The good firm, for Hunter, should require far more from employees – 'loyalty, co-operation, a sense of mutual purposes'.

Hunter had commenced his work sensing the inadequacy of existing management precepts. Others concerned with personnel management also felt much the same. Professor Drever's address at the 1961 I.P.M. National Conference was the signal for a considerable amount of heart-searching discussion among members of the movement. He had spoken of the dangers likely to result when joint consultation remained but a mere pretence of participation and democracy, a shadow rather than the substance. He felt that such deception left employees uncertain of where they stood; whatever their immediate apparent contentment at such an arrangement, in the long-run it led to apathy or unrest.[85] Similarly, a prominent member of the personnel management movement, who also holds an academic post, expressed a keen awareness of the problem that what was 'good' in industrial relations depended on where one was placed in industry: 'What are good industrial relations? We speak of "the two sides" and the need to identify their common rather than their conflicting interests, but we recognize that employees are the means and not the ends of industry.'[86]

Other spokesmen have come to recognize that personnel managers have to face two conflicting pressures – cost-consciousness and employees' claims to both security of tenure and improved standards of remuneration.[87] The Institute of Personnel Management in 1963 issued a 'Golden Jubilee Statement' which clearly recognized the difficult implications arising from social science findings. In fact the editor of its journal at the time was herself a prominent industrial sociologist – Miss Joan Woodward. In the preamble to the Statement one finds an acknowledgement that:

'. . . in personnel management different methods may be right in different circumstances. What is appropriate will differ according to current social values and custom, the size and traditions of an undertaking, its product or service, and its state of technical development.'[88]

Yet once again, when it came to formulating some generalized practical aims and recommendations for personnel managers – some guides for action – the honest recognition of social science findings inhibited the laying down of any precise or universalized precepts. The I.P.M. Statement in fact took refuge in superficially attractive, yet question-begging labels such as 'fair and reasonable' payment differentials, the seeking of 'both efficiency and justice', the provision of 'fair terms . . . and satisfying work for those employed', and the need for 'sound' organization and 'sound' relationships.[89]

There is a necessary postscript to this discussion on human relations and the personnel management movement. For if many writers were at least attempting to face up to the complexities of industrial relationships which social science had indicated, there also remained others who continued to show ignorance of such research and who instead still took refuge in what was fast becoming a discredited mode of analysis. For instance, in 1960 Munro Fraser argued for:

'. . . a "human relations" approach . . . looking at industry not so much in terms of the economic, technical or engineering processes which it involves, but rather in terms of the attitudes and aspirations of the individuals who make their living in it.'[90]

That there might be some connection between the wider 'processes' and employee 'attitudes' was overlooked. In his analysis of these attitudes Munro Fraser asserted that they were moulded as much by emotion as by objective evaluations, that the cause of much industrial conflict lay in 'misunderstanding', and that a striving for 'status and appreciation' frequently possessed greater significance for employees than did monetary rewards. As generalizations these statements would require qualification in the light of findings suggesting the contrary – Munro Fraser fails to do this. He makes a further explicit and plainly misleading assumption that worker effort is 'directly proportional' to task satisfaction. These assertions on worker behaviour and attitudes are universalized into a 'typical citizen' who constantly re-appears through Munro Fraser's discussion. This approach might be understandable in so far as the author is primarily an industrial psychologist, but in his book he goes further and claims to draw upon the 'theories' of sociology and anthropology as well. Finally, it is instructive to notice that the values which he openly acknowledges – the preservation of 'our established institutions' and the maintenance of 'social cohesion' – are clearly derived from Elton Mayo. There is no question that they colour his subsequent analysis.

There are other examples of a largely unqualified Mayoist human relations approach to be found during the 1960s. Two books which still adhere to this line of thought are Tredgold's revised *Human Relations in Modern Industry* (1963) and the second edition of Brech's textbook, *The Principles and Practice of Management*, also issued in 1963.[91] This latter reproduces apparently unchanged a section on 'Personnel' by R. M. Aldrich which sees fit to discuss little social science research other than the original interpretations of Hawthorne. It is not surprising to find that it presents readers with a number of human relations assumptions which have been discredited by the results of more recent research.[92]

There has been in recent years, if anything, a revival of

interest in another concern of human relations – 'communications'. This comprises one of the main themes in Moonman's
textbook on *The Manager and the Organization*, while among
others the then Minister of Labour, Mr Godber, energetically
expounded this set of techniques during the early part of 1964.[93]
It is not always clear just how much its supporters expect from
communications. Is its purpose merely to forestall misunderstandings through keeping employees informed of new developments and through ascertaining their views on such matters,
or is it expected to go further and actually to persuade employees
to accept managerial decisions which are handed down to
them? In any event phrases commonly associated with communications, such as 'goodwill', 'understanding', and 'loyalty',
carry with them an ambiguity which suggests that their per-
petrators have made but a superficial analysis of the factors
influencing organizational relationships. Certainly, this has
been felt by some who would seek to warn managers against
attaching too many expectations to communications as a
technique. For instance, Bowker and Hall, writing in *The
Manager* late in 1963, elaborated a point in this connection,
which we saw Hunter had made earlier. Namely, communications faced a range of barriers arising from the role of power
and conflict within enterprises. These barriers were reinforced
by the different values, language, and expectations held by those
with different social backgrounds between whom communication would be passed.

The conclusion these two management teachers reached
deserves extensive quotation. For it well illustrates the radical
assault upon cherished beliefs in management thought which
was being effected in some quarters by the growing influence
of social science analysis:

'To talk about "good" and "bad" communication is to conceptual-
ize the problem wrongly, for it assumes that communication needs to
be improved in order to improve a whole set of other phenomena.
We do not have evidence to show that communication is a causal
variable. Furthermore, to think in terms of "good" and "bad"
industrial communication is to assume that its improvement lies
exclusively within the competence of executives, which again is not
necessarily true. And finally, what may be "good" communication
from one organizational standpoint, may certainly not be good from
another. It depends upon who you are and what you are trying to
do.'[94]

(2) *Management thought on the study of organization*

Brech's *The Principles and Practice of Management*, on its re-appearance in 1963, largely repeated the exposition of manage-ment principles which he had put forward in the early 1950s. Another, lesser known textbook published in the same year also affirmed its support for the principles.[95] Those who still support this approach to organizational analysis, and who rely upon it to the exclusion of others, must today adopt what is necessarily a conservative stance. Their formulations have advanced little further than Urwick's work of the 1930s. Moreover, their pro-vision of supposedly 'practical' guides for managers relies for its plausibility on the rejection of social science research as unhelpful for everyday organizational practice.

Other management thinkers are today prepared to face up to the primarily sociological critiques levelled against the management principles. Nevertheless, they have to admit their perplexity with the position this leaves them in. For example, in a work of 1962 entitled *Management Principles*, Puckey expressed this feeling:

'Organization is, in some ways, even more complex than other aspects of management. There are a few laws, principles, or one-best ways available to managers interested in better organization, although those that exist are little known. There are many varying and apparently successful organizational forms existing, yet all they seem to have in common is their difference.'[96]

In this book, and in his *Organization in Business Management* which followed it the next year, Puckey attempts to combine useful tips for managers on organization with a continuing recognition that studies such as Woodward's have shown such generalizations to be particularly perilous. As a result in both books he frequently allows advice to pass out to his readers without being able to afford them much idea of how to put it into practical effect. In some cases, the advice rests rather more on aspiration than on careful analysis; for instance – 'It is important that every individual is encouraged to identify himself with his organization', with the rather sweeping corollary that 'both suffer if this is not achieved'.[97] In other cases, there is an attempt to cover up imprecision with jargon. Again the result would appear far from helpful to the ordinary practising manager:

'Because of constantly changing anti-cohesive and cohesive changes, in individuals and in groups, and in external conditions, "cohesive

N

balance" cannot be maintained unless the group leader exercises constant vigilance and constant adjustment of many factors. Cohesion, like its big brother, organization, is a continuing process.'[98]

In quoting these examples our intention is not to single out writers such as Puckey for any particular censure so much as to indicate some of the difficulties which sociological work has presented to the older type of management thinker with his tradition of passing on fairly definitive advice to men in the field. And indeed we shall record later how a similar uncertainty and imprecision has recurred in the opinions of many management teachers, whose occupational role requires them to provide some lead to their manager-students. These examples from the study of organization, together with those we quoted above from the personnel management field, illustrate the current transitional phase in management thought and education. Older precepts are being slowly discarded in the light of a rapidly expanding body of empirical research, while the construction of a new body of reliable knowledge is still in its infancy.

No writer who attempts to set out a full, comparative, and standard work on management can afford to ignore the current change in ideas and outlook. Some who prefer, like Harold Whitehead, to treat merely of the 'art' in management, and who claim to do no more, may be within their rights to ignore comparative social science research. Having been successful men themselves, such authors wish merely to pass on to younger men some homely wisdom distilled from their personal experience.[99] But other authors, who aspire to write standard texts on management, can today plead no such excuse. We have already criticized parts of Brech's work on these grounds. As a further example we might take W. S. Barry's *The Fundamentals of Management* (1963), a work which received a number of favourable reviews.[100] On the one hand, this book does recognize some underlying problems in industrial relationships. For instance, diverging interests between parties to the enterprise, and the difficulties which might accompany the authority of managers as selected leaders in a society dedicated to principles of elected leadership. Yet, at the same time this work fails to refer to available empirical research in industry and for this reason its discussion remains a purely personal point of view. Consequently, while its Preface claims that it will emphasize 'the importance of organization in the work of management', the book follows this up with no sustained analysis of organization either as structure or as system. And the section on personnel management presents the reader with so-called 'laws of human nature'. These are wholly unspecific and couched in terms such as 'justice and fair play'. The sociologically meaningless nature of Barry's formulation on these matters may be assessed by its professed point of departure: 'We have a unique means of getting to know about men. We are men. We have the inside story.'

(3) The Glacier Project

The Glacier Project occupies a unique place in recent British management thought and requires a separate discussion. It is of particular interest to this chapter since it provides an example of the use of social science for management consultancy purposes, one which is comparable, to the Hawthorne programme. It illustrates the strengths of this approach, and the weaknesses which can derive from investigation based on purely managerial assumptions. It also indicates the problems which arise when generalizations are attempted from a single or small number of cases.

In Chapter 5 it was seen that Wilfred Brown, chairman of the Glacier Metal Company, had even in the late 1940s adopted a broader analysis of industrial relationships than was allowed for in human relations. One reason for his dissatisfaction with the human relations approach was due to the way in which it tended to blur lines of authority and responsibility through the organizational hierarchy. In fact, the greater part of the long programme of research at Glacier centred on the clarification of what is called 'executive' authority. In the first place, members of the project team, led by Elliott Jaques, attempted to identify the constraints acting on this authority. They recognized that other parties, such as shareholders, customers, and worker representatives, had the power to prevent managers from successfully introducing change. Thus a set of formal arrangements were established within the company to institutionalize this system of power into what is called a 'Legislative System'. This involves shareholders (through the managing director) and employee delegates in the formation and review of policy. By means of this arrangement, which amounts to a variant of Follett's notion of 'depersonalizing orders', the company attempted to secure a wide basis of support for the managerial execution of agreed decisions.

In the second place, there was a continuing analysis of formal positions (or 'roles' in Glacier language) within the firm with a view to finding structural arrangements which would increase the operational effectiveness of executive command. For instance, in order to free this command from extraneous obstruction, 'representation' from employees, and their 'appeal' against executive actions, were both channelled into separate formal systems of communication. A careful analysis of Glacier's managerial organization led to a further clarification of executive command by separating from it all specialist advisory roles. Methods of communication and co-ordination within the 'executive system' were standardized and set down in writing. An attempt was made to clarify and strengthen executive authority at shop-floor level by concentrating this into one managerial role. Piece-rate payment systems were abolished, largely with a view to increasing direct executive control on the shop floor.

Finally, Jaques' studies on the content of work and on 'equitable payment' represented an attempt, first, to improve a manager's ability to regulate and review the quality of his subordinates' performances and, second, to substitute managerial control over payment differentials for the less predictable and conflict-inducing operation of market and institutional forces. Once managers were able to maintain a stable system of differentials within a firm, not only might a source of employee opposition to executive authority be avoided, but it would also become possible to plan the progression of an individual's earnings as his capacity grew for undertaking work with a higher 'discretionary' content.

The strengths of the Glacier Project are apparent from the brief description we have just given. It continually refined its analytical model during a lengthy investigation of the social structure of a particular factory. It always attempted to give a careful definition of the terminology used during the course of this research. The Project's progress has been regularly recorded in published works.[101] Members of the Glacier research team have been at pains to explain their concepts and findings to others. A teaching organization, the Glacier Institute of Management, was set up in 1962 for this purpose. The Project as a whole suggested that, from a managerial point of view, applied social science research could bring considerable practical benefits.

However, the Glacier approach suffers as well from a number of serious weaknesses which have only occasionally received the attention they deserve. These deficiencies relate first to the actual industrial research itself, and second to subsequent attempts to generalize the research findings, and concepts associated with these, into a new system of management thought.

The Glacier Project has relied on a derivation of the 'clinical' method of investigation. This method has been used extensively in the work of the Tavistock Institute of Human Relations, and it was this Institute which was actively involved in the earlier stages of the Glacier investigations. This clinical method employs a personal observation and diagnosis of organizational or individual problems. An example is Jaques' so-called 'social-analytic relationship' which entails the gathering of research information by means of strictly confidential, personal meetings with respondents.[102] This method of investigation may be contrasted with the normal comparative methods used in social science, which to some extent allow interested students and critics to examine the validity of data and the strength of associations. Such examination is not possible with the Glacier investigations. One is forced to take the researchers' word for practically every event which they have reported. The opinions of those who are studied – workers or managers – are never presented in a direct manner, while comprehensive statistical reporting is also lacking from the Glacier writings. It is known that men such as Brown and Jaques are committed to pronounced views on a wide range of industrial matters. The methods of investigation which they have used do not enable them to counter any possible suspicion that research data has been presented selectively so as to support preconceived theories. In short, the methodology which has been used in the Glacier Project is suspect. This deficiency cannot fail in turn to cast doubt over some of the findings which have been recorded in the Glacier reports.

The second major set of weaknesses associated with the Glacier Project concerns attempts to generalize from its highly specific findings. We have noted in connection with other management writing how an attempt to generalize from scattered or situational research findings is understandable from the viewpoint of management education, yet how it remains at best a hazardous operation. The Glacier team, particularly following its establishment of a separate institute of management, does not appear to have recognized this problem at all adequately. In fact, there is today a considerable danger that its analysis of a single case – perhaps a unique factory situation – is being 'universalized' into a new management dogma. If this process were to develop, the highly ironic situation would be reached in which managers from other factories might be inhibited from carrying out the fresh and original diagnosis which has characterized work at Glacier, because of their uncritical absorption of subsequent Glacier theory.

The limitations of the conclusions which have been drawn from the Glacier research should be brought to the notice of managers attending Glacier Institute of Management courses. For example, Brown's sweeping condemnation of piece-work payment systems involves a generalization from extremely limited experience. Marriott's review of a large number of studies into financial incentive schemes allowed of no such dogmatic conclusion.[103] It is, however, perhaps Jaques' system for 'equitable payment' that provides the clearest instance of how an unproven theory has been translated into supposedly sound 'practical' procedure, and passed on as such to managers. Indeed, a handbook on the subject has been published.[104]

The Jaques payment system has already received considerable criticism, largely on the question of its practicability.[105] We shall therefore add only a few brief comments here. There are three areas in which it is particularly difficult to accept the Jaques thesis. The first concerns the nature of the evidence used to support the notion of 'felt-fair pay', a concept which forms the starting point for Jaques' theory as a whole. We have already discussed the major difficulty here, namely that Jaques' 'social-analytic' method of investigation does not allow for a critical scrutiny of the data used to support his claim that there exist unconsciously felt norms of equitable payment levels.

The second problem concerns Jaques' framework of analysis around the concept of 'felt-fair pay' and his views on the meaning of remuneration in modern industry. Jaques regards

unconsciously felt norms of payment as largely autonomous, so
that they can be presented as an alternative basis for an incomes
policy instead of the prevailing system of collective bargaining.
A possibility which he does not face is that any such unconscious
norms are themselves moulded by the 'consciously' prevailing
systems of income allocation. If this were in fact the case, then
it would not be possible to view the Jaques system and collective bargaining as alternatives – which Jaques implies is the
choice facing us. And if they are not true alternatives, then
Jaques' aim of regulating differentials on the basis of 'felt-fair
pay' could only be achieved upon the elimination of employees'
rights consciously to bargain for the highest rewards they can
obtain. We return to this point shortly, when we discuss Jaques'
values.

Jaques' limited analytical perspective also leads him to overlook several important aspects of the part played by remuneration in modern industry. This deficiency casts serious doubt on
the practicability of his ideas, assuming that they rest upon an
adequate scientific foundation in the first place. For example,
Jaques minimizes the importance of some labour market
features which would in fact appear to be fulfilling quite
essential economic requirements. One case is the attraction of
labour to tasks which possess low intrinsic satisfaction (and
normally a low discretionary content as well) by rewarding
deprivations on the job with high levels of pay. Jaques' 'time-
span' analysis does not cope with this kind of situation, which
may be quite common with mass-production, assembly-line
technologies. In this situation, a manufacturer is not necessarily
concerned to reward high levels of discretion among his
employees; but he is interested in rewarding sustained effort
on their part. In fact, the Jaques system does not deal at all
adequately with this problem of effort, and in this connection
one should recall that, like Brown, Jaques rejects financial
incentive schemes.

There are further practical difficulties arising from Jaques'
analysis. It ignores the fact that differentials are only one of
several focal points for conflict within industry. In other words,
any regulation of differentials to the satisfaction of all parties
might only serve to shift the focus of conflict on to other points
of difference. A final and most obvious difficulty with the Jaques
system is that, in seeking to replace current collective bargaining

procedures, it must face the power of the trade union move-ment to prevent any such change. And when we now discuss the third set of difficulties in accepting the Jaques thesis, it will become clear that its underlying values and implications would lead the trade unions to accept his system only at their own peril. Indeed, its rejection by the Glacier Metal Company's own manual employees will become fully understandable.

The third set of criticisms concerns the way in which Jaques' proposals are heavily influenced by his own, freely-admitted, values. We shall discuss this point at some length, for it is of considerable interest to a review of British management thought. Whatever the difference in their practical recom-mendations, the values expressed by Jaques the management consultant at Glacier come close to those of Elton Mayo, the consultant at Hawthorne. As with Mayo, a fundamental point in the Jaques system is the avoidance of conflict. And both have legitimized this goal in terms of social welfare. For instance, Jaques has described his search for 'equitable payment' as one for 'a solid foundation for society'. He hopes that it will help to eliminate 'social tension', and to contribute towards 'sound national morality and social health'. For, 'My experience leads to the impression that . . . strong constructive forces of social co-operation lie waiting to be released if income were equitably distributed.'[106]

With both the Jaques system and Mayoism, the reduction of industrial conflict is to be achieved by means of an increase in managerial control over employees. The managerial contribu-tion to what these writers define as 'social health' derives from techniques to avoid tensions within the industrial enterprise. In other words, it coincides conveniently with the furtherance of managers' chosen purposes within firms. And as with human relations, the Jaques proposals contain their own legitimation for the extension of managerial control. Jaques claims to have found that employees feel discomfort and guilt if their earnings are markedly above the 'felt-fair pay' level for the discretionary content in their work, and acute dissatisfaction if they are below.[107] As a result he suggests that payment differentials should be related to the discretionary content in work as measured by the maximum length of time over which a person is required to exercise discretion in his job without this being reviewed by a superior.

It should be noticed that Jaques' scheme opens the road to a managerial control just as manipulatory in nature as was Mayoism. For the so-called 'time-span of discretion' is itself a variable that management has some power to alter. Thus Jaques is in effect advocating a very substantial managerial control over employee incomes. Moreover, the Jaques system would freeze differentials in the sense that employees would be deprived of the right collectively to bargain for a relative improvement in their incomes. Whatever one's personal views on the use and abuse of bargaining power to further sectional interests in society, one should clearly recognize that, for Jaques, the elimination of economic conflict in industry is to be achieved by giving management the right to define the interests and due rewards of others. As with Mayoism, the Jaques policy rests upon a fundamental anti-pluralist bias.

Although the nature of Jaques' evidence for norms of 'felt-fair pay' is such that it cannot readily be scrutinized, he has sufficient confidence in its validity to have recently expressed his willingness for an independent survey to check his methods of measurement and his general findings.[108] Granted that his findings are valid, it is worth recalling that in terms of straight recording there was little to criticize about the Hawthorne results. It was their interpretation and subsequent policy recommendations which led to controversy. The Mayoist perspective contained values which were oriented towards the fulfilment of a social programme. Consequently it failed to account fully for the worker behaviour which was so carefully observed in the first place. In Jaques' case there is a comparable confusion between underlying values of social cohesion and the objective analysis of remuneration. Indeed, he is more concerned to put over a normative point of view than a straight-forward analysis of behaviour. He urges that the intuitive feeling of income equity which he claims to have found should replace institutional and market forces as the basis for the determination of remuneration:

'How much any given section of the population should receive in wages or salaries cannot be *equitably* settled by reference to productivity, or efficiency, or profitability, or strength of union organization, or capacity of an industry to pay'[109] (Jaques' emphasis).

Both Jaques and Mayo also share a tendency to overlook the role of behavioural determinants which derive from forces

beyond the physical limits of the enterprise, and which therefore lie beyond managerial regulation. They have both restricted their analysis of industrial attitudes and behaviour to
determinants which managers can to some extent utilize for
their own ends – Jaques has concentrated on 'intuition', while
Mayo stressed 'sentiment'. Both have been prepared to assume
away those more consciously held, rational and socially determined influences on worker action, which research has indicated
to be of considerable importance in some work situations at
least.

Jaques' thesis provides an interesting and subtle example of
the inter-play between managerial values and the analysis of
employee behaviour. While his arguments, with their underlying hostility to collective bargaining, may represent an aberra-
tion from the trend of much recent British management thought,
they do strongly express an understandable desire which in
some form has run through this thought from its very beginning
– namely, to increase the scope of managerial regulation
within industry. In fact, Jaques has described his approach in
words which might have come directly from F. W. Taylor's
Principles:

'What is required is to supplant custom and practice by principle –
or at least to give them a firm footing in principle; to bring the
sophistication of rule of law into an area of social and economic
life where rule of thumb largely prevails.'[110]

However, it would appear that for Jaques, as for Taylor,
this 'rule of law' is to remain under exclusively managerial
definition. In that case, given that the present structure of
industry contains conflicting as well as common interests, this
'law' could be interpreted so as to conflict with what employees
consider to be their best economic interests. This possibility
continues, of course, to provide the *raison d'être* for trade
unionism. It is their neglect of this point which explains the
hostility towards collective bargaining common to Taylor,
Mayo, and now Jaques. Tension between the managerial
aspiration to regulate and employee rights to contest executive
decisions is a fundamental characteristic of industrial life. The
Glacier Metal Company in fact attempted to ease this tension
by separating out an 'executive' from a 'representative' system.
But Jaques, in his more recent work on payment, has chosen to
focus on what he describes as employees' 'intuitive' feelings. In

so doing he has moved away from the recognition that employees may wish to challenge managerial regulation over pay and other matters in quite conscious and rational terms as well. For this reason, so long as industry remains structurally a system of power and diverging interests, Jaques' approach to payment differentials can strictly speaking be no more 'objective' than Taylor's time-study was 'scientific'.

In short, the Jaques system of 'equitable payment' provides a good illustration of how a managerial value-orientation can distort an analysis of the industrial behaviour which managers are in fact likely to meet in practice. Jaques' views are a reminder of the dilemma which, in some form, has been present throughout the history of British management thought. Namely, that any legitimation of managerial control in terms of values such as 'common interests' or 'social cohesion' tends to ignore the grounds for conflict between managers and other social groups. The presence of this conflict may render a purely managerial definition of common interest too subjective a foundation upon which to base practical policies for coping with all the facets of industrial behaviour.

However, Jaques' writing on payment cannot be said to lie within the main stream of recent British management thought. We noted how a considerable number of management writers are today beginning to appreciate some of the implications arising from social science research. They are coming to recognize the presence of diverging interests in industry, and the value of working with representatives of labour rather than attempting to by-pass them. Nor is Jaques' approach, with its sweeping and normative social programme, typical of most modern industrial social science. If anything, his ideas attempt to return to the climate of the later 1940s when Mayoism and human relations were at the height of their influence.

SUMMARY AND DISCUSSION

Industrial social science today commands considerable attention in discussion on the 'human' problems of management. It has presented increasing evidence to show that previous management thought requires substantial revision. It has indicated that industrial behaviour is both less uniform and subject to a considerably more complex network of determinants than management writers generally had assumed. Social science research has illustrated that analysis must relate to particular industrial situations rather than depend on the normative generalizations offered by management thought. Thus social scientists now insist that questions such as the relative importance for motivation of material and non-material rewards, the means to greater productivity, and the requisite system of managerial control, can only be answered after a review of the circumstances of particular enterprises and of the social characteristics possessed by their employees.

Current industrial social science does not question the importance of studying the work group, or of the managerial emphasis on effective organization and a 'scientific' process of administration. But it qualifies all these. It has shown the limitations of analysing work groups in isolation from the wider social system of the enterprise or from the expectations and images held by their members. It has shown that certain production technologies may even inhibit the formation of cohesive work groups in the first place. Equally, it has stressed that the structure of organization should not be designed in isolation from the requirements of particular firms. The scientific process which it recommends managers to follow is no longer to attempt to apply universalized rules or 'principles' to their local problems, but rather to make a careful review of the situation in which these problems have arisen before planning out a course of action.

Of the social sciences, sociology has had a particularly disturbing influence on British management thought. It has argued the inadequacy of focusing too narrowly on the purely consensual aspects of industrial relationships, and of treating enterprises as closed systems. Sociologists have questioned the long-term effectiveness of any system of industrial control which attempts to deny the presence of different interests within firms, or to prevent a constructive process of conflict-regulation and negotiation through constitutional procedures between employee representatives and management. For research studies have indicated that employees, whether organized into unions or not, frequently have the ability to counter managerial control if they wish, and that they can use this power quite rationally to further interests at variance with those of management. Indeed, it is today becoming clear that the process of management is liable to far greater frustration by various groups in the enterprise than was acknowledged by earlier writing. This realization may itself have been encouraged by the continuing strength of labour in a full employment situation and the persistent scarcity of trained technical personnel. In any event, sociologists have illustrated how an acceptance of final managerial authority in principle is no guarantee that this authority will not be distorted or even resisted during the process of being translated into action. And the comforting notion that standard techniques were available whereby managers could regulate behaviour in the enterprise, and which could be passed on to new managerial recruits as established knowledge, is today being fast rejected.

This challenge to the precepts of management thought has tended to reverse those trends towards generalization about techniques and principles which were evident from at least the 1920s onward. In fact, social science findings have led some management writers back to some of the broader analytical perspectives of the 1920s. For instance, back to recognizing that workers' interests are not identical with management's, that for this reason trade unions possess a legitimate role in industry, and that the industrial enterprise contains contractual as well as solidary elements. British management thought developed slowly over the best part of a half-century. It grew confident in the utility of its constantly repeated themes, and their demise within the space of a decade at the hand of social scientists represents a revolution.

Social science has come as an external influence on management thought, and has greatly increased the quantity of research evidence available to management writers. In this process, several value-elements in management thought have been brought to light. To the extent that these values were performing a legitimatory function in presenting management as the embodiment of wisdom and paternal benevolence, the work of social scientists has in a sense been performing an 'anti-ideological' role. However, this view requires some qualification. For the purpose and the effect of most social science writing has not been to challenge the legitimacy of managerial authority so much as to point out the limits to that authority, and even to improve its effectiveness by analysing the barriers to managerial control. Social scientists have, in the main, accepted managerial authority rights as given – indeed, we noted how one or two such as Paterson have even advocated that those rights should be extended, and have added appropriate justifications for their suggestions. Some left-wing sociologists have in fact accused their colleagues of carrying a consistent pro-managerial bias in their researches.[111]

Industrial social science has followed a primarily technical orientation. When it has exposed value distortions, this has normally been part of the process of scientific investigation. Social science research has in various countries received financial support from governmental agencies on the grounds of its technical utility. It is meaningful to view this research in relation to the wider post-war social climate with its emphasis on economic growth, competitive industrial performance, and management training. We argued earlier that in response to this environment, which is conducive to a widespread acceptance of managerial authority rights, management thought had itself shifted towards a concentration on technical purposes once the political uncertainties of the 1940s had passed. These considerations help to explain why many management thinkers are today attempting to absorb social science findings and to face up to the difficulties they present. For these thinkers, social science is recognized as a technical aid – the means to a better understanding of industrial behaviour which managers should try to utilize. On the other hand, we noted the continued presence in recent years of older perspectives and of analyses distorted by managerial values, among some writers whose work remains either coloured by a legitimatory purpose (as with Jaques) or marred by ignorance.

The pattern of management thought is far from clear at the present time. Its content shows considerable variety and uncertainty. In the areas of study which we have been reviewing, its boundaries *vis-à-vis* academic social science have become blurred. Overall, British management thought today is disorganized and in decline.

NOTES

1. T. Lupton, 'Industrial Conflict', *New Society*, 14th Nov. 1963, pp. 11-13; cf., L. Coser, *The Functions of Social Conflict*, London: Routledge & Kegan Paul 1956.

2. J. R. Tréanton and J.-D. Reynaud, 'Industrial Sociology 1951-1962', *Current Sociology*, XII, 2, 1963-64, p. 123 ff. For a general review of current progress in industrial sociology see S. R. Parker, R. K. Brown, J. Child and M. A. Smith, *The Sociology of Industry*, London: Allen & Unwin 1968; on industrial and organizational psychology see B. M. Bass, *Organizational Psychology*, Boston: Allyn & Bacon 1965.

3. Cf., the American critics listed in H. A. Landsberger, *Hawthorne Revisited*, Ithaca, N.Y.: Cornell University Press 1958, chapter III; G. Friedmann, *Problèmes Humaines du Machinisme Industriel*, Paris: Gallimard 1947, pp. 300-309; M. Argyle, 'The Relay Assembly Test Room in Retrospect'. *Occupational Psychology*, 27, 2, April 1953, pp. 98-103; A. H. Richmond, 'Conflict and Authority in Industry'. *Occupational Psychology*, 28, 1, Jan. 1954, pp. 24-33; J. Woodward, 'The Social Sciences and Industry' (a paper of July 1954) in ed. D. C. Thomson, *Management, Labour and Community*, London: Pitman 1957, pp. 77-87.

4. H. A. Landsberger, *op. cit.*, chapter III.

5. Cf., T. Hariton, *Conditions Influencing the Effects of Training Foremen in Human Relations Principles*, unpublished Ph.D. thesis, University of Michigan 1951; E. A. Fleishman, E. F. Harris, and H. E. Burtt, *Leadership and Supervision in Industry*, Monograph no. 33, Columbus: Ohio State University Bureau of Educational Research 1955; J. D. Handyside, *An Experiment with Supervisory Training*, London: N.I.I.P. Report no. 12, 1956; F. C. Mann, 'Studying and Creating Change: a Means to Understanding Social Organization' in ed. C. M. Arensberg *et al.*, *Research in Industrial Human Relations*, New York: Harper 1957, pp. 146-167.

6. P. Blau and W. R. Scott, *Formal Organizations*, London: Routledge & Kegan Paul 1963, esp. pp. 153-157; N. C. Morse and E. Reimer, 'The Experimental Change of a Major Organizational Variable', *Journal of Abnormal and Social Psychology*, 52, Jan. 1956, pp. 120-129; E. S. Stanton, 'Company Policies and Supervisors' Attitudes Toward Supervision', *Journal of Applied Psychology*, 44, 1, Feb. 1960, pp. 22-60; H. L. Wilensky, 'Human Relations in the Workplace: an Appraisal of Some Recent Research' in ed. C. M. Arensberg, *op. cit.*, p. 32.

7. A. H. Brayfield and W. H. Crockett, 'Employee Attitudes and Employee Performance', *Psychological Bulletin*, 52, 5, 1955, pp. 415-422; W. F. Goode and I. Fowler, 'Incentive Factors in a Low Morale Plant', *American Sociological Review*, XIV, 5, Oct. 1949, pp. 618-624.

8. S. E. Seashore, *Group Cohesiveness in the Industrial Work Group*, Ann Arbor: University of Michigan Press 1954.

9. D. J. Hickson, 'Motives of Workpeople who Restrict their Output', *Occupational Psychology*, 35, 3, July 1961, pp. 111-121; T. Lupton, *On the Shop Floor*, London: Pergamon Press 1963, chapters 8-11, and p. 189; D. Roy, 'Quota Restriction and Goldbricking in a Machine Shop', *American Journal of Sociology*, LVII, 5, March 1952, pp. 427-442.

10. E. Gross, 'Some Functional Consequences of Primary Controls in Formal Work Organizations', *American Sociological Review*, 18, Aug 1953, pp. 368-373; D. Roy, 'Efficiency and "the Fix": Informal Intergroup Relations in a Piecework Machine Shop', *American Journal of Sociology*, LX, 3, Nov. 1954, pp. 255-266.

11. D. J. Hickson, *op. cit.*

12. J. Mills, *The Engineer in Society*, New York: Van Nostrand 1946, p. 93; L. Baritz, *The Servants of Power*, Middletown, Conn.: Wesleyan University Press 1960, p. 100. See also note 16 below.

13. C. Argyris, 'The Organization: What Makes it Healthy?', *Harvard Business Review*, 36, 6, Nov.-Dec. 1958, pp. 107-116; S. Cotgrove & S. Parker, 'Work and Non-Work', *New Society*, I, 41, 11th July 1963, pp. 18-19; R. Dubin, 'Industrial Workers' Worlds: a Study of the Central Life Interests of Industrial Workers', *Social Problems*, 3, Jan. 1956, pp. 131-142; J. H. Goldthorpe, 'Attitudes and Behaviour of Car Assembly Workers: a Deviant Case and a Theoretical Critique', *British Journal of Sociology*, XVII, 3, Sept. 1966, pp. 227-244.

14. L. R. Dean, 'Union Activity and Dual Loyalty', *Industrial and Labor Relations Review*, VII, 1954, pp. 526-536; T. V. Purcell, *The Worker Speaks his Mind on Company and Union*, Cambridge, Mass.: Harvard University Press 1954; T. V. Purcell, *Blue Collar Man: patterns of dual allegiance in industry*, Cambridge, Mass.: Harvard University Press 1960.

15. A. Carey, 'The Hawthorne Studies: A Radical Criticism', *American Sociological Review*, 32, 3, 1967, pp. 403-416; Cf., M. Argyle, *op. cit.*

16. A. J. M. Sykes, 'Economic Interest and the Hawthorne Researches', *Human Relations*, 18, 3, Aug. 1965, pp. 253-263.

17. D. C. Pelz, 'Influence: a Key to Effective Leadership in the First-Line Supervisor', *Personnel*, 29, Nov. 1952, pp. 209-217.

18. J. C. Worthy, 'Organizational Structure and Employee Morale', *American Sociological Review*, XV, April 1950, pp. 169-179.

19. C. B. Frisby, 'Psychology Applied to Organization', *The Human Factor*, VII, 6, June 1933, pp. 224-231; D. McGregor, *The Human Side of Enterprise*, New York: McGraw-Hill 1960.

20. J. C. Worthy, *op. cit.*, pp. 172-173. See the review of studies on plant size and morale in: G. K. Ingham, 'Organizational Size, Orientation to Work and Industrial Behaviour', *Sociology*, 1, 3, Sept. 1967, pp. 239-258. On work group size see: R. Marriott, 'Size of Working Group and Output', *Occupational Psychology*, 23, Jan. 1949, pp. 47-57.

21. J. Woodward, *Industrial Organization: Theory and Practice*, London: Oxford University Press 1965.

22. R. Blauner, *Alienation and Freedom: the factory worker and his industry*, University of Chicago Press 1964; J. H. Goldthorpe, 'Technical Organization as a Factor in Supervisor-Worker Conflict', *British Journal of Sociology*, X, 3, Sept. 1959, pp. 213-230; L. R. Sayles, *Behavior of Industrial Work Groups*, New York: Wiley 1958;

E. L. Trist *et al.*, *Organizational Choice*, London: Tavistock 1963; C. R. Walker and R. H. Guest, *The Man on the Assembly Line*, Cambridge, Mass.: Harvard University Press 1952; J. Woodward, *Management and Technology*, London: H.M.S.O. 1958, pp. 18, 29-30.

23. Cf., M. Argyle *et al.*, 'Supervisory Methods Related to Productivity, Absenteeism and Labour Turnover', *Human Relations*, XI, 1, 1958, esp. pp. 24-25.

24. W. Baldamus, 'Type of Work and Motivation', *British Journal of Sociology*, II, 1, March 1951, pp. 44-58; R. Bassoul, P. Bernard, and A. Touraine, 'Retrait, Conflit, Participation: Trois Types d'Attitudes Ouvrières au Travail', *Sociologie du Travail*, II, 4, Oct.-Dec. 1960, pp. 314-329; G. Friedmann, *The Anatomy of Work*, London: Heinemann 1961; E. Mumford, 'Research in Progress – the Assembly Line', *The Technologist*, II, 1, Winter 1964-65, pp. 26-36.

25. J. P. Davison *et al.*, *Productivity and Economic Incentives*, London: Allen & Unwin 1958; T. Lupton, *Money for Effort*, London: H.M.S.O. 1961; R. Marriott, *Incentive Payment Systems*, London: Staples, 2nd ed. 1961; S. Melman, *Decision-Making and Productivity*, Oxford: Blackwell 1958.

26. J. P. Davison *et al.*, *op. cit.*

27. O. Collins, M. Dalton, and D. Roy, 'Restriction of Output and Social Cleavage in Industry', *Applied Anthropology*, V, 3, Summer 1946, esp. p. 14; D. Kipnis, 'Mobility Expectations and Attitudes Toward Industrial Structures', *Human Relations*, 17, 1, Feb. 1964, pp. 57-71; R. C. Stone, 'Mobility Factors as They Affect Workers' Attitudes and Conduct Toward Incentive Systems', *American Sociological Review*, 17, 1, Feb. 1952, pp. 58-64; Cf., R. H. Guest, 'Work Careers and Aspirations of Automobile Workers', *American Sociological Review*, 19, 2, April 1954, esp. p. 163.

28. A. Bird, 'A Sociological Analysis of Management-Worker Conflict in Industry', unpublished M.A.(Econ.) thesis, University of Manchester, April 1960; W. F. Goode and I. Fowler, *op. cit.*; T. Lupton, *On The Shop Floor, op. cit.*, pp. 194-201.

29. R. Sainsaulieu, 'Pouvoirs et Stratégies de Groupes Ouvriers dans l'Atelier', *Sociologie du Travail*, VII, 2, April-June 1965, esp. pp. 171-174.

30. M. Dalton, 'The Industrial "Rate-Buster": a Characterization', *Applied Anthropology*, VII, 1, Winter 1948, pp. 5-18; N. Dennis, F. M. Henriques and C. Slaughter, *Coal is Our Life*, London: Eyre and Spottiswoode 1957; J. H. Goldthorpe and D. Lockwood, 'Affluence and the British Class Structure', *Sociological Review*, 11, 2, July 1963, esp. pp. 146-148; R. A. Katzell, R. S. Barrett and T. C. Parker, 'Job Satisfaction, Job Performance, and Situational Characteristics', *Journal of Applied Psychology*, 45, 1961, pp. 66-72; C. Kerr and A. Siegel, 'The Interindustry Propensity to Strike – an International Comparison', in eds. A. Kornhauser, R. Dubin, and A. M. Ross, *Industrial Conflict*, New York: McGraw-Hill 1954,

pp. 189-212; G. L. Palmer, 'Attitudes Toward Work in an Industrial Community', *American Journal of Sociology*, LXIII, 1, July 1957,
pp. 17-26; S. Shimmin, 'Extra-Mural Factors Influencing Behaviour
at Work', *Occupational Psychology*, 36, 3, July 1962, pp. 124-131;
A. N. Turner and P. R. Lawrence, *Industrial Jobs and the Worker*,
Boston: Harvard University Press 1965; F. Zweig, *The British
Worker*, Harmondsworth: Penguin 1952, chapter 3.

31. M. W. Herman, 'Class Concepts, Aspirations, and Vertical
Mobility', chapter V in G. L. Palmer *et al.*, *The Reluctant Job
Changer*, Philadelphia: University of Pennsylvania Press 1962, esp.
pp. 134-152.

32. G. V. Rimlinger, 'International Differences in the Strike
Propensity of Coal Miners: Experience in Four Countries', *Industrial
and Labor Relations Review*, 12, 3, April 1959, pp. 389-405; A. M.
Ross and P. T. Hartman, *Changing Patterns of Industrial Conflict*, New
York: Wiley 1960.

33. D. J. Levinson, 'Role, Personality, and Social Structure in
the Organizational Setting', *Journal of Abnormal and Social Psychology*,
58, 2, March 1959, pp. 170-180.

34. A. Etzioni, *A Comparative Analysis of Complex Organizations*,
Glencoe, Ill.: Free Press 1961.

35. C. Argyris, *Personality and Organization*, New York: Harper
1957, pp. 205-208, and cf., W. W. Daniel, 'How Close Should a
Manager Be?', *New Society*, 7th Oct. 1965, pp. 6-8; K. E. Thurley
and A. C. Hamblin, *The Supervisor and his Job*, London: H.M.S.O.
1963, pp. 35-37; J. H. Goldthorpe and D. Lockwood, *op. cit.*

36. H. A. Simon, *Administrative Behavior*, New York: Macmillan,
2nd ed. 1957, p. xxxiv.

37. J. Woodward, *Management and Technology*, *op. cit:* I. Blain,
Structure in Management, London: N.I.I.P., Report no. 17, 1964,
p. 36; R. L. Payne and D. J. Hickson, 'Measuring the Ghost in the
Organizational Machine', *European Business*, 13, May 1967, pp.
41-45.

38. T. Burns and G. M. Stalker, *The Management of Innovation*,
London: Tavistock 1961; T. Burns, 'Industry in a New Age', *New
Society*, 31st Jan. 1963, pp. 17-20.

39. E. Litwak, 'Models of Bureaucracy which Permit Conflict',
American Journal of Sociology, LXVII, 2, Sept. 1961, esp. pp. 178-179.

40. N. C. Morse and E. Reimer, 'The Experimental Change of
a Major Organizational Variable', *Journal of Abnormal and Social
Psychology*, 52, Jan. 1956, pp. 120-129.

41. R. H. Hall, 'The Concept of Bureacracy: an Empirical
Assessment', *American Journal of Sociology*, LXIX, 1, July 1963,
pp. 32-40.

42. I. Blain, *op. cit.*, p. 28; R. Stewart, *The Reality of Management*,
London: Heinemann 1963, pp. 31-35.

43. T. Burns and G. M. Stalker, *op. cit.*, pp. 233-234.

44. C. Argyris, *Personality and Organization*, New York: Harper
1957; C. Argyris, *Understanding Organizational Behavior*, London

Tavistock 1960; C. Argyris, 'The Integration of the Individual and the Organization' in ed. G. B. Strother, *Social Science Approaches to Business Behavior*, London: Tavistock 1962, pp. 57-98; C. Argyris, *Integrating the Individual and the Organization*, New York: Wiley 1964; E. W. Bakke, 'The Function of Management' in ed. E. M. Hugh-Jones, *Human Relations and Modern Management*, Amsterdam: Nth-Holland Pub. Co. 1958, pp. 221-254; M. Haire, 'The Concept of Power and the Concept of Man' in ed. G. B. Strother, *op. cit.*, pp. 163-183; R. Likert, *New Patterns of Management*, New York: McGraw-Hill 1961; D. McGregor, *The Human Side of Enterprise*, New York: McGraw-Hill 1960; A. Zaleznik, C. R. Christensen, and F. J. Roethlisberger (with the assistance of G. C. Homans), *The Motivation, Productivity and Satisfaction of Workers: a Prediction Study*, Boston: Harvard Graduate School of Business Administration 1958, chapter XI; cf., C. B. Frisby, 'Psychology Applied to Organization', *The Human Factor*, VII, 6, June 1933, pp. 224-231; J. C. Worthy, 'Organizational Structure and Employee Morale', *op. cit.* 1950.

45. C. Argyris, *op. cit.* 1964, pp. 15-19, 58, 78-86.

46. *Ibid.*, pp. 61-62.

47. T. Burns and G. M. Stalker, *op. cit.*, chapters 7 and 9, esp. p. 175; and more particularly: H. Croome, *Human Problems of Innovation*, London: H.M.S.O. 1960, pp. 24-25.

48. D. McGregor, *op. cit.*, chapter 12.

49. G. Strauss, 'Some Notes on Power-Equalization' in ed. H. J. Leavitt, *The Social Science of Organizations*, Englewood Cliffs, N. J.: Prentice-Hall 1963, pp. 39-84; B. Davies, 'Some Thoughts on "Organizational Democracy" ', *Journal of Management Studies*, 4, 3, Oct. 1967, pp. 270-281.

50. A. Etzioni, *op. cit.*

51. E.g., T. Burns, 'The Reference of Conduct in Small Groups: Cliques and Cabals in Occupational Milieux', *Human Relations*, VIII, Nov. 1955, pp. 467-486; M. Crozier, *The Bureaucratic Phenomenon*, London: Tavistock 1964; M. Dalton, *Men Who Manage*, New York: Wiley 1959; eds. R. L. Kahn and E. Boulding, *Power and Conflict in Organizations*, London: Tavistock 1964; A. J. M. Sykes, 'The Effect of a Supervisory Training Course in Changing Supervisors' Perceptions and Expectations of the Role of Management', *Human Relations*, XV, 3, Aug. 1962, pp. 227-244.

52. R. Stewart, *Managers and their Jobs*, London: Macmillan 1967 (pp. 12-19 reviews some previous studies).

53. For a review of some major studies see: R. Dubin, 'Business Behavior *Behaviorally* viewed', in ed. G. B. Strother, *Social Science Approaches to Business Behavior*, London: Tavistock 1962, pp. 11-55.

54. P. B. Smith, 'The T-Group in Industry', *New Society*, 6th Aug. 1964, pp. 11-13; 'Behaviour of Budding Managers', *The Times*, 3rd June 1965. Cf., C. Argyris, *Interpersonal Competence and Organizational Effectiveness*, London: Tavistock 1962, esp. part IV.

55. E.g., eds. R. L. Kahn and E. Boulding, *op. cit.*, pp. 115-126.

56. B. M. Bass, *Organizational Psychology*, *op. cit.*; R. C. Cooper, 'The Psychology of Organizations', *New Society*, 22nd April 1965, pp. 14-17.

57. D. S. Pugh, 'Modern Organization Theory: a Psychological and Sociological Study', *Psychological Bulletin*, 66, 4, Oct. 1966, esp. pp. 244-246.

58. J. H. Goldthorpe, *op. cit.*, *British Journal of Sociology*, Sept. 1966; A. Willener, 'Payment Systems in the French Steel and Iron Mining Industry' in eds. G. K. Zollschan and W. Hirsch, *Explorations in Social Change*, London: Routledge & Kegan Paul 1964, esp. p. 616.

59. F. E. Emery and E. L. Trist, 'Socio-Technical Systems' in eds. C. W. Churchman and M. Verhulst, *Management Sciences*, London: Pergamon 1960, vol 2, pp. 83-97.

60. Cf., R. K. Brown, 'Research and Consultancy in Industrial Enterprises', *Sociology*, 1, 1, Jan. 1967, pp. 33-60.

61. T. Burns, 'Research and Development in the Firm', *Journal of the British Institute of Management*, I, 3, Jan. 1958, pp. 182-190; J. Woodward, *Management and Technology*, London: H.M.S.O. 1958.

62. N. C. Hunt, 'Second Thoughts on Management Education', *The Manager*, May 1960, p. 351.

63. W. H. Scott, 'The Scientific Study of Human Relations in Industry – II. General Findings of Current Research', *Personnel Management*, XXXIV, 321, Sept. 1952, pp. 143-149.

64. E. Goubitz, 'Research in Human Relations in American Industry', *The Manager*, Oct. and Nov. 1954, esp. pp. 728-731.

65. J. D. Handyside, 'The Effectiveness of Supervisory Training – a Survey of Recent Experimental Studies', *Personnel Management*, XXXVIII, 336, June 1956, pp. 97-107.

66. R. Likert, 'Developing Patterns in Management', *Personnel Management*, XXXVIII, 337, Sept. 1956, pp. 146-161.

67. N. Bamforth, 'The Effects of Training in Human Relations', *The Manager*, July 1958, pp. 518-520, 548.

68. A. T. M. Wilson, 'Some Contrasting Socio-Technical Production Systems', *The Manager*, Dec. 1955, pp. 979-986.

69. R. W. Revans, 'Is Work Worthwhile?', *Personnel Management*, XL, 343, March 1958, pp. 12-21.

70. R. Marriott, 'Work Motives and Financial Incentives', *Personnel Management*, XL, 345, Sept. 1958, pp. 151-156.

71. R. Stewart, *The Reality of Management*, London: Heinemann 1963.

72. British Institute of Management, *New Concepts in Management*, London: B.I.M. 1963.

73. W. B. D. Brown and W. Raphael, *Managers, Men and Morale*, London: Macdonald & Evans 1948; J. J. Gillespie, *Free Expression in Industry*, London: Pilot Press 1948; E. L. Trist and K. W. Bamforth, 'Some Social and Psychological Consequences of the Longwall Method of Coal-Getting', *Human Relations*, IV, 1, Feb. 1951, pp. 3-38.

74. Editorial, *Personnel Management*, XXXV, 323, March 1953 p. 1.

75. G. Hutton, *We Too Can Prosper*, London: Allen & Unwin 1953, p. 138 ff.

76. D. McMahon, 'The Psychologist and Personnel Manager', *Personnel Management*, XXXVII, 331, March 1955, p. 25.

77. G. Hunter, *The Role of the Personnel Officer: A Group Review*, London: I.P.M. Occasional Paper no. 12, 1957, quotation from p. 8.

78. Editorial, *Personnel Management*, XXXIX, 341, Sept. 1957, p. 134.

79. E.g., "Bystander", 'Personal Viewpoint', *Personnel Management*, XXXIX, 339, March 1957, pp. 50-52.

80. Cf., M. B. Forman, 'The Personnel Function of Management', *Personnel Management*, XXXVIII, 335, March 1956, p. 16; J. O. Blair-Cunynghame, 'Management and Trade Unions' in ed. D. C. Thomson, *Management, Labour and Community*, London: Pitman 1957, pp. 91-103; D. L. Nicholson, 'Leadership and Industrial Relations', *The Manager*, Jan. 1959, esp. pp. 33-34; R. H. S. Turner, 'Industrial Relations: Management's Responsibilities', *Personnel Management*, XLV, 366, Dec. 1963, pp. 168-171.

81. Cf., J. Woodward, 'Industrial Behaviour – Is There a Science?', *New Society*, 8th Oct. 1964, esp. p. 14; T. Lupton, *Industrial Behaviour and Personnel Management*, London: I.P.M. 1964.

82. G. Hunter, 'Ideals and Reality: Some Thoughts about Ethics in Industry', *Personnel Management*, XLIII, 355, March 1961, p. 20.

83. G. Hunter, *Studies in Management*, University of London Press 1961, p. 7. Other references in order are from pp. 23, 34-36, 88-89, 93-94, 97, 99 ff, 113-115, 126, 92.

84. *Ibid.*, chapter X. Cf., R. Marriott, *Incentive Payment Systems*, London: Staples, 2nd ed. 1961.

85. Editorial (by Joan Woodward) on Drever's paper, *Personnel Management*, XLIII, 358, Dec. 1961, pp. 219-222.

86. A. Crichton, 'A Persistent Stereotype? The Personnel Manager: the Outsider', *Personnel Management*, XLV, 336, Dec. 1963, p. 163.

87. E.g., L. Stephens, 'The Institute and the Personnel Manager: a Stock-taking', *Personnel Management*, XLV, 363, March 1963, esp. p. 31.

88. 'Statement on Personnel Management and Personnel Policies', *Personnel Management*, XLV, 363, March 1963, p. 11.

89. *Ibid.*, pp. 11-15.

90. J. Munro Fraser, *Human Relations in a Fully Employed Democracy*, London: Pitman 1960, p. 330. Other references in order are from pp. 27, 330-331, 17, 162, 253, 340, 1, 23.

91. Ed. E. F. L. Brech, *The Principles and Practice of Management*, London: Longmans, 2nd ed. 1963; R. F. Tredgold, *Human Relations in Modern Industry*, London: Duckworth, 2nd ed. 1963.

92. Ed. E. F. L. Brech, *op. cit.*, part III, esp. chapter 1.

93. E. Moonman, *The Manager and the Organization*, London: Tavistock 1961; J. Godber, reported in *The Times*, 2nd March and 28th April, 1964.

94. N. C. Bowker and M. F. Hall, 'Not by Words Alone', *The Manager*, Nov. 1963, pp. 36-38. See also: C. Argyris, *Personality and Organization*, New York: Harper 1957, pp. 142-145, 154-155, 157-160.

95. Ed. E. F. L. Brech, *op. cit.*, 'Introduction' by Brech; C. S. Deverell, *Business Administration and Management*, London: Gee 1963, pp. 26-27.

96. Sir W. Puckey, *Management Principles*, London: Hutchinson 1962, p. 10.

97. *Ibid.*, p. 178.

98. Sir W. Puckey, *Organization in Business Management*, London: Hutchinson 1963, p. 223.

99. H. Whitehead, *How to Become a Successful Manager*, London: Allen & Unwin, 2nd ed. 1963.

100. W. S. Barry, *The Fundamentals of Management*, London: Allen & Unwin 1963. References in order are from pp. 42-43, 80, 83, 119, 11, 168.

101. W. Brown, *Exploration in Management*, London: Heinemann 1960; *idem, Piecework Abandoned*, London: Heinemann 1962; W. Brown and E. Jaques, *Glacier Project Papers*, London: Heinemann 1965; E. Jaques, *The Changing Culture of a Factory*, London: Tavistock 1951; *idem, Measurement of Responsibility*, London: Tavistock 1956; *idem, Equitable Payment*, London: Heinemann 1961. A full bibliography of the Glacier Project is given in *Glacier Project Papers, op. cit.*, pp. 253-255.

102. E. Jaques, *Equitable Payment, op. cit.*, pp. 123-124.

103. W. Brown, *Piecework Abandoned, op. cit.*; cf., R. Marriott, *op. cit.*, 2nd edition 1961; J. H. Goldthorpe, review of W. Brown, *Piecework Abandoned*, in *The Economic Journal*, LXXIII, 292, Dec. 1963, pp. 747-750.

104. E. Jaques, *Time-Span Handbook*, London: Heinemann 1964.

105. E.g., T. T. Paterson, 'The Jaques System: Impractical?', *New Society*, 19th Dec. 1963, pp. 9-11; A. Fox, *The Time-Span of Discretion Theory: an Appraisal*, London: I.P.M. 1966.

106. E. Jaques, 'A System for Income Equity', *New Society*, 12th Dec. 1963, pp. 10-12.

107. E. Jaques, *Equitable Payment, op. cit.*, pp. 131-133.

108. E. Jaques, 'Time Span: A Reply', letter to *New Society*, 26th Dec. 1963, p. 26.

109. E. Jaques, 'An Objective Approach to Pay Differentials', *The Manager*, Jan. 1961, p. 27.

110. *Ibid.*, p. 27.

111. E.g., V. L. Allen, 'A Failure of Method: the Inadequacy of Present Research as a Basis for Understanding the Nature of Management', *Technology*, Jan. 1963, pp. 14, 23.

PART III

ASSESSMENT AND IMPLICATIONS

CHAPTER 7

ASSESSMENT: BRITISH MANAGEMENT THOUGHT AS A BODY OF KNOWLEDGE*

Internal Structure: (1) compatibility of major propositions; (2) ideology and science – Functions and Developmental Influences: (1) developmental cycle of management thought; (2) functions of management thought; (3) influence of socio-industrial context; (4) the autonomous influence of ideas; (5) a diagrammatic summary – Intellectuals and Practitioners – Summary, the Sociology of Knowledge.

THE preceding review of British management thought falls within the ambit of what Merton has labelled the 'European species' of the sociology of knowledge.[1] It has dealt with a structured and relatively sophisticated system of ideas, which was the work of an intellectual élite.

Merton has distinguished a number of interpretative difficulties which beset historical research into systems of thought.[2] The present study has faced several of these. Although British management thought is clearly recorded in numerous sources, a considerable degree of personal judgement is still involved in generalizing about it, particularly regarding changes over time. It is frequently difficult to assess the degree of unanimity shared by a range of sometimes highly individual writers. There is always a danger of taking ideas out of their intended contexts – one cannot check one's own interpretation by interviewing figures of the past. A further problem lies in the necessary, but to some extent arbitrary, delimitation of management thought in relation, for instance, to what could be called 'business ideology' or to the contributions on industrial affairs of academic social scientists.

These problems should be borne in mind when reading the present chapter which assesses British management thought

*Part of the substance of this chapter has appeared in a paper by the author on 'British Management Thought As a Case Study Within the Sociology of Knowledge', *Sociological Review*, July 1968, 217-239.

as a body of knowledge. They render such assessment suggestive rather than definitive. This chapter begins by considering the composition, or internal structure, of management thought. It then discusses factors which shaped the development of management thought, and which were closely linked to the functions performed by that thought. This is followed by a section which discusses the relations between management intellectuals and the general run of practising managers – a discussion which also throws further light on the functions of management thought.

I. INTERNAL STRUCTURE

(1) *Compatibility of major propositions*

We noted that during its early stages of development, British management thought contained certain logical inconsistencies which subsequently were largely resolved. In recent years, management thinkers have exhibited increased confusion and disagreement due primarily to the impact of social science. For the purposes of clarity, we shall for the moment concentrate on some of the predominant themes in management thought as they were expressed when it exhibited the greatest degree of structural integration – during the 1930s and 1940s.

Within the limiting assumptions of British management thought, most of its prominent ideas were highly compatible. For instance, we noted how the management principles and human relations were in large part complementary and mutually supportive, once the industrial enterprise was assumed to be a closed system. In fact, although 'classical organization theory' and human relations are sometimes seen as rival models of industrial organization, management thought tended to regard the latter conception as a complement to the formal structural approach of the former.

Given the tendency to view the enterprise as a closed system, it was easy to understate the role played by employees outside the factory as bread-winners and consumers. That is, management thought under-emphasized the force of employees' economic needs in comparison with others, such as those for belonging, social esteem and self-actualization. The emphasis on social rewards implied a solidary view of industrial enterprises, and suggested that employees necessarily desired a high degree of personal involvement in their activities. This view treated conflicts of economic interests as of minimal importance, and even ignored them. Once this step was taken, trade union activities, often expressed in terms of material demands, could be regarded as constituting unwarranted interference and trouble-making.

Comparable reasoning supported the notion of managers as professionals. It could be argued that, in attempting to cater for employees' material and non-material needs, managers were in effect serving a client group whose primary interests were complementary to their own. Similarly, a further attribute of professionalism appeared to be met by the acceptance of management principles and human relations as generally applicable precepts, and by the assumption that these were founded upon systematic investigation and proven experience. This attribute was the grounding of practice upon a systematic and codified body of knowledge. This body of knowledge was supplemented by the range of standardized procedures available to management, such as costing and work study. In this way, the process of managing appeared to rest upon a scientific basis. In addition, the management movement undertook to record and to publicize new methods. Thus to some extent it filled another professional requirement, one which was notoriously lacking among managers generally, namely the exchange of technical information.

The idea of a profession implied the direction of industry by those possessing a distinct 'managerial' skill, resting on knowledge that was something more than just a collection of specialisms such as accountancy or engineering. It also encouraged the notion of managerial prerogatives. Whatever might be argued to the contrary by legal or political theorists, industry had to be directed by those best suited to perform this function. The pursuit of efficiency thus required that absentee owners relinquish direct control, that managers possess the right to final command within the enterprise, and that managerial recruitment be restricted to those with clearly proven abilities. The claim of managerial professionalism was intimately linked to the recognition of a 'divorce' from ownership. Management spokesmen were encouraged to seek this kind of legitimation for their growing assumption of industrial authority. At the same time, this development enabled them to argue that managers would now pay regard to wider interests than merely those of shareholders. Managerial responsibility could thus be presented as a social one, subsumed under the notion of service. The pursuit of this goal by personnel recruited on the basis of widely accepted criteria, and then carefully trained in a body of managerial knowledge, was thought to be an acceptable foundation for managerial authority.

This sketch of some prominent ideas which we found within British management thought is sufficient to indicate their considerable integration within a consistent scheme of reasoning. It shows that we have been dealing with a well-structured system of knowledge rather than with a mere collection of scattered ideas and opinions. Another dimension of consistency within British management thought became apparent during the review of its historical development. Namely, the continuity of many important themes over the course of time – a longitudinal consistency. Indeed, at the point of its maturity, there was relatively little new in management thought. Its underlying assumptions were well established, and were only seriously challenged by the widespread development of social science research.

Nevertheless, there were also some inconsistencies within management thought which its exponents tended to ignore. For example, the emphasis on managerial expertise and selective recruitment was not completely harmonious with that on the solidary nature of the enterprise. Given the process of educational differentiation, selective recruitment to managerial positions tends to restrict very severely the promotion opportunities available to operative employees. If employees were in this way denied the chance of advancing up a career hierarchy, and if their educational (let alone social) background were at variance with management's, then the comforting claim put out by Mond and others, that managers were much the same kind of employees as operatives, was plainly misleading. For a long period of time, management thinkers also tended to ignore the incompatibility between the technical requirements of competitive industry and notions attached to a solidary view of the enterprise, such as serving employee's social needs. Technical constraints – among them the necessity for a flexible labour force (implying the possibility of redundancies), the apparent economies in some. industries of an advanced division of labour and of repetitive, 'deskilled' tasks, or the pressures placed upon workers by scientific management devices such as work study and incentive schemes – were typically overlooked during expositions of 'team-work', 'social satisfaction', and 'a sense of belonging'.

(2) *Ideology and science*

A system of knowledge may contain ideas that in varying degree derive from values on the one hand, and from scientific observation on the other. These two elements may be seen as representing poles of a continuum. They correspond to Pareto's distinction between 'non-logical' and 'logico-experimental' factors which he made in his classic analysis of thought and action.[3] Between these two categories, it is for present purposes useful to distinguish two more possibilities. The first allows for empirical observations, the assessment of which is distorted by the presence of values. The second allows for a refinement which Pareto also made. He pointed out that ideas and conclusions departing from a scientific standard did not necessarily reflect the influence of prior values. They could arise randomly from 'genuine' errors in observation or from a faulty interpretation of data.[4] Thus it may be postulated that British management thought could draw upon four broad categories of ideas: (1) scientific observation, (2) erroneous observation, (3) distorted observation, and (4) pure value statements. These four positions represent a progression from the scientific to the ideological.

It became apparent during our review of British management thought that its technically-oriented content rendered it far more than just an ideology designed to support the purposes of a certain group against possible challenge from other groups. On the other hand, we also suggested that ideological elements might prejudice this technical content. For instance, they might encourage managerial techniques to be developed on the basis of a biased and unrealistic analysis of behaviour in industry. To some extent social science research and analysis can serve as a point of reference when attempting to separate out the more scientific from the more ideological or erroneous elements within management thought. Indeed, it became apparent in Chapter 6 that some social scientists have already contributed quite considerably to this process. Nevertheless, this does not by itself necessarily provide any clear distinction between our two middle categories of ideas – observations which were heavily influenced by values, and those which were more 'genuinely' mistaken. Thus one could attempt to go a stage further and to differentiate between (i) ideas which, *at the time of their exposition*, might readily have been seen as incomplete, over-simplified, distorted, or in some other way analytically inadequate; and (ii) ideas which today, with the advantage of hindsight and further knowledge, we can see to be inadequate, but which (on a generous interpretation) may not have been so readily open to criticism given the state of knowledge prevailing when they were first formulated. This distinction is a tenuous one. However, it may help us to compare aspects of British management thought which were rather more ideological in origin than put forward simply in good scientific faith. Such a distinction may clarify the intent with which elements of this thought were expounded.

Ideas falling into the first category tended to contain a heavy value component, and we shall suggest that primarily they served management thought's legitimatory purposes. An ideological standpoint was clearly expressed in claims to adopt an ethic of 'service', or in the notion of a managerial 'social mission', especially when these accompanied attempts to extend the scope of managerial control. The idea that management was, or could become, a recognized profession also enters this first category. For it was strenuously put forward at a time when it was quite possible to analyse the attributes of full professional status possessed by occupations such as law, medicine, or the clergy, and then to note how far management was from being able to fulfil these. Management might, admittedly, aspire to satisfy some professional criteria without a drastic restructuring of its industrial role – for instance, a controlling central organization, or regulated recruitment based upon some fairly standard entrance requirement. Yet other criteria were clearly beyond its reach, given the prevailing conditions of private competitive industry and a system of industrial finance which normally ensured that the interests of capital were not disregarded with impunity over any length of time. These structural constraints inhibited any widespread public acceptance that managers could take as their primary goal a purely impartial pursuit of 'public interest'. They also tended to militate against a further professional attribute, namely a common sub-culture involving the open exchange of technical information among members of the occupation. Indeed, in 1937 P. A. Wilson, joint author of a classic work on the professions, made it plain to members of the Oxford Management Conference that industrial management lacked several key attributes of a recognized profession.[5]

A further instance of fairly deliberate ideological bias was seen with the later version of human relations. In putting this forward some authors chose to ignore or to denigrate the role of trade unionism in representing workers' interests – they also chose to overlook the possibility that these interests could diverge from those of management. A related idea was that there was something amiss if managers did not succeed in securing the total commitment of employees to their own purposes. Even the most cursory unbiased observation of industrial life would have shown up the analytical deficiencies in such ideas when they were originally formulated.

It is also apparent how the ideas we have just discussed stressed elements of consensus in industrial relationships rather than those of conflict. They implied that management represented common interests and aspirations, so that given its technical competence there was no reason for workers or other groups to question its right to authority. The values contained in these ideas were in this way allied to the legitimatory purpose within British management thought. It is arguable that the same ideology came to distort other observations which were incorporated into management thought. One example was the comparison between the process of management and the leadership of an army at war. For we have seen how, in most cases, the different social situation of the latter was conveniently ignored – in particular, the far higher normative consensus as to means and ends of the organization which prevails at all levels in the typical combat army. Another example was the considerable exaggeration, especially in early management writings, of the extent to which managers as a whole were free from ownership control and able to adopt independent, socially appealing objectives.

The second category of ideas comprised those which today can be seen as deficient, but which may not have readily appeared so at an earlier date. These ideas present far greater difficulties when we wish to assess whether their inadequacies were the result primarily of genuine error or of ideological distortion. Any precise evaluation of the ideological content in such ideas is not possible, though it is probably safe to assume that it is relatively less than for those in our first category.

A number of ideas in this second category were in fact largely designed to meet the more technical purposes of management. We may take as an example the problem of employee motivation and productivity. We noted within British management thought a growing emphasis on social rewards and employee-centred leadership, associated with the concept of integration and contained within a human relations frame of reference. On the one hand, this trend of thought was supported by limiting assumptions of an ideological nature regarding the structure of relations within business enterprises. Yet, on the other hand, it was also a move towards what appeared technically the most effective methods of motivating employees, particularly in situations where trade union activity was no longer focused on the plant level or where it was felt that growing physical distance between managers and men (with increasing scale and complexity) should be offset.

This type of approach was supported by the interpretations of the Hawthorne experiments at the hands of the Mayo school. It is reasonable to assume that the reports of Mayo and his colleagues were, at the time, accepted in all honesty by the British management movement as being scientifically legitimate. The limitations of Mayoism have only become apparent with the benefit of subsequent reflection and investigation. Consequently, we are able today to appreciate how it followed most ideological systems in putting forward a subtle combination of facts and values. That is, it allowed a prior philosophical 'world-view' to take its interpretations of research to a point far beyond that warranted by the original data, and to erect from these a normative system which had nothing strictly to do with scientific investigation. This poses an important question: how far was the influence of Mayoism over British management thought due to its sympathy with values already present in that thought, and how much was due to its status as 'scientific' research? Although we are unable to provide an answer, this question touches on the kind of issue which should concern sociologists of knowledge in their current work into the formation and content of opinion. For the use of systematic survey methods ought to make possible some clarification of the processes whereby values and factual information are together incorporated into thought.

In turning to the management principles, there is a similar difficulty in separating out merely erroneous analysis from distortion associated with the instrusion of values. In the first place, there is little evidence to question that those formulating the principles, and claiming a universal applicability for them, believed they were following a legitimate comparative approach to organizational analysis. When a work of scholarship such as that of Mooney and Reiley supported their ideas, they had no inducement to think otherwise. And the search for generalizations on organizational structure and on managerial functions was in large part motivated by a technical purpose. This was to provide some guidance for practising managers in a form which they might readily understand and utilize – the span of control principle is an example. In addition, the formulation of general propositions was not merely an attempt to create some order from a range of scattered data or of personal experience. It also represented the type of analytical construction which its exponents doubtless believed would stimulate further the progress of management as an area of study. Although today the principles may be viewed as an over-confident elaboration of precepts from what was largely impressionistic evidence, it may well be that, by encouraging critical evaluative studies of their propositions, they have contributed to the further advance in organizational knowledge we now enjoy.

Yet, in the second place, it is possible to argue that the formulation of the principles was influenced by those values which we have already distinguished in British management thought. Management's claim to professionalism, for instance, was only plausible if it could be shown to possess some uniform and generalized system of knowledge upon which its practitioners could draw. The so-called 'principles of management' could be presented as the theoretical base upon which the subject of 'management' rested. Furthermore, by ignoring problems of conflict, change and uncertainty within administrative organization, the principles gave management an appearance of cohesion and rationality which it did not often possess in practice. Indeed, to be able to put forward a convincing claim for unchallenged prerogatives based upon functional expertise, management had

P

to appear to follow a rational logic of 'efficiency and costs'. If, as the Mayo school argued, this logic contrasted with worker 'sentiment', in fact a non-logic, then this provided so much the more support for the managerial claim to authority within the factory. Thus the analytical omissions of the principles and the rather grandiose claims attached to them may not have been entirely the result of genuine error or over-enthusiasm, but also the manifestation of some legitimatory purpose.

Similarly, some of the so-called 'scientific management' techniques, the possession of which was taken as a further technical reason for detailed managerial control in the workshop, can today clearly be seen to rely upon subjective judgement. Techniques such as rate-setting and time-study may quite justifiably be challenged by workers, since far from being scientific their operation depends upon the setting of an 'effort-bargain' which forms a focal point of the conflicting economic interests between management and workers.[6]

In short, the management principles and many elements in scientific management presented an appearance of established knowledge and unchallengable expertise which subsequent analysis and investigation has shown to be largely spurious. In so far as these aspects of management thought were incorporating ideology under the guise of science, managerial values under the cover of technical advance, then it is perhaps fruitful to compare this with the similar situation Marx claimed to find in nineteenth-century political economy.[7]

II. FUNCTIONS AND DEVELOPMENTAL INFLUENCES

(1) *Developmental cycle of management thought*
Within the total field of knowledge pertaining to the organization and operation of business enterprise, management thought passed through a cycle of emergence, predominance and decline. This developmental cycle represented a phase in the overall and long-term evolution of thought on business organization. To a large extent, the cycle of British management thought reflected a similar cycle of influence through which the management movement as an intellectual élite has also progressed.[8]

Prior to the formation of the management movement, prevailing thought on the operation of business enterprise had derived from owner-entrepreneurs, aided by the theoretical contributions of laissez-faire economists and by moralists such as Samuel Smiles. Management thought developed as the expression of an emerging would-be professional management movement. This movement was in its early stages acutely aware of the need to differentiate itself from a system of industrial control based upon rights of ownership – it claimed control on the basis of professional impartiality and expertise.

Management thought thus emerged with the evolution of a distinct managerial role, and in particular with the differentiation of the role of management intellectual. Similarly, management thought declined when this role differentiation was eroded, with the recent movement of the intellectual management power centre into the academic sphere. The difficulty of distinguishing today a body of contemporary management thought of high and independent status has coincided with the shift of major managerial educational efforts away from institutes such as the B.I.M. towards new schools attached to the British university framework. It is not true to say as yet that there has been a complete circulation of intellectual élites in this sphere, but the present status of management thought indicates that the process is well under way.

A historical review of the development of British management thought has also indicated how its content changed in emphasis, particularly with respect to the balance of attention given to the social morality of management and to more strictly technical concerns. We shall now elaborate on a feature that is critical for an understanding of previous chapters; namely, that the content of management thought related to its functions and through these to its wider socio-industrial context.

(2) *Functions of management thought*

Management, it was suggested in Chapter 1, is a technical function of organizing and administering economic resources, which is performed by particular groups through systems of authority. The purely technical aspect of management has probably always secured a considerable degree of social acceptance. However, the question of who should perform the managerial function and with what powers has met with substantially greater contention. The problematic status of managers in control of commercial assets which they frequently do not own has been reinforced by the fact that this control impinges on matters, such as the determination of working conditions and the distribution of income, which have been grounds for bargaining and areas of wide public concern.

Given the nature of management, those intellectuals who sought to represent and support it were faced with two primary requirements. First, they had to show that managerial authority was socially legitimate. Second, they had to develop knowledge which would aid the technical performance of those managers.[9] These needs, as *perceived* by members of the management movement in the light of the prevailing socio-industrial context, in effect operated as a kind of 'substructural' base for management thought – though the use of this term is not intended to convey any narrow sense of economic determinism.

The *legitimatory content* in management thought was chiefly directed at non-managerial groups. In large measure it amounted to a dialogue with other intellectuals who might challenge managerial goals and activities. It is possible to suggest at least two main functions which the legitimatory aspects of management thought performed for members of the management movement. The first was the securing of social approval for managerial control by asserting that managerial objectives and behaviour were in accord with widely accepted social values. In so far as this was a strategy aimed at the defence of a particular occupational group, it came close to what Mannheim has termed a 'particular ideology'. To the extent that the legitimatory content of management thought went beyond the mere 'defence' of the managerial role and developed more aggressive ideas aimed at industrial change, it also contained certain 'utopian' elements, to follow Mannheim again.[10] The explicit intention of early management thought to discredit and weaken owner control, though aiming at industrial change, was primarily a defence of an emerging managerial role. More recently, with the Mayoist version of human relations and with Jaques' consultancy proposals for a new payments system, there have emerged techniques aimed at a substantial increase in managerial control within work organizations, which have been cloaked with the notion that managers have the duty to initiate widespread 'improvements' in the existing social order. The legitimation in such cases has been of a more clearly 'utopian' nature.

Secondly, the legitimatory values expressed by management thinkers derived to some extent from psychological 'strains' in their role. The proponents of management thought were on the one hand linked with the occupation they represented, while on the other hand they faced prevailing currents of intellectual opinion. In consequence, they suffered from the typically severe discrepancy between the demands which leaders of opinion made on industry and the reality of industrial practice. The post-1918 era and the early 1940s provide particularly notable instances of such discrepancy. Thus not only were management thinkers defending those they represented; they were also in effect justifying their own position before other intellectuals. At the same time, the values which were utilized for this defence – such as service to the community and the satisfaction of employee needs – were directed back at industrial practice in order that this should accord more closely to the picture which was being presented to intellectual opinion. The more that managerial practice was reconcilable with these values, the less the 'role-strain' facing members of the management movement.

Moreover, it is probable that legitimatory values served the subsidiary socio-psychological function of sustaining the management movement in its work by providing it with a set of common aspirations. Such support was particularly necessary in view of the continued indifference shown by most practising managers towards the movement's activities and output – an observation to which we return later. In short, the process of representing managerial interests set up psychological strains for management thinkers, which in turn provided an impetus to the legitimatory aspects of their work. In this way, the psychological function performed by legitimatory values was closely linked with the social function of supporting managerial interests. This connection appears sufficiently close to lend support to those who have criticized Sutton and his colleagues for implying that the defence of interests and 'role-strain' are two distinct and rival explanations for the formation of ideology.[11]

The *technical content* in British management thought was directed almost entirely at managers themselves. Bendix has indicated how the process of industrial bureaucratization presented new problems of co-ordination, and of securing

among employees what he calls an 'ethic of work performance'.[12]
The technical content in management thought has sought to
meet problems such as these. It has aimed to provide improved
modes of organization, a greater understanding of employee
motivation, and other technical means to superior business
performance.

Before examining more closely available evidence on the
relationships between British management thought and the
socio-industrial context in which management thinkers worked,
it is necessary to qualify two assumptions which have been
implicit in our previous analysis.

The first assumption has been that where management
thought reflected the legitimatory and technical purposes of the
management movement, the former would be manifested by
value elements and the latter by more objective and factual
observation. This assumption should not be taken as excluding
cases where features in management thought derived, at least
initially, from circumstances other than an assessment of the
management movement's interests and requirements. We shall
shortly illustrate instances whereby important elements in
management thought derived from ideas or precepts applied
quite outside the industrial sphere, and where they were introduced by virtue of non-industrial experience on the part of
management thinkers. However, we would still suggest that
an examination of the evidence indicates that most of the values
in management thought were directly associated with its legitimatory purpose, while most of its more scientific elements were
directly associated with its technical purpose. Hence in this
study we have tended to use the terms 'legitimatory content'
and 'technical content' without further qualification.

The second assumption concerns the clarity with which the
legitimatory and technical purposes of the management movement were reflected in British management thought. Employing
the previous assumption that these two main purposes were
largely reflected in ideological and scientific contents, then we
have already in this chapter touched on one of the problems
involved here. Namely, the difficulties encountered in an
attempt to separate out ideological and scientific elements in
management thought, and the possibilities of achieving this by
using social science findings as a scientific standard. There is
also a further qualification which needs to be applied to our

second assumption. It is not entirely correct to assume that legitimatory and technical purposes were always distinctly reflected within management thought. In practice, some ideas could serve both purposes simultaneously. This was because the two purposes were themselves to some extent interdependent. Effective managerial technical performance might itself serve as an important legitimation of managerial authority. A certain minimum acceptance of managerial control as legitimate is necessary for managers to perform their technical functions at all. Moreover, certain management techniques may conflict with wider social values or contain latent social costs, and hence themselves require legitimation. Thus there is a close relationship between managerial legitimation and technical performance, and the distinction of these points of reference within management thought may be quite subtle.

(3) Influence of socio-industrial context

Management thought was directed at a range of publics, comprising the reference groups for members of the management movement. Through these publics, this system of thought was linked to the wider social environment. The proposition that thought is in some way related to prevailing social conditions is the starting point for the sociology of knowledge. It is not a major point of dispute. What is open to considerable contention, and remains a largely unresolved question, is the nature of the causal relationships between reflective thought and social structure. The development of British management thought can serve to provide some illustration of these relationships at the level of a specific system of knowledge. For there are two indications that the prevailing socio-industrial context within which management thinkers operated did exercise a direct influence over their work.

The first indication is relatively straightforward – the open admission by management thinkers that their formulations *were* influenced by the social environment. In particular, management writers recognized the changes in prevailing socio-industrial conditions which followed both World Wars, and argued explicitly that these changes required managers to adopt new attitudes and techniques. Indeed, an open admission of this nature was necessary if practising managers were to be persuaded of the wisdom of adopting new approaches in the changed social and industrial climate.

The second indication is the way in which the balance of attention within management thought between legitimation and technique, and the nature of the legitimation itself, tended to alter in conjunction with significant changes in its context. The extreme difficulties in assessing such a subtle relationship, particularly when using historical data, need emphasizing. Nevertheless, we would argue that the parallel shifts of existential environment and management thought are most meaningful when taken together, and that this suggests some kind of causal process from the former to the latter.

Within management thought over the last 50 years, there has been an overall shift of emphasis from legitimatory concerns to a more technical concern with processes of organizational control. We noted, for instance, how British management thought moved from the concept of service, in which different interests would be impartially respected, to an assumption that managers should take the lead in defining those interests in relation to their goal of organizational effectiveness. Similarly, there was a shift of emphasis from 'democratic' constitutional procedures towards neo-paternalistic methods, and from a free negotiation of material rewards to a stress on other rewards which managers themselves should determine. The claim of managerial professionalism was less forcefully advanced as time went on, and certainly its ethical implications were increasingly kept in the background. This long-term trend has been paralleled by a more widespread public acceptance of the necessity for a managerial function in modern British society. Equally significant was the changing nature of legitimatory content within management thought from the attempt to secure the *principle* of managerial control – to establish the managerial role – towards the justification of techniques designed to intensify the *operation* of managerial control. This changing legitimatory content itself, in effect, signified a growing emphasis in management thought on technical requirements.

These two overall trends in management thought – the move away from a legitimatory emphasis, and the changing nature of that emphasis – accompanied certain contextual developments. These include the growth in scale, technological complexity and bureaucratization of work organizations which has heightened the technical problems of management, as well as the increase of economic difficulties in Britain which has focused attention on to industrial performance. The decline in legitimatory content has also accompanied a growing acceptance of managerial authority by organized labour, by shareholder interests, and by political groups. Although the shift from legitimatory content has undoubtedly been hastened by the anti-ideological impact of academic research, it should be remembered that this last is only a recent development in the total history of British management thought.

The one important deviation from this long-term decline in legitimatory content appeared during the 1940s when the management movement faced new threats to its position due to low managerial prestige, a rapid shift in the industrial balance of power to labour, and a greatly accelerated rate of sociopolitical change. This particular case would appear to re-affirm our general contention that the formulation of British management thought was influenced by the prevailing social environment. It also supplements Coser's proposition that ideology can sharpen conflict between collectivities by indicating that conflict may itself encourage the formulation of ideology.[13]

(4) *The autonomous influence of ideas*

The analysis of 'managerial ideology' by writers such as Bendix, McGivering, Matthews and Scott, has largely been contained within a Marxist type of framework in which systems of thought are seen to be shaped by the interests of particular social groups and classes.[14] The analysis of British management thought offered so far has also followed a comparable model of interaction between knowledge and relevant 'substructural' requirements. However, this type of analysis is not in itself sufficient to account for a full explanation of management thought, and we shall attempt to illustrate this view.

Bendix has more recently gone beyond a purely Marxist analysis (though as he shows not beyond that of Marx himself) in admitting that the historical legacy of ideas might also play something of an independent role in fashioning current thought: '. . . ideologies of management can be explained only in part as rationalizations of self-interest; they also result from the legacy of institutions and ideas which is "adopted" by each generation much as a child "adopts" the grammar of his native language.'[15] A full analysis of British management thought requires us to go one stage further than Bendix. We would suggest that management thought recorded at any particular moment of time was influenced not only (i) by ideas formulated by earlier management writers (comparable to Bendix's 'legacy of ideas'), but also (ii) by ideas deriving from sources which were in the first place not closely connected with the management movement and its needs.

To take the first category, it would probably be little disputed that ideas previously formulated by management writers had some influence over subsequent thought – in the sense of creating a 'school' of thought. Thus many subsequent writers made frequent reference to ideas put forward by pioneers such as Fayol, Follett, and Taylor. Recurrent patterns within management thought indicate a considerable historical legacy of ideas. For instance, the notion of universal principles of management can be traced at least as far back as Taylor, that of a managerial social mission to the Quaker employers and even to Robert Owen, and many human relations assumptions to the First World War period. It is also likely that previous management thought held some influence over the perception of substructural needs by management writers at any given point of time. These propositions do not, in any case, necessarily break with the Marxist concept of substructural determination. This makes some allowance for 'cultural' lags, while it could also be argued that the historically previous ideas were themselves the product of similar substructural forces.

There are, however, indications that the second class of ideas – those deriving from independent sources outside the management movement – also held some autonomous influence over the development of British management thought. The Quaker employers, for example, first advanced new concepts and methods of labour management when this placed them at odds with the great mass of entrepreneurial spokesmen and when there was no clear proof that their innovations would bring any material gains. The role of these employers in bringing religious principles to bear on management thought has been discussed in detail elsewhere.[16] The impact of social science on management thought in recent years provides a further instance of ideas from an external source having a profound influence on the shape of management thought. Not all management writers have given equal attention to the implications of social science research, but so far as they have done so, a system of knowledge deriving from outside the management movement proper has been able to influence the form of management thought, even though this influence has often been discomforting. Moreover, the whole trend towards a more pronounced technical content within management thought has to be viewed not only with regard to the changing needs perceived by the management movement but also to the general development of science in fields relevant to industrial operation. One may suggest, with less certainty, other examples of the same process. There is reason to believe that the personal backgrounds of pioneering writers influenced the values incorporated in their work – Taylor's Quaker background, Follett's training in political philosophy and social work, Mayo's early philosophical training and interest in Pareto. A number of ideas deriving from military practice, for example the 'staff officer' concept, were incorporated into management thought through the medium of writers such as Urwick who had a distinguished military background.

In short, the case of British management thought illustrates how existing concepts and ideas may exercise an independent role in the formation of systems of thought. This is not to deny that such ideas may subsequently be adapted to suit the requirements of those formulating thought. It is, however, to assert that ideas can, through their own appeal, autonomously influence the content of that thought.

(5) *A diagrammatic summary*
The main strands of the analysis presented in the present chapter are represented in the following model. This serves to summarize the processes which we suggested were operative in the formation of management thought at a given point in time. The model links these processes to the range of ideas which were incorporated into management thought, and which may be categorized in respect of their scientific status. The diagram also draws attention to an important process which may affect all systems of knowledge; namely, that thinking aimed at the solution of technical problems could incorporate value elements or limited perceptions which cripple its intended practical utility.

FIGURE I

The Formation of British Management Thought

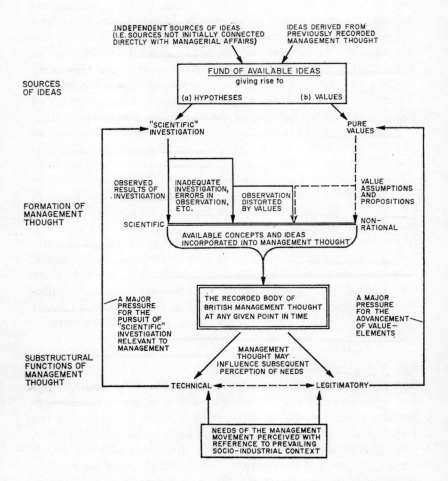

N.B. The representation of the influx of ideas as a downward flow, and the placing of substructural needs at the foot of the diagram, is purely a matter of graphical convenience. It implies no priority in time between available ideas and substructure.

III. INTELLECTUALS AND PRACTITIONERS

The sociology of knowledge, at least in its 'European' tradition, has tended to neglect the question of how acceptable the work of intellectual spokesmen has been among those groups it was intended to represent and support. At the level of occupational groups, how well do the activities and views of the professional spearhead reflect those of the general run of practitioners?

Others have indicated that American business or managerial ideology does not necessarily find acceptance among all business-men or managers.[17] In the British case, there is also evidence that management thought, a system of knowledge superficially so attractive ideologically and technically, was never in fact wholeheartedly accepted by most practising managers. Not only did managers openly express their criticism of manage-ment thought, but equally management intellectuals themselves expressed their exasperation at managers' lack of concern for their ideas.[18] The continuing low membership of management institutes over many years also indicates the distance between intellectuals and practitioners.

Several factors may have encouraged this lack of sympathy for management thought. A considerable section of British industry has always been noted for its resistance to new ideas in any case. Secondly, the notion of 'the feel of a trade' militated against the generalizations of management thinkers. This notion is not too far removed from the current emphasis in industrial social science on the need to analyse organizational situations on their own account before deciding on appropriate action within them. Thirdly, it would appear that many managers regarded the labour management techniques proposed in management thought as too costly for their uncertain returns – they were too peripheral. The commercially schooled practi-tioner found little sympathy for the sweeping legitimatory claims and moral exhortation that frequently accompanied writing on personnel management. University educated men might be more inclined to accept ethical values of this kind, but such men have only been recruited in large numbers to managerial positions since the Second World War.

Recent social science research has indicated that a great deal of management thought was grossly over-simplified and hence unrealistic. It is apparent today that many of these analytical weaknesses derived from the influence of legitimatory values, and were ideological in nature. A considerable part of the indifference and even opposition shown by practising managers towards management thought may have stemmed from their closer contact with the actual complexities and exigencies of organizational life. This suggests that, for practising managers, legitimatory claims designed to justify their authority were of less moment than the practical maintenance of their position through presenting acceptable financial results, offering adequate rewards, and returning an adequate overall record of business performance. And this would not have been an unrealistic position for most managers to have adopted. For there is little question that management thought tended to underplay the financial exigencies faced by managers. The extent to which most management intellectuals assumed practising managers to enjoy independence from ownership, and to be free from the financial pressures exerted by capital and product markets, was for much of British industry an exaggerated one.[19] Such exaggeration was most pronounced in the earlier stages of British management thought. It manifested the desire of management intellectuals to assert the ability of managers to play a socially responsible and financially impartial role in industry. It may also in part have been due to an excessive focus on large-scale industry, with which most management intellectuals were associated.

Management thought reflected a professional awareness among members of the management movement and it represented an attempt to spread a sense of professionalism among practising managers. Its failure to achieve this was due to the lack of importance which most practitioners attached to the notion of a managerial profession. Certain professional criteria, such as the adoption of service to all sectors of the community as a primary goal, or the frank exchange of technical knowledge were not merely considered unnecessary, but went against the whole tenor of management in private competitive industry. The universalistic outlook inherent in professionalism was countered by the particularism which tended to dominate managerial outlooks in practice – the sense of belonging to, and working within conditions peculiar to, particular firms or particular industries. Thus management thought in its attempt to sustain professionalism with a systematic, cohesive body of knowledge tended to appear too generalized, abstract and idealistic for immediate practical application. Indeed, much management thought was not only the creation of consultants, but it required considerable interpretation and adaptation by them during the course of their everyday work. It was just this distance between management thought and practice which encouraged the widespread industrial disinterest in management education for a long time in this country.

These considerations suggest in turn that the ideological elements in British management thought were of greater functional consequence for management intellectuals than for practitioners. We have already indicated the role-strain of management thinkers. The most prominent management spokesmen were of above average education and were in contact with contemporary intellectual currents, including that particular hostility towards industry and commerce which has persisted in many intellectual circles. Some of them, for instance, worked closely with men such as the Quaker employers, who were themselves peculiarly sensitive to contemporary debate of moral issues. Managers out in business organizations may have felt reasonably assured of their position, and that they possessed the necessary rewards and sanctions to secure compliance with their authority. Management intellectuals could not so easily admit this blunt power perspective; they had to soften or to justify it. And in the event, the situation was reached where (as we saw in Chapter 5) an approach such as human relations probably carried more weight among other intellectuals, including academics and even labour spokesmen, than it did among the rank and file of British management.

SUMMARY – THE SOCIOLOGY OF KNOWLEDGE

The assessment of British management thought has required reference to the theoretical perspectives of the sociology of knowledge. At the same time this has enabled the study of management thought to illustrate usefully some important concerns of this branch of sociological enquiry. An analysis of the content of management thought led to a four-fold classification of ideas with respect to their scientific or ideological nature. Management thought was linked to the role of management intellectual; its cyclical progress reflected a phase in the

circulation of intellectual élites concerned with the business
sector. An explanation of the formation of management thought
required an analytical framework allowing for the role of substructural functions, for the influence of pre-existing ideas, and
for the 'contamination' of observation by ideology. This broad
framework, summarized in Figure 1, may be applicable to
systems of knowledge associated with other occupational groups.
Finally, the nature of relationships between management
intellectuals and practitioners was seen to imply that sociologists of knowledge should take account of the influence held by
systems of thought not only over groups which these systems
seek to persuade, but also over groups which they ostensibly
represent.

Some commentators have expressed a deep pessimism concerning the contributions of the sociology of knowledge. Aron,
for instance, has gone so far as to claim that its theoretical
contributions have been virtually nil.[20] Some of this disappointment perhaps stems from an expectation that this branch of
sociology should contribute a composite theory of knowledge
rather than just a sociological mode of analysis of knowledge.
But another important cause of pessimism lies in the empirical
difficulties of adequately testing and developing those theoretical
explanations which are already available. In this regard, it is
clearly more difficult to deal with 'total' systems of thought
rather than the much more limited, coherent, well-defined
and accessible type of system which has been the subject of
our study. This is particularly the case if account is to be taken
of the changing relations between thought and social context
over time, and it is primarily from cases of change that causal
inference may be drawn. In short, if one still accepts that the
sociology of knowledge can provide valuable insight, then one
has also to accept that more rigorous empirical research must
be undertaken to develop that insight. The areas of thought
which are most accessible for such research lie nearer to Mannheim's 'particular' level, pertaining especially to occupational,
political, or small religious groups.

NOTES

1. R. K. Merton, *Social Theory and Social Structure*, Glencoe: Free
Press, rev. ed. 1957, pp. 439-455.
2. *Ibid.*, pp. 442-453.

3. V. Pareto, *The Mind and Society*, London: Cape 1935, vol. I.
4. T. Parsons, *The Structure of Social Action*, Glencoe: Free Press 1949, pp. 269-277.
5. P. A. Wilson, reported in *British Management Review*, II, 4, Oct.-Dec. 1937, pp. 121-124.
6. H. Behrend, 'The Effort Bargain', *Industrial and Labor Relations Review*, X, 4, July 1957, pp. 503-515.
7. Eds. T. B. Bottomore and M. Rubel, *Karl Marx: Selected Writings in Sociology and Social Philosophy*, London: Watts 1961, pp. 165-166.
8. For a general discussion on the circulation of élites see: T. B. Bottomore, *Elites and Society*, London: Watts 1964, chapter III.
9. R. Bendix, 'Industrial Authority and its Supporting Value Systems', in ed. R. Dubin, *Human Relations in Administration*, Englewood Cliffs: Prentice-Hall 1961, p. 271.
10. K. Mannheim, *Ideology and Utopia*, London: Routledge 1936, chapters II and IV.
11. F. X. Sutton, S. E. Harris, C. Kaysen, and J. Tobin, *The American Business Creed*, Cambridge, Mass.: Harvard University Press 1956, chapter 15; D. Rogers and I. E. Berg, Jr.: 'Occupation and Ideology, the Case of the Small Businessman', *Human Organization*, 20, 3, Fall 1961, esp. pp. 106-108.
12. R. Bendix, *Work and Authority in Industry*, New York: Wiley 1956, p. 204.
13. L. Coser, *The Functions of Social Conflict*, London: Routledge & Kegan Paul 1956, chapter VI.
14. R. Bendix, *op. cit.* 1956; I. C. McGivering, D. G. J. Matthews, and W. H. Scott, *Management in Britain*, Liverpool: The University Press 1960, pp. 91-101.
15. R. Bendix, 'Industrialization, Ideologies and Social Structure', *American Sociological Review*, 24, 5, Oct. 1959, p. 619.
16. J. Child, 'Quaker Employers and Industrial Relations', *Sociological Review*, 12, 3, Nov. 1964, pp. 293-315; Cf., the classic study suggesting the influence of religious ideas on commercial practice – M. Weber, *The Protestant Ethic and the Spirit of Capitalism*, London: Allen & Unwin 1930.
17. R. Bendix, *op. cit.* 1956, esp. pp. 331 ff; D. Rogers and I. E. Berg, Jr., *op. cit.*, p. 108.
18 E.g., J. A. Bowie, *Education for Business Management*, London; Oxford University Press 1930, pp. 115-136.
19. J. H. Westergaard, 'The Withering Away of Class – A Contemporary Myth', in eds. P. Anderson and R. Blackburn, *Towards Socialism*, London: Fontana 1965, pp. 95-97.
20. R. Aron, *German Sociology*, New York: Free Press 1964 ed., p. 62.

CHAPTER 8

IMPLICATIONS: FOR MANAGEMENT EDUCATION

The Implications of Social Science – Management Teachers – Use of Social Science for Management Education – Problems with the Use of Social Science – Management Education, Industrial Studies and the Universities.

CONTRIBUTORS to British management thought had always held as one of their objectives the foundation of management education upon a body of systematic knowledge. In so far as they aspired to have management recognized as a profession, they had to seek the establishment of appropriate training courses as a necessary prerequisite. Urwick, for instance, chaired the committee set up in 1945 by the Minister of Education, whose report on *Education for Management* was a milestone in the development of management studies. Many years previously, writers such as John Lee had urged the establishment of regular and comprehensive management courses within the universities and other colleges.[1] Management literature, with its complement of ethical precepts, general principles and functional techniques, was regarded as the main support upon which this educational programme would rest.

The foregoing review of British management thought has indicated that it possessed serious deficiencies for educative purposes. It lacked an adequate empirical base, which also partly explains the relatively slow development of its concepts and ideas. It tended to merge values with factual observations, so that in management thought the desirable was frequently confused with an appreciation of the actual. Management thought appeared to attract little regard from most practising managers, and it would seem that some of this scepticism has remained in respect of current British management education. It is therefore quite apposite to ask what implications for management education may be drawn from recent develop-

242

ments in management thought and social science. In particular, what can social science offer in place of previously established ideas, and what relevant conclusions may be derived from our earlier assessment of British management thought?

There is considerable agreement that management education is concerned essentially with improving the ability of managers to reach appropriate decisions and to implement them effectively. Its focus, in other words, should be on the decision-process.[2] Management education in that case comprises the imparting of knowledge relevant for decision making, as well as the development of appropriate skills. It is possible to categorize a great deal of current activity within management education into three areas:

(1) Teaching the organizational applications of relevant academic disciplines, primarily the social sciences – economics, psychology, sociology – and relevant aspects of engineering technology.

(2) Teaching relatively standardized techniques, the application of which is often the province of particular functional areas of management. For example, various costing systems, critical path analysis, investment analysis, sales forecasting techniques, work study.

(3) Providing the means for management students to develop and exercise appropriate skills. This includes business exercises, role-playing, T-groups, and case-studies.

British management thought was intended to furnish knowledge appropriate chiefly to the first two areas of activity. The first area is concerned with providing a framework of analysis so that industrial and organizational behaviour can be better understood and predicted. Such analysis must derive from the theoretical and empirical content of relevant academic disciplines. Management thought represented an early attempt to furnish an analysis of industry and organization by drawing eclectically upon available disciplines and supplementing these with ideas derived from personal experience and instilled wisdom. From these available contributions, it developed a range of administrative precepts and techniques appropriate to the second activity area of management education.

It is of limited value to teach techniques and to exercise skills without affording managers the analytical means to appreciate the particular organizational needs for which techniques and skills may be utilized, and the particular circumstances in which they may be applied. Reference to the academic disciplines in the first area of management education is necessary in order to specify the context in respect of which a choice between available techniques is made. Equally, any training exercise which is used to develop skills represents a particular situation which ultimately must be defined in terms of concepts and variables deriving from relevant academic disciplines. Thus in a very real sense, management education is founded upon these disciplines, comprising the social sciences together with an appreciation of technology.[3]

Not only is the means to analyse organizational behaviour (in its widest sense) the most critical aspect of management education, it is also the most problematic. It is in this area that, failing adequate comparative and inter-disciplinary research, unwarranted assumptions can readily be incorporated into writing and teaching. It is an area where the discrediting of management thought by industrial social science has left an apparent dearth of propositions which can be advanced to students with confidence.

The present chapter will concentrate on this area of management education and will discuss some of its problems. Following a review of the main implications of developments in social science, the practical problems these have posed for management teachers are illustrated by reference to a survey undertaken by the author. A third section outlines an approach to management education which utilizes social science analysis, and which is increasingly being adopted today. Fourthly, we consider some problems involved in this new approach. A final section discusses some fundamental issues which are raised by the status of management education in relation to social science. The more general intention of this chapter is to review a number of important matters which the recent course of management thought and social science has shown to require further discussion.

THE IMPLICATIONS OF SOCIAL SCIENCE

In Britain, most publicity has been given to developing the structure of management education, in terms of its physical and institutional location, lengths and titles of courses, techniques of teaching, and types of student to be admitted. Neverless, at least some commentators have been aware that the really fundamental problem in management education today concerns the actual content of teaching.[4] For it remains a truism that education is concerned with the creation and passing on of *knowledge*.

The development of social science has presented difficulties for the content of teaching on the social and organizational aspects of management. Social science has largely discredited an established body of 'management' knowledge which was intended to apply to practical managerial problems in all circumstances. Yet social science has so far not substituted a new and equivalent set of prescriptions for administrative practice, although some social scientists might appear to claim otherwise. Indeed, to the extent that social science is concerned with the comparative analysis of complex, varied and changing situations, it is difficult to see how it can ever be expected to produce exact prescriptions rather than probabilitarian assessments for those who wish to apply its insights to practical purposes.

Social science research has indicated that the influences upon, and processes of, behaviour at all levels of organization are considerably more complex than had been allowed for by most management writers. This research has exposed a large number of independent, or semi-independent, determinants of behaviour, only some of which are likely to be open to managerial regulation. This is to say that social science has pointed to various constraints upon managerial control which had previously been overlooked by management thinkers. Further, social science findings have implied that optimum organizational structures and arrangements, together with the behaviour of those filling organizational roles, can only be analysed and predicted in the light of the specific circumstances and requirements – the particular situations – of given enterprises.

Social scientists have tended to specialize in studying the role played by different organizational features, such as workflow technology, plant size, rates of change, market forces, or leadership styles. Moreover, they have tended to confine the scope of their researches to limited empirical areas, such as informal employee practices or job satisfaction. This specialization can be understood as a strategy for coping with a new and complex area of research prior to the availability of unifying concepts or statistical methods for dealing with multi-variate analysis. With the growing favour of concepts such as 'role' or 'system' which encourage an inter-disciplinary and multivariate analysis, and the availability of powerful new methods of analysing data, there are signs of a move away from this fragmentation of research interests.

However, the present situation still presents the student of organizational behaviour with a considerable diversity of emphasis, some of which was noted in Chapter 6. For example, the key variables which have been proposed as the basis for comparative organizational analysis range from membership compliance (Etzioni), decision-making (Simon), prime bene-ficiary (Blau and Scott), to technology (Perrow).[5] What is really required as a basis for the comparative study of organiza-tions is not just a single supposedly 'critical' dimension but a whole range of salient variables.[6] With the present development of industrial social science it is possible to single out a given variable such as technology, which research has indicated as being likely to exert some influence on behaviour or to impose a condition upon the most effective type of organizational structure. There is, so far, much less knowledge of how the influence of technology may be mediated by other variables, such as employee expectations or types of production control systems, or of the relative importance of technology vis-à-vis other variables in different situations. In short, the present diversity of research within social science is, from one point of view, an indication of the subject's promise and vitality. Yet those who might wish to utilize its findings for purposes of educating managers are faced with an apparent lack of synthesis, quite apart from a considerable confusion of terminology.

The restricted empirical scope of many social science findings (much sociological work, in particular, has tended to take the form of single case studies), their present lack of duplication, follow-up and validation, and the failure to synthesize them in terms of inter-disciplinary analytical models, all make it very difficult to use this research for management teaching. Manage-ment education is a process necessarily oriented towards admin-istrative practice. Because it caters for students drawn from, or going to, a range of organizational backgrounds, management teaching searches for knowledge that has a wide application. It is probably the hope of many industrial social scientists that sufficient comparative evidence will eventually be accumulated to allow for reliable qualified generalizations which could then be passed on to managers.

It is extremely important for managers to be made aware that this stage of social science development is still some distance away. It is very tempting for social scientists, particularly when they have connections with management education or consultancy, to offer solutions which are not always so well founded as they are made to appear. We noted earlier how some schools of thought, such as the neo-human relations and Glacier approaches, were offering general precepts to managers on the basis of what appears to be inadequate evidence.

Thus writers such as Argyris, Likert and McGregor have based their recommendations on values regarding styles of management which may, in the first place, be held much less widely in non-American cultures. In focusing on systems of management authority as a major influence on organizational behaviour, these writers attempt to set up general recommendations for managerial practice which ignore the possible countervailing influence of other factors. In stressing that self-actualization opportunities should be given to employees with the intention of securing their greater commitment to organizational activities, the neo-human relations school fails to recognize that certain types of employee may not seek social or task involvement as a major reward from work. In addition, this approach gives insufficient attention to the fact that certain forms of technology, and certain tasks, are not in any case conducive to high employee involvement. To modify the situation in order to improve the possibilities for involvement may entail substantial costs for uncertain gains.

The Glacier school is also open to criticism, for attempting to expound general rules for management on the basis of a single case. It is worth noting, with reference to later sections of this chapter, that both neo-human relations and Glacier approaches have been linked closely with management consultancy. This has undoubtedly given rise to pressures for recommendations of a supposedly 'practical' nature, with the result that over-simplified, over-confident and potentially misleading conclusions have been offered to managers.

MANAGEMENT TEACHERS

Not surprisingly there are signs that problems of teaching material in management education have been reflected in disagreement and even bewilderment among management teachers. For example, a study group on *Management Studies*, meeting at the Further Education Staff College in 1963, recorded their failure to agree on 'the best basis for management education' or on 'what should be taught'.[7]

A survey which the author carried out in 1964 to ascertain the teaching material used by, and the views of, management teachers in colleges of technology also indicated a wide range of different approaches towards subjects such as organizational behaviour and labour relations. In this survey information was obtained by postal questionnaire from 126 teachers in 46 colleges of technology, all of which were running courses for the Diploma in Management Studies or for a comparable college diploma. There were also personal interviews with 35 senior management teachers in 27 of these colleges. The results of the survey, and characteristics of the sample, have been recorded in detail elsewhere.[8] It is only possible here to use this survey sparingly in order to illustrate some of the problems which recent developments have posed for management teachers.

The literature which these management teachers recommended to their students indicated that nearly all of them were well aware of the critiques of classical organization theory. On the other hand, writing following a human relations analysis predominated in the literature used for courses on personnel management and organizational behaviour. Few teachers knew the available critiques of human relations, and few appeared to make use of relevant social science research studies.

To a large extent the views of management teachers on the behavioural content of management education tended, as might be expected, to reflect the kind of literature they recommended to their students. This was, for instance, the case regarding their views on the value of the 'management principles' advanced by classical organization theorists. The majority of teachers were critical of these principles. However, the distance between those who wholeheartedly attacked and defended management principles was very considerable. On the one hand, the head of a management studies department commented in an interview that:

'Management principles have been taught as arising from writers' own experience. They are a mixture of this and folk-lore. On the face of it they appear reasonable, simply because they are empty, and therefore give one nothing to argue about.'

A senior lecturer in another college maintained, on the contrary, that:

'You can't get away with teaching managers just the background aspects of industry without drawing up any principles. . . . Practical men will insist that there are principles of management, and I think that the social scientists who attack this idea are being academic and unconstructive.'

A third position, between these extremes, was adopted by the majority of senior management teachers who were interviewed as part of the survey. This last position, which at the time probably represented the majority view among management teachers, reflected the dilemma they faced. These teachers acknowledged the powerful criticisms which had been made of classical organization theory. But they also felt it was necessary to formulate generalizations on organizational structure of practical use to managers. Not only would such propositions offer something that the management student could readily grasp, but their very existence would provide a challenge for the further development of research. Nevertheless, those who took up this middle position often seemed to feel great uncertainty in face of the conflict between management theorists and social scientists.

Turning to the analysis of organizational behaviour, most management teachers appreciated the limitations of human relations in respect of phenomena such as conflict, but a majority also thought that 'social skills' could play an important part in reducing the incidence of conflict. There was a marked and almost equal division of opinion as to the influence upon behaviour exerted by factors such as social differences and promotion opportunities. There was substantially more agreement that the nature of managerial control was a feature which could reduce co-operation in industry through its restriction of employees' self-actualization needs. This last result, taken together with reachers' views on 'social skills' and the popularity of neo-human relations literature among those in the sample, suggests that at the time considerable emphasis was given in courses to discussions about increasing the discretionary content of work and employees' participation within organizational affairs. This strongly supports the view that neo-human relations has become the new 'orthodoxy' in management education.[9]

In Chapter 6, we observed how British management thought has in recent years exhibited uncertainty and divided opinion, largely due to the critical impact of social science. The survey of management teachers confirmed that substantial dispute existed on several important issues and that many teachers were left in a state of considerable uncertainty. Nevertheless, this survey also suggested that, as a whole, management teachers were moving away from the older a prioristic standpoints. While the majority of teachers were in 1964 still unacquainted with any substantial range of social science sources, many had become sceptical of the established management literature. Nor did these teachers show any appreciable concern for the more legitimatory aspects of management thought. For example, most regarded the question of management's 'professional' status as irrelevant. Although by today the orientations of management teachers are likely to be more research minded than in 1964, the substantial differences of opinion which they exhibited may well still be felt within British management education. This would represent a measure of the present immaturity of management education and of the problems it still faces.

If it is accepted as desirable for management education to utilize the developing body of social science, two questions must be answered. What kind of management teacher appears to be most receptive to using social science, and how can it be put across to the management student? The second question will be discussed in the next section of this chapter, while our survey can begin to throw some light on the first.

Among the sample of management teachers by far the strongest and most consistent predictor of opinion and use of literature proved to be whether the respondent had specialized in sociology during his own academic training. Sociologists made relatively the most use of research-based literature, followed by those with a specialized training in psychology. In addition, younger teachers knew of and used significantly more social science research studies. Age and a specialized training in sociology were almost completely independent of each other. No other features of teachers' backgrounds, such as length of experience in management education or type of previous organizational experience, showed any independent predictive power (i.e., with $P = < \cdot 02$ on an X^2 test).

The views expressed on teaching for organization and labour relations were strongly correlated with teachers' knowledge and use of different types of available literature. It is thus reasonable to suppose that an acquaintance with research-based literature has a considerable influence on the management teacher's opinions and on the content of his teaching. Our survey suggests that if the use of social science is considered necessary in management education, steps should be taken to acquaint many more management teachers with the appropriate literature. We have already mentioned that few of the teachers in our survey appeared to make use of relevant social science research studies. And although these teachers would not be representative of staff in the new business schools, it is worth remembering that the great majority of British management students are still attending colleges running the Diploma in Management Studies.

The familiarizing of more management teachers with the social science literature is only the first, and perhaps not the most difficult, problem that is involved. There remains the question of how to apply social science, in the teaching process, to matters of managerial concern. This is the subject of our next two sections.

USE OF SOCIAL SCIENCE FOR MANAGEMENT EDUCATION[10]

Social science research is the source of most empirical data now available on the behaviour of organizations and on behaviour within organizations. As such, it must be taken into account by management educators. At the same time, for their purposes, the scattered findings and differing emphases of social scientists require presentation in a form that managers can find relevant to the decisions they have to take. This requirement means that the use of social science for industrial or organizational purposes must take the form of applying the contributions of all the constituent disciplines, plus relevant aspects of other fields such as engineering, to the analysis of given empirically-defined areas. That is, an integrated inter-disciplinary use of social science is called for.

Landsberger has recently argued that the most creative development of social science applied to industry, work and organizations will, in any case, lie in this direction. He urges the student to take a single problem, such as unemployment or conflict, and to see how the different social sciences have approached its analysis. This, he feels, is likely to prove more enlightening than concentrating on a single one of the social sciences and reviewing all the possible and highly diverse issues to which it is relevant. Even though it may not at present be possible to weld together in a single theory the contributions of different social sciences to the analysis of a particular area, Landsberger argues that each contribution nevertheless gains greatly through being compared with the others. This kind of analytical approach has in recent years been adopted by many working under the umbrella of 'organization theory', though Landsberger thinks that this is still a too broadly-defined field.[11]

The inter-disciplinary problem-oriented use of social science would normally proceed on the basis of conceptual schemes and analytical models appropriate to the issues being studied. For this purpose a systems framework is coming to prove useful as a device to integrate the variables and processes suggested by different disciplines. The systems concept may encourage integration, as may that popular construct 'role'. but it remains true that for explanatory power one must revert back to the contribution of the underlying disciplines. The use of a systems framework enables one to cope more adequately with the nature of relationships between variables possessing different degrees of influence, and the concept of 'role' enables one to relate these patterns of influence to a given social position. Yet it is the various social sciences themselves which afford some explanation for the sources of influence on what is being studied.

Some social scientists have already gone some way towards adopting at least a multi-variate approach to analysing particular phenomena. For instance, Ingham has classified different types of employee involvement in and attachment to organizations as a function of the factors determining (a) orientation to work, and (b) organizational size and its structural correlates.[12] Pugh and his colleagues have adopted an inter-disciplinary approach to the analysis of organizational structure, context, administrative roles, and individual characteristics which is already considerably advancing prediction in this field.[13] There is great scope for the further synthesis of already available social science research findings within analytical frameworks that are centred on given problems. There appears to be some progress in this respect in areas such as the study of consumer behaviour.

At the level of management teaching, the inter-disciplinary approach could allow for managers to be presented with the range of variables which research has indicated are operative upon given phenomena. Our own, extremely brief, review of some social science research in Chapter 6 itself indicated variables which were relevant to employee behaviour and administrative organization. The object would be to highlight factors which managers are advised to take into account when formulating decisions, and to keep under review at other times. Moreover, the identification of relevant variables may be complemented by an appreciation of which ones are subject to managerial regulation and which are not. In this way the limits to managerial control may be clarified.

This particular use of social science analysis goes some way towards reconciling the scattered and situational nature of research findings with the need to set out some specific instruction for management students, who will themselves be returning to a wide range of organizational circumstances. This approach means that the management teacher does not have to lay down any set of a prioristic rules supposedly relating to any organization. Instead, a working appreciation of the multiple dimensions of organizational structure and behaviour provides a means by which managers themselves can subsequently survey the requirements of the enterprises in which they must operate. Being empirically-based and remaining essentially non-prescriptive, this analytical approach is a realistic one. For this reason alone, it should prove of greater long-term benefit to managers than many precepts in the existing management literature. It does not place preconceived notions before students, which may be inappropriate or over-simplified, as was the case with management principles or human relations. On the contrary, this approach encourages managers to form their *own* appreciation of the circumstances in which problems happen to arise. Hence it stimulates them to formulate solutions appropriate to those circumstances. It is in this way suitably flexible.

The application of social science analysis to management problems allows discrete variables operating within an organizational situation to be identified. It encourages, as a further step, their subsequent sub-division into constituent items which may then be open to fairly precise measurement. An accurate assessment of the parameters of management decision, whether by academic researchers or by managers themselves, requires these two preliminary stages of clear analysis and careful measurement. Such assessment is a necessary prerequisite for decision-making that is to have any consistent success in attaining desired objectives. In other words, from the point of view of forward planning and general managerial prediction, the emphasis on measurable variables which is encouraged by applied social science is likely to improve the possibilities of an accurate evaluation of the consequences stemming from alternative policies and procedures.

A further advantage of the broad inter-disciplinary application of social science is that it stresses the wide range of variables which managers should consider in respect of organizational behaviour. It implies that an analytical focus upon one or two dimensions only can lead to a distorted evaluation of organizational phenomena. Thus it encourages the management educator to warn students against becoming over-attached to schools of thought which may appear to offer attractive solutions, but which base their teaching on too restricted an analytical foundation. It is precisely for this reason that, at various points in this study, we have criticized some recent managerial and social science writing.

A multi-variate and inter-disciplinary approach to management education does not merely enable the various parameters relating to a problem to be placed before managers. Equally important, it encourages managers to appreciate that they will have to balance a range of considerations brought out by the various disciplines when deciding upon a course of action. For instance, a production layout for a given product may be 'optimum' in terms of engineering economics, but it may also set up pressures towards employee frustration which then prejudices production levels or is in other respects 'undesirable' from a managerial point of view. In such an event, managers must consider the alternative costs of, say, (1) modifying the technology, (2) attempting in other ways to alleviate employee frustration, or (3) accepting the undesirable behaviour. Similarly, in different circumstances, different combinations of personal supervision (a factor stressed by social psychologists) and impersonal controls (of an engineering or economic nature) may be required to give managers the results they require.

In short, the grounding of management education upon a study of the fundamental processes of organizational life should encourage students to appreciate the need to diagnose causal factors rather than merely attempting to offset their symptoms. From this point of view, the analytical 'academic' approach should take precedence over the teaching of specific techniques, the application of which at best alters only one set of variables in a complex situation, and possibly dependent variables at that. By helping teachers to outline the likely limits to managerial choice, this approach should spare students frustration and wasted energy in the future. It should encourage students to reflect critically upon panaceas such as 'better communications' which sources such as the popular press sometimes find it their duty to put forward. It should assist managers to assess the requirements posed by changing conditions, particularly if these are already being indicated by organizational malfunctioning or by informal adaptive practices.

PROBLEMS WITH THE USE OF SOCIAL SCIENCE

A prerequisite for the extensive use of social science is, of course, that institutions of management education should employ well-trained social scientists. This may not present too much of a problem for the business schools or for university departments. However, in so far as the results of the author's survey are still representative today, it would appear to pose a problem for some colleges of technology. Certainly the approach outlined in the previous section requires a much more extensive appreciation of relevant social science research than the majority of management teachers in our survey appeared to enjoy. It would not necessarily prove easy for present teaching staff in those colleges to take up a study of social science. This would entail not just a seeking out of recorded research findings, but an appreciation of available theoretical approaches. For, if management students are themselves to utilize the analytical methods of social science, they must be presented with considerably more than simply the results of previous investigation. They have to learn how to investigate problems themselves, or at least how to evaluate any investigations they commission in the future. It might well prove difficult for older teachers to adapt to the requirements of using social science – in our sample older staff tended to be the least familiar with social science literature. The long-term solution lies with the recruitment of trained social scientists by colleges of technology, although at present good recruits may be difficult to secure.

Even if suitable staff are available, the application of social science to management teaching is not straightforward. It allows teachers little of the satisfaction which can derive from the passing-on of clear-cut and well-established precepts. Instead, the management teacher has to deal largely in terms of probability and uncertainty. Equally, this approach is arduous for the management student. It demands a considerable length of formal study, and a mental agility which can appreciate the concepts, methods and findings of several academic disciplines. Even then, students would have acquired not so much rules of conduct as guide-lines for the collection and assessment of information, on the basis of which they would have to form their own conclusions. The further burden of formulating appropriate policies is thus thrown back squarely on to managers' own shoulders.

Management studies departments, at least outside the business school ambit, face the very practical problem of attracting industrial support for their courses. They seek to maintain or expand the numbers of management students attending their courses, to persuade organizations to release and finance those students, and to secure sufficient recognition for management diplomas when students return to industrial life. It may be very salutary to emphasize to management students that certain features of industrial behaviour lie beyond their control, or that they may be faced with unpleasant choices during the course of their work. These are the implications of social science when, for instance, it presents a comprehensive analysis of industrial conflict or of the balance between economic interest and social welfare. However, sponsoring organizations may regard this type of instruction as 'unhelpful', adopting the view that any alert manager would appreciate the existence of such problems in any case. In other words, while the social science approach to management may appear realistic, this could encourage the feeling that the painstaking findings of social scientists were known to managers all the time. In addition, the more academic content of management education faces the disadvantage that it cannot compete with specialized short courses on standardized techniques in terms of offering the possibility of an immediate return for a relatively small investment of time.

This last point suggests a further difficulty concerning an extensive use of social science in management education. Organizations are most likely to release younger men for longer courses containing a relatively high academic content. Indeed, many of those attending such courses may come directly from universities. Such students will normally be some way removed from the policy-making roles for which academic analysis, as opposed to a routine application of techniques, is probably most relevant. To the extent that a grounding in social science analysis remains a permanent acquisition, this problem is not such a serious one, except that it may create frustration in younger managers if they cannot fully apply their extensive training. It may well prove of advantage to organizations to set up specialist sections, whose members could be sent to longer, more academic management courses. They could subsequently apply the methods of investigation so acquired in order to collect information, submit forecasts required by senior management, analyse particular organizational problems and trouble spots, and generally give advice. Sections such as these might prove valuable training grounds for younger managerial personnel.

There is a final difficulty with the application of social science to management education which it is only possible to discuss very tentatively. Woodward has recently suggested that while factual knowledge about industrial life is being built up, managerial 'ideology' (exemplified by human relations) serves a positive function in sustaining management 'as a social institution'.[14] It is possible that, given the general inability of social science to offer unqualified prescriptions for managerial problems, managers feel that it is better to follow some codes of action rather than none at all. An ideology may in this way

R

encourage managers to take some action where otherwise none would be forthcoming. In addition, the availability of such ideology might make it easier for managers to secure compliance with their instructions, by presenting their decisions with some supporting legitimation. In other words, there is perhaps for the time being some risk that the teaching of industrial social science would undermine these purported functions of managerial ideology, without substituting alternative guides for action.

It is difficult to evaluate this argument, but one should probably not set too much store by it. For some of the items which Woodward includes in this managerial ideology, such as human relations, appear to have belonged to the realm of management thought rather than to the views of most practising managers. We suggested in Chapter 7 that for this reason they may not have exercised the functions for managers which Woodward ascribes to them. More important, if managerial ideology obscures an objective evaluation of organizational processes, then any action which it stimulates managers to take will not necessarily be constructive. Nonetheless, the role of values in relation to managerial performance does remain a subject deserving some further study.

The problems attending the use of social science in management education enable one to appreciate the continuing popularity of courses which are confined to standard techniques or to the exercising of specific skills. Courses on techniques such as work study, and the various business exercises, are shorter in length and appear to bear directly and unambiguously upon everyday managerial operations. These management training activities relate to aspects of organization over which managers appear to have most personal control, and attention to which promises the most immediate returns. Courses on techniques allow for instruction that is forceful, pragmatic and can deal in firm generalizations. The standardized and apparently proven nature of most techniques lends them an aura of science which not only attracts industrial support, but is presumably also psychologically satisfying for many teachers. Yet whatever the attractions of courses on techniques and business exercises, we have suggested that these may be of limited value if they do not make reference to the organizational contexts which are relevant for management students, and which appropriate academic disciplines help to define. This is not only the case with a new development such as group exercises, but is equally true of a well-established technique such as work study.[15]

Thus the supposed divorce between the 'academic' approach in management education and 'practical' industrial requirements, which appears to have been felt by those who criticised the academic basis of the new British business schools,[16] is seen to be a misleading idea. The opposition of so-called 'practical' men to academic business education overlooks the point that the process of management does not consist merely in the application of techniques. More fundamentally, management concerns the establishment of policies related to an assessment of the whole organizational situation, which themselves govern the choice of appropriate techniques to be employed. The further criticism that academic research in industry has merely 'discovered the obvious' is also hardly tenable in view of the devastating effect which such research has had upon management thought. Although it appears that many practising managers may have been more realistic in their views than most management thinkers, at the level of written educational material the 'obvious' has *had* to be discovered by academics. Indeed it is the further development of comparative research by academics which offers management the best chance of clarifying the correlates of organizational effectiveness.

In short, the attempt to apply social science and other relevant disciplines to management education is difficult yet necessary. In the long-term it should promote steady progress towards more reliable conclusions about the processes of organizational life. Such progress towards an organizational 'science' will be the more rapid if the academic training of managers encourages them to be more receptive to researchers seeking their co-operation, and if it fosters an increase in research carried out by companies themselves.

MANAGEMENT EDUCATION, INDUSTRIAL STUDIES AND THE UNIVERSITIES

During the 1960s there has been a considerable expansion of management education within British universities. A number of universities have established management courses for the first time. Colleges of Advanced Technology with a tradition of management education have been upgraded to university status. Two business schools, attached to the universities of London and Manchester, have been founded.

It would appear today that the development of management education within the universities is favoured by many spokesmen for management, by many universities themselves, and by a wide range of political opinion. Management education is regarded as a vital factor in the hoped-for national economic recovery, and its extension within the university orbit is generally felt to carry several advantages. For instance, the study of management problems will benefit from the high quality of university teaching and research. The prestige which university patronage adds to management education serves to emphasize publicly its national economic importance. Nevertheless, some commentators have expressed misgivings about the role of management education in the universities, both at an operational level and at the level of basic principles. A brief consideration of these problems, particularly the objections of principle, will subsequently be seen to relate to other fundamental questions concerning the status of management education which arise from our review of management thought and social science in previous chapters.

At the operational level, some spokesmen with close industrial connections, such as Sir Paul Chambers and the authors of the Bow Group memorandum on British Business Schools, fear that the products of university courses may be too abstract or indecisive in their approach to cope successfully with the practical exigencies of industrial life.[17] To some extent we have discussed this objection in the previous section, in connection with the role of academic social science in management education. Commenting from the university side, Loasby and Robertson (then tutors in management studies at the University of Bristol) admitted that co-operation between industry and the universities was often not an easy process.[18] Organizations faced the problem of releasing key personnel for longer courses, and there was insufficient knowledge of the benefits which could derive from broadly-based university courses. Industrialists felt that management courses should be able to provide clear 'management rules', and that they should be practical in the sense of producing immediate and visible improvements in managerial performance. Equally, there were difficulties in adapting the universities to the requirements of management courses. University teaching has traditionally conformed to the demands of the separate disciplines rather than to the vocational requirements of the market. For university staff have traditionally derived prestige from professional peers working securely within the confines of a given discipline.

However immediate these problems may be, they do not defy possible solution. They should be ameliorated if, with the passage of time, there is an improvement in understanding between industry and the universities together with a further development of management teaching as a discrete professional activity, and hence as a point of reference for occupational prestige and status. Support is already growing for an inter-disciplinary approach to the study of industrial and organizational behaviour, and this represents an important advance upon traditional thinking. Indeed, the universities already manage quite successfully in other areas to provide courses which are both vocational and inter-disciplinary, such as on medicine and social studies, without apparently lowering any of their academic standards or prejudicing their research activities.

A more fundamental problem relates both to the nature of the material available for management education and to the social role of management. In a broadcast of 1961, V. L. Allen went some way towards setting out the problem we have in mind, albeit from an extreme standpoint. Allen felt that 'management studies in their present form represent a travesty of the traditional, proper, and unique role of universities'.[19] He argued, first, that as the conceptual framework of management studies was set by the existing structure of industrial relationships, this would inhibit that questioning of assumptions which was essential to the universities' charter of advancing and disseminating all types of knowledge and experience. Secondly, Allen argued that management studies were not suited to university teaching since they did not possess their own distinct theoretical framework and body of knowledge. As vocational *training*, management education should be left to colleges of technology and to companies' own courses. Whereas the *study* of management should form part of an objective, comparative study of industrial behaviour as a whole to which the universities could legitimately devote their energies. The results of this study would be of value to managers, and also to trade unionists or any other interested parties. The subject which would emerge – a 'sociology of industry' – would stand in its own right as an academic discipline and 'could be taught openly and honestly and usefully in our universities'.

Allen's remarks brought forth critical replies from several sources, notably J. H. Smith, S. Hyman, and A. J. Odber.[20] All three denied that management teachers, or those carrying out associated research, adopted the biased frame of reference which Allen had implied was a necessary concomitant of their particular role. Smith made the important point that a study of management problems presented the universities with a valuable oppportunity to bring together different specialist disciplines into a 'unity of learning'. Moreover, he felt that the distinction between a liberal and a vocational education, which formed part óf Allen's case, was an artificial one. In any event, a managerial élite was steadily forming – that was a social fact. Thus, in Smith's view, the question one should be asking was: 'What sort of an élite will it be?' If the managerial élite were to be encouraged to adopt socially responsible policies and to be technically proficient as well, then it was far better for the universities to educate its members and to study its needs than for it to be left to its own devices.

This particular controversy raised an issue of considerable importance. It is correct to point out that the academic contributions to management education in no way represent a discipline which is exclusively managerial. Bechhofer has joined Allen here in arguing that the academic content of management education in effect amounts to a study of industrial and organizational processes.[21] As such this study is of interest and relevance for all who are concerned with organizations – civil servants, hospital administrators, politicians, trade union officers and other groups, in addition to business managers. The analysis, techniques and skills taught on management courses are relevant to these other groups because they too may be in a position to use them, as administrators of one kind or another. In addition, if other parties to business affairs, such as civil servants or trade union officers attended courses with business managers, all might find it easier at a later stage to view each other's problems with greater understanding and sympathy.

The failings in British management thought, and the role of

social science in exposing these, raise a second point. Namely, while it is reasonable to argue the pressing need to educate further those who are or will be in control of our national economic resources, it does not follow that these managers will be better educated if they attend courses within universities or colleges from which other types of student are excluded. We noted earlier how the technical value of British management thought was seriously prejudiced by considerations of managerial legitimation. Indeed, it has taken the efforts of many social scientists, some of them possessing a marked antipathy to the managerial point of view, to bring management thought and education to a position where they are prepared to face more realistically the complex problems of organizational behaviour. There would seem to be a good case for suggesting that educational institutions admitting students from a variety of organizational roles might be more successful in presenting their business manager students with a balanced appreciation of industrial and organizational life. That is, they might more readily avoid the temptation to adopt a restricted managerial perspective and the over-simple assumptions that can accompany this.

This argument applies not only to the quality of the educational experience from the student's point of view, but also to the quality of university research on industry and organization. It has been an assumption underlying this book that the greatest benefit for managers and others is provided by the most scientific analysis of industry. In this connection, academic investigators, as well as management thinkers, have sometimes failed to maintain sufficient objectivity because of their over-close association with purely managerial objectives. Baritz provides a comprehensive record of how this affected American social science.[22] The best-known example is the Hawthorne research, particularly in respect of the interpretations which the Mayo school placed on its findings. We have also suggested that a recent instance can be seen with some of the Glacier Project writings, especially by Brown on piecework payment systems and by Jaques on equitable income determination.

It is extremely important to note that the most powerful critics of Mayoism were academics who were not tied exclusively to the managerially-oriented activities of American business schools. Jaques' work on incomes has also been developed, like Mayoism, into a programme for social change. This programme claims to rest on scientific findings which it is the role of academics to feel free to examine critically, and if necessary to challenge. There is some danger, if the universities choose to support a narrowly bounded 'management education' rather than a more broadly defined 'industry studies', that teaching and research may be tied so closely to managerially defined problems as to prejudice this process of free criticism.

In sum, we have suggested that the exact form of 'management education', particularly within the universities, should not yet be regarded as a closed issue. The progress of British management thought and the critiques which can be levelled against recent writing exclusively tied to managerial definitions should sound a note of caution. If it is considered necessary for the general good that the study of industrial problems should steadily discard ideology and conjecture for meaningful fact, then the context of relevant teaching and research is of fundamental importance.

NOTES

1. J. Lee, *Management*, London: Pitman 1921, pp. 12-13.

2. A. F. Earle, address to B.I.M. National Conference on 'Management Education: the Next Five Years', reported in *The Manager*, April 1965, p. 40; D. C. Hague, 'What Should the Business Schools Teach?', *Times Review of Industry*, May 1965, pp. 78-80; B. J. Loasby, 'The Substance of Management Education', *District Bank Review*, Dec. 1966, pp. 41-56.

3. Cf., D. C. Hague, *op. cit.*, p. 79.

4. E.g., B. W. Denning, 'What Should the Business Schools Teach?', *Times Review of Industry*, July 1965, pp. 14-16; H. W. Fordham, 'On Training Managers', *Personnel Management*, XLV, 364, June 1963, pp. 55-59; D. C. Hague, *op. cit.*; N. C. Hunt, 'Second Thoughts on Management Education', *The Manager*, May 1960, pp. 348-353, 383; C. F. Kearton, 'What Should the Business Schools Teach?', *Times Review of Industry*, June 1965, pp. 20-22; *Management Studies*, Further Education Staff College, Blagdon, Nov. 1963, p. 10.

5. A. Etzioni, *A Comparative Analysis of Complex Organizations*, Glencoe: Free Press 1961; H. A. Simon, *Administrative Behaviour*, New York: Macmillan 1947; P. M. Blau and W. R. Scott, *Formal Organizations*, London: Routledge & Kegan Paul 1963; C. Perrow, 'A Framework for the Comparative Analysis of Organizations', *American Sociological Review*, 32, 2, April 1967, pp. 194-208.

6. D. S. Pugh, *et al.*, 'A Conceptual Scheme for Organizational Analysis', *Administrative Science Quarterly*, 8, 3, Dec. 1963, pp. 289-315.

7. *Op. cit.*, p. 3.

8. J. Child, *British Management Thought and Education: Their Interpretation of Industrial Relationships*, unpublished Ph.D. thesis, University of Cambridge 1967, Part II *passim*.

9. B. Davies, 'Some Thoughts on "Organizational Democracy" ', *Journal of Management Studies*, 4, 3, Oct. 1967, pp. 270-281.

10. Cf., T. Lupton, *Management and the Social Sciences*, London: Hutchinson 1966; D. S. Pugh, 'The Social Science Approach to Management', *Scientific Business*, 4, 13, Summer 1966, pp. 23-31.

11. H. A. Landsberger, 'The Behavioral Sciences in Industry', *Industrial Relations*, 7, 1, Oct. 1967, pp. 1-19.

12. G. K. Ingham, 'Organizational Size, Orientation to Work and Industrial Behaviour', *Sociology*, I, 3, Sept. 1967, pp. 239-258.

13. R. L. Payne and D. J. Hickson, 'Measuring the Ghost in the Organizational Machine', *European Business*, 13, May 1967, pp. 41-45.

14. J. Woodward, *Industrial Organization: Theory and Practice*, London: Oxford University Press 1965, pp. 254-257.

15. A. E. Mills, 'Don't be Dogmatic About Methods', *The Manager*, Dec. 1964, pp. 43-45.

16. E.g., R. G. A. Boland, letter to *The Times*, 2nd Dec. 1963; The Bow Group, *British Business Schools*, London, Feb. 1964.

17. Bow Group, *op. cit.*; Sir P. Chambers, Chuter Ede Lecture to the National Union of Teachers, reported in *The Times*, 3rd June 1964.

18. B. J. Loasby and N. Robertson, 'Industry and the Universities: the Assumption and the Reality', *The Manager*, July 1965, pp. 50-52.

19. V. L. Allen, 'Management and the Universities', *The Listener*, 13th July 1961, pp. 51-52.

20. J. H. Smith, 'Management and the Universities', *The Listener*, 20th July 1961, pp. 89-90; S. Hyman, 'The Role of the Universities', *The Manager*, Sept. 1962, pp. 49, 51; A. J. Odber, letter to *The Listener*, 20th July 1961.

21. F. Bechhofer, 'Why Not Industrial Studies?', *New Society*, 2nd April 1964, pp. 19-20.

22. L. Baritz, *The Servants of Power*, Middletown, Conn.: Wesleyan University Press 1960.

INDEX

Administrative, Technical and Clerical Employees, 15
Albu, A., 136
Aldrich, R. M., 191
Allen, V. L., 261-2
American Business Creed, The, (F. X. Sutton *et al.*), 25-6
Anglican Congress 1912, Sir Benjamin Browne's Address to, 39
Appleby, R., 153
Argyris, C., 90, 177, 178, 247
Army, Analogy with, 57, 90, 123-4, 136, 152, 223
Aron, R., 240

Bakke, E. W., 177
Bamforth, N., 138, 139, 184
Baritz, L., 263
Barnard, Chester, 116, 144
Barry, W. S., 194-5
Bechhofer, F., 262
Behrend, H., 21
Bendix, R., 25, 26, 229-30, 233-4
Bevin, E., 111
Blain, I., 176
Blau, P. M. and Scott, W. R., 246
Bow Group, 260
Bowker, N. C. and Hall, M. F., 192
Bowie, J. A., 103, 133, 137, 143
Brassey, T., 34
Brech, E. F. L., 24, 51, 115, 139, 140, 144-6, 147, 183, 193
Briggs, Henry (firm), 34
British Business Schools (Bow Group), 260
British Institute of Management (B.I.M.), 113-14, 143, 146, 185, 227
Membership, 113
British Management Review (journal), 88, 153
Brown, J. A. C., 115, 127, 147
Brown, Wilfred, 13, 137, 148-51, 185, 195-9, 263
See *also*: 'Glacier Project'
Browne, Sir Benjamin, 39, 46
Burnham, J., 137
Burns Morton, F. J., 115, 119, 123, 125, 128
Burns, T., 183
Burns, T. and Stalker, G. M., 60, 91, 176-7, 178-9

Business Enterprise, Conceptions of, 21, 55n, 56, 58, 60, 61, 62, 65, 74, 117-8, 131-2, 156, 178-9, 182
Environment, 18, 89, 90, 156-7, 174-5, 176-7, 178, 182, 199, 202
Scale, 14-15, 25, 37-8, 58, 72, 78, 119, 132-3, 173, 176, 184
Social Differences in, 20-1, 74-5, 133, 179
Byng, E. S., 96

Cadbury, Edward, 37, 38, 39, 40, 53, 54, 75, 123
Cadbury, Lawrence, 131
Cadbury Brothers Ltd. (Bournville), 36, 37, 38
Cameron, M. A., 123
Cammell, Lairds Ltd., 46
Capital, 39-40, 56-7, 72, 74
And Labour, 44, 56-7, 80
See *also*: 'Entrepreneurial Philosophy', 'Ideology, Business', 'Managers and Industrial Ownership'
Casson, H. N., 42, 53, 58, 75, 76, 123
Chambers, Sir Paul, 260
Chelioti, G., 152-3
Chief Inspector of Factories, Report for 1940, 111
Clarke, Mrs. V. M., 115, 123, 128
Coal Industry Commission 1919, 52
Collier, H. E., 97
Common Interests, 18, 22, 33, 37, 57, 64, 73, 118, 119, 121, 136, 147-8, 153, 157, 190, 203
Communications, 36, 76, 119, 136, 192
See *also*: 'Joint Consultation'
Comparative Analysis of Complex Organizations (A. Etzioni), 175
Conflict, 17-18, 20-1, 39-40, 49, 50, 53, 55n, 65, 72, 73, 74, 75, 77, 87, 90, 93, 95, 97, 117, 143, 146, 174-5, 180, 185, 188, 190, 192, 199-203
Analysis in Management Thought, 40, 55-7, 62, 80-2, 122, 130-5, 150
Types, 20
See *also*: 'Restriction of Output'
Co-operation, 17-18, 37, 45, 53, 61, 64, 75, 77, 78, 95, 116, 118, 119, 136, 142, 189
Cooper, A. R., 122
Coser, L., 20, 233